INDIAN WATER RESOURCE DEVELOPMENT FOR IRRIGATION:
ISSUES, CRITIQUES, REVIEWS

INDIAN WATER RESOURCE DEVELOPMENT FOR IRRIGATION :
ISSUES, CRITIQUES, REVIEWS

B.D. DHAWAN

Commonwealth

Indian Water Resource Development for Irrigation

Edition : 2019

ISBN 81-7169-259-1

Published by **:**
COMMONWEALTH PUBLISHERS (P) LTD.
4831/24, Govind Lane,
Ansari Road, Darya Ganj,
New Delhi - 110002
Ph. : 23272541, 23242541
e-mail : commonwealthpublishers2016@gmail.com

Distributed by :
ARJUN PUBLISHING HOUSE
4831/24, Govind Lane,
Ansari Road, Darya Ganj,
New Delhi - 110002
Ph. : 23272541, 23242541
e-mail : arjunbooks2001@gmail.com

Laser Typesetting by :
Dimple Computers
Delhi

Printed at :
Milan Enterprises
Delhi**9**

PREFACE

I am pleased to offer this collection of my recent writings on the Indian irrigation sector. These were written over the last three years or so, and have already been published in abridged or full form. The abridging became necessary whenever a newspaper or a periodical could not accommodate the full text of a paper for reasons of space and style, e.g., detailed footnotes obviously could not be carried in the popular media.

Water is a very complex resource. This hinders easy comprehension of issues related to it even by a keen person, who is further frustrated by the technicalities used in the writings of researchers on water and water-related subjects. Also, researchers, like myself, are prone to address fellow researchers in the same area, mainly through journals and less often through general purpose books. This is understandable because the needed-critical appreciation of research results can come forth from one's own research fraternity only. But the esoteric content and form of research papers grossly restricts readership to the few initiated in modern methods of research and analysis.

This restrictiveness diminishes when a researcher makes a deliberate effort simultaneously to diffuse his ideas in a simple, intelligible form free from jargons and technicalities. Opportunity to do so these days is not inconsiderable as both the print and electronic media of mass circulation are evincing interest in carrying writings by scholars on matters of public concern and importance. Many of the writings in this volume originated mainly as a result of (a) my keenness to propagate my research-based irrigation knowledge, and (b) two invitations received from editors of one economic daily and one monthly periodical to publish my views on Indian irrigation, my area of research over the last two decades or so. I am really grateful to Prof. A.M. Khusro who after taking over the editorship of the *Financial Express* afforded me the opportunity to publish six articles on Indian irrigated farming in that daily. A like opportunity to write more frequently for the monthly periodical, *Facts for You*, came from its editor Mr. S.P. Chopra, a former editor of the economic weekly *Eastern Economist* with which I did a short stint back in 1960.

Besides these media writings, the volume includes nine reviews: *Economic and Political Weekly* (four) and *the Journal of Indian School of Political Economy* (three) and one each is from *International Journal of Development Banking,* and *Indian Journal Agricultural Economies*. I am thankful to the editors of these journals.

Many papers in this volume emerged when the author got the opportunity either to attend some national symposium on water resources or to offer a critique of some newly released documents and reports relating to Indian water resources but meant for wider readership. For example, the paper in chapter 2 tries to react to the proceedings of a national symposium on tall and small dams. Likewise, the large comment on the irrigation sector of the Eighth Five Plan, set out in chapter 4, was made when the final version of this plan was released last year. In a like manner, the author chose to comment on the two, much-cited evaluation studies on Tehri and Narmada dams by INTACH which entrusted this task to Vijay Paranjpye, a noted critic of the big dam idea.

The big dam issue figures in many chapters. Much has been getting reported on this issue in the Indian print media, thanks mainly to the intense controversies on Tehri and the Narmada dams. An irrigation research economist like myself could hardly remain a bystander to the raging controversies. However, it is necessary to clarify one aspect of my interventions, so to speak. This was not so much because of a particular expertise in the big dam economics as such. What prompted me to write on this matter was my grave reservation about the alternatives to big dams in the realm of minor irrigation, especially the option of groundwater-based irrigation. During the course of the debate

I noticed glaring misperceptions or misunderstandings about Indian irrigation in general and groundwater irrigation economics in particular. These are precisely the topics wherein I had gained some credentials through sustained research work over several years.

I am happy to dedicate this volume to my former colleague, Professor Dharm Narain, the thorough research scholar with a gentle, helpful disposition towards fellow scholars, especially the younger ones.

Special mention needs to be made of the Institute of Economic Growth, where I have been working as a full time researcher since 1961. I really feel a sense of privilege to be associated with this institution which offers excellent facilities for gainful research activity - and for publications arising out of this activity. I am pleased to put on record the research support provided by its staff, notably the ones manning the computer unit and the library.

B.D. Dhawan

20th May, 1993

CONTENTS

Part II. REVIEWS OF REPORTS / STUDIES

PART I

STATE OF INDIAN IRRIGATION

CHAPTER 1

INTRODUCTION

The subject of water interests every one. Water meets human needs in a number of ways. In India, bulk of the water, tapped from rivers, ground water, natural lakes and springs, is utilised for irrigation purpose. Thus nearly nine-tenths of the water consumed in our country is for the production of crops in the agricultural sector.

Industrial and urban growth, being faster than that of agriculture, has given rise to more rapid expansion in non-agricultural demand for water. But in the Indian conditions this disparity in growth rates is not likely to result in non-agricultural uses of water eventually acquiring a dominant status as we observe in the developed economies of Europe and North America (Table 1). This is because irrigation in these temperate economies, unlike ours, is not an essential requirement for practising intensive farming based on modern bio-chemical technology.

Development of irrigation facilities has been central to India's agricultural planning right from the commencement of the first Five Year Plan. This development has taken place both within the public and the private sectors. Whereas major and medium irrigation works, being large scale in size, are wholly under the public aegis, minor or small scale irrigation works are predominantly under private ownership, individual as well as communal. Over time, both categories of works have increased greatly in numbers, but each category maintaining, more or less, its own relative position as determined by its own share in total irrigation capacity. Needless to say, such balanced growth in irrigation expansion, highly desirable as it is from the standpoint of integrated irrigation planning whose hallmark is conjunctive use of water resources, could be achieved more at the national than at the state level.

TABLE 1

SECTORAL USE* OF WATER IN SELECTED COUNTRIES

S.No.	*Country*	*Quantity of water used (km³)*	*Percentage for agricultural use*
1.	India	380,000	93
2.	China	460,000	87
3.	Egypt	45,000	98
4.	Libya	1.5	83
5.	South Africa	9.2	83
6.	Canada	30,000	10
7.	U.S.A.	472,000	41
8.	Belgium	8.3	10
9.	Finland	4.6	8
10.	Poland	15.9	25

Source : Based on Table 4.2 of Adriant T. Mcdonald and David Kay's book Water Resources: Issues and Strategies (Longman Scientific and Technical, U.K., 1988).
The word 'use' means water tapped or withdrawn from natural water bodies. Such use does not apply to hydro power generation.

By now a pretty large investment has taken place in irrigation sector. However, definite estimates on this account are lacking. There are several difficulties in deriving such estimates from our plan documents. For one, the investment outlays reported in these documents against the minor irrigation head are exclusive of investments on farmers' own account - one surmise is that such investments on private account could be as sizeable as those on public (and institutional) account. For another, there is no mention of capital already invested in irrigation sector by the beginning of the five year planning process in 1951. Of the total irrigation capacity existing at the beginning of the ongoing Eighth Five Year Plan (1992-97), almost one-fourth is of pre-1951 vintage. Thirdly, the estimates in respect of plan outlays lack temporal comparability because of persistence of price inflation during the period of planning.

In view of these limitations of the plan data on investments in the irrigation sector readers should beware of all estimates derived from the use of such data. Thus neither their cumulation nor comparison over plans would be sensible so long as these are first not corrected for the price inflation effect that otherwise grossly exaggerates the scale of step up in irrigation investments from one plan to the next. Likewise, contrasting plan investments on minor irrigation with those on major and medium irrigation is inappropriate either for judging this comparative planning emphasis on these two categories of irrigation or for assessing comparative capital requirements for establishing irrigation capacity for one hectare area.

Outline and Overview of Book

The book consists of two parts. Besides the introductory chapter 1, the eleven chapters in part I aim at apprising the reader with the state of Indian irrigation. Chapters 2 and 3 focus on the proceedings of a national symposium on the issue of large and small dams, and the Third National Water Convention. This author was present at both these widely attended congregations, also making a keynote presentation at the Convention. The big dam issue loomed large at both the meetings, one organised by the Central Board of Irrigation and Power and the other by the National Water Development Agency (in collaboration with the Indian Water Resources Society, Nagpur Centre).

In the early phase of anti-big dam movement in India, ground water-based irrigation programmes, as well as small dams, were both commended to Indian planners as attractive alternatives to large dams for fulfilling India's pressing irrigation requirements. It was not long before it was realised by the critics of big dams that there were really not enough of groundwater resources to meet our potential irrigation needs. In other words, they began showing appreciation of the apprehension of groundwater experts that groundwater stock could deplete as a result of excessive preoccupation with well irrigation, especially in the low rainfall regions of the country. So, the big dam debate veered round to the issue of tapping our bounty of surface water resources through tall or small dams. In chapter 2 the author reports on the discussions which took place on this issue at a national symposium organised by the Central Board of Irrigation and Power which had invited speakers from both sides of the controversy to review the strengths and weaknesses of both types of dams.

Unfortunately, the discussions at the symposium became almost one-sided, mainly because of poor representation from the side of the big dam critics. As a result, the plus points of large dams and weak points of small dams (height below 15 metres) got highlighted in the floor discussions. Still, the proceedings are worth noting, as this was probably the first occasion when protagonists of the big dam idea set out to tell their part of the story on Indian water planning, for which they were time and again urged upon by their critics — and this author. Particularly noteworthy are submergence and earthquake hazard aspects of tall vis-a-vis small dams as these run quite counter to common perceptions or big dam critics' claims. Furthermore, proponents of big dams have shown much better appreciation for small dams by conceding their due place in the upper reaches of a river where flows are, unlike in the down reaches, small. Construction of multitude of such small dams plays a vital role in sustaining irrigated agriculture based on big dams, by minimising the siltation process of big reservoirs as the small dams check the silt and debris from reaching the downstream reservoirs. Obviously, big river flows cannot be technically impounded through small dams which would be wiped out every season when the huge monsoonal flood waters overtop these dams.

At the Water Convention, once again, the pro-big dam participants outnumbered others, but the difference was not as glaring as in the Delhi symposium on tall and small dams three months earlier. Still the transactions merit attention. One is struck by the wide disparity in perceptions and perspectives — and even about facts. Thus, whereas critics of big dams presented untenably high estimates of land degradation due to canal irrigation, the defender engineers cited incredibly low figures in this regard for some specific projects.

The release of a five year plan report has so far been a momentous occasion in the annals of Indian economic development. In chapter 4 the author offers his own critical appreciation of the irrigation sector encompassed in the Report of Eighth Five Year Plan for the period 1992-93 to 1996-97. The investment for this vital sector of Indian farm economy is placed at Rs. 32,500 crores, of which nearly Rs. 22,000 crores is for major and medium irrigation development. The investment of nearly Rs. 6,000 crores proposed for minor irrigation segment appears comparatively small. But it is to be remembered that this is a partial estimate as it is not inclusive of *(a)* investment from farmers' own funds for wells and other minor irrigation works and *(b)* supporting investments on public account in rural power supply system-nearly Rs. 4,000 crores are earmarked for rural electrification which would benefit primarily electric pumpsets used for lift irrigation from both groundwater and surface water sources.

The anticipated addition to irrigation capacity from these investment programmes is reckoned at 15 million hectares of crop area, of which over two-thirds is expected from minor irrigation works. This scale of addition in capacity would mean 18 per cent expansion in irrigated acreage. Knowing as we do know about the one-to-one correspondence or relationship between foodgrains production and total irrigated area, the resultant 18 per cent increase in domestic foodgrains production should well take care of the anticipated increase in demand for foodgrains of the same order over the Eighth Plan period. So, food security of the nation is reasonably well provided for by the planners' continued emphasis on irrigation expansion in the ongoing Eighth Plan.

The area of real concern here, however, is whether the needed investment funds would be forthcoming for the programmed expansion of the irrigation sector. On the one hand, investment resources for public sector activities are becoming increasingly scarce, partly due to the mounting burden of many subsidies provided by the central and state governments through direct and indirect means. On the other hand, some of the large irrigation projects continue to be bedevilled with controversies which have even spilled over to international arena. For instance, first came the highly adverse Morse-Berger report on the Sardar Sarovar Project (SSP), which is slated to add 1.8 million hectare capacity by the end of the 8th Plan. More recently (March 1993), the Government has decided to forego the rest of the 170 million dollars of World Bank assistance for this project, presumably because the international standards in respect of rehabilitation of dam oustees and other displaced persons are much more exacting to comply with than those being followed here in India. Now, the Centre has assumed responsibility for making available funds and foreign exchange to the government of Gujarat in lieu of the World Bank aid.

In view of the vagaries of Indian monsoons the imperative need for irrigation development for protecting crops during drought time has been much highlighted. As against these agronomical compulsions, the dire economic compulsions arising from a large and steadily growing population are not so widely appreciated. The Indian planners have been under terrible pressure to expand substantially and urgently the agricultural output so as to meet the rising needs of food and fibre of the Indian masses. These needs are rising because of growth in human population, as also its purchasing power owing to developmental planning which is an instrumental factor in causing a continual reduction in mortality - thereby aggravating the rate of growth of population. Without irrigation, dependence on dryland farm technologies can prove disastrous. For one, such technologies perform well under temperate conditions. For another, in the Indian conditions these have not shown such encouraging results as to warrant a major reliance being placed on them for meeting our rising food needs. In chapter 5 we take a closer look at the comparative yield and stability performance of the irrigated *vis-a-vis* dryland farming. As the paper was written as a keynote address on the occasion of a national seminar on 'Large Reservoirs - Environmental Loss or Gain?', it also contains some observations on large versus small-scale irrigation, and on environmental degradation due to large reservoirs.

Except for the few protagonists of "natural" farming and dryland technology, the case for irrigation development is indisputably accepted by most people. There is, however, not that kind of unanimity when it comes to developing different types of irrigation works. In chapter 6 the author has tried to de-emphasise this issue that otherwise has exercised many minds. The issue of developing this or that irrigation resource loses significance in an ultimate analysis. When the exploitable water resources, taken as a whole, happen to be far from bountiful - these would hardly provide irrigation cover to two-thirds of our crop area even on full exploitation say, by the year 2010 A.D. — eventually we have per force to develop all categories of irrigation works: mega dams, big dams, small dams, check dams, tanks, dugwells, tubewells, borewells, etc. And once we begin to show due appreciation of the inherent complementarities or inter-linkages between irrigation sources, the issue of choice among irrigation sources becomes really a non-issue in a pragmatic sense. If at all priority to groundwater irrigation is to be accorded, it should be in the high rainfall areas of the east Gangetic plains and Madhya Pradesh where much of the groundwater resource is unexploited.

This paper was originally written for a seminar on Economics of Land Water Resources at Pune where both economists and non-economic experts were to congregate. Because of this wider character of the participants, the author decided to comment upon a wide range of issues in his writeup. Many of these issues again cropped up at the Third National Water Convention at Nagpur, a summary view of whose salient proceedings is presented in chapter 3.

In chapter 7 we take up the question of improving groundwater availability for well irrigation through artificial recharge measures. First the natural process of groundwater replenishment is expounded. Then, how this process can be strengthened through man-made measures is highlighted. In the Indian conditions the key to groundwater augmentation for low rainfall states lies in developing an extensiive system of surface water based irrigation works, especially canal and tank irrigation. The role of seeped-in canal and tank waters in the thriving groundwater based agriculture of the states of Punjab and Tamil Nadu is delineated.

The central objective in chapter 8 is to dispel the myth that minor irrigation is a low-cost option for the Indian economy. This is done by taking a macro or total view of costs, irrespective of the fact as to whether the individual or the government incurs such costs. Recent empirical researches have highlighted the huge, hidden subsidies borne by the State Electricity Boards while supplying electricity to agricultural pumpsets which have become so necessary in modern-day minor irrigation works. Farmers hardly bear one-tenth of the cost of resources expended on public account in supplying power to the countryside. Supporting investment funds required to erect the necessary infrastructure of power generation, transmission and rural electrification are greater than the corresponding outlays utilised in establishing minor irrigation structures themselves. When these supporting investments are duly taken into account, the capital requirements for establishing irrigation capacity for one crop hectare area could be as high as Rs. 39,000 in the case of a dugwell equipped with an electric pumpset. The same would be nearer Rs. 17,500 in the case of a private electric tubewell.

Admittedly, the aforesaid cost estimates do turn out to be lower than the comparable estimates for major irrigation works. However, we should not rush to the hasty conclusion that minor irrigation is less capital using than major irrigation. Here, we have to reckon also with another pertinent parameter of capital, namely, the life aspect of a capital asset. Whereas a shallow tubewell would need fresh replacement investment every fifteen years or so, a major irrigation work typically lasts for 100 years or thereabout. Finally, which of these two irrigation works for a nation is more cost effective (as distinguished from economy in the use of scarce capital) has to be sorted out within the framework of rigorous benefit-cost analysis involving the use of discounting procedures and shadow pricing, as also reckoning with the external effects of each category of irrigation.

Water management is the watchword of our times, attention to which is drawn for resolving many an ill of Indian irrigation: water shortages, pollution of water bodies like rivers, lakes, streams and drains. Water management in the context of technological progress in Indian agriculture is briefly dwelt upon in the short chapter 9. Economy in water use is not likely to be practised so long as it is not widely appreciated that it is a scarce resource whose tapping cost too is not low. Before long, water can become a truly binding constraint in sustaining agricultural development.

In chapter 10 we explore the issue of capacity utilisation in the case of small-scale irrigation works. Fascination for such works is quite strong but outside the Indian engineering circles, more so within the environmental groups where a sort of romantic view about 'small is beautiful' pervades. The limited objective is to dispel the myth of full capacity utilisation in the case of minor irrigation works. The investigation has been carried out with the help of a fresh set of data gathered through a census of minor irrigation works.

Leaving aside the rather ticklish issue of measuring correctly irrigation capacity itself, the incidence of unutilised capacity does exist also in minor irrigation segment of Indian irrigation sector. That is to say, this problem is not something unique to Indian large scale irrigation works, which have been much berated on this count. Somewhere between 7 and 17 per cent of the total minor irrigation capacity remained underutilised during 1986-87, the reference year for the census of minor irrigation. This picture is highly aggregative indeed, and could vary considerably from state to state, as also by type of minor irrigation. The same picture for the state of Gujarat was very dismal, with the rate of underutilisation of minor irrigation capacity lying somewhere in-between 45 and 63 per cent. This was because of serious constraints on the supply side, not on the demand side - the latter kind of constraints are equally germane in the case of state-managed, large-scale irrigation works. That is to say, because of severe shortfall in natural precipitation during 1986-87, there was acute paucity of water availability in dugwells, small streams and small reservoirs. This paucity of water was so acute that as many as half the minor irrigation works in the state could not be used at all by the farmers, precisely at a time when the need for irrigation was utmost owing to the state's rainfall recording barely half its normal level which in itself is naturally on the low side. This extremely high vulnerability to drought of minor irrigation is not so well recognised by the lobbyists of the minor irrigation cause.

Within the minor irrigation segment, privately owned tubewells reveal a performance that truly goes well with the lustrous image of small-scale irrigation. Hardly one per cent of such tubewells were found to be out of use during the survey year — the corresponding percentage for dugwells was 20, and for surface flow irrigation works (mainly tanks) was 12. For the drought-affected state of Gujarat these very percentages stood at much higher levels: 55 per cent for dugwells, 68 per cent for surface flow irrigation works, and 6 to 14 per cent for private tubewells. Again, the capacity of these tubewells was, more or less, fully utilised. But, then, tubewell irrigation cannot be deemed synonymous with minor irrigation.

In Indian geological conditions, hardly one-third of our land is of non-consolidated (i.e., non-rocky) formations in which alone tubewells can be effectively installed. For our rest of the land mass dugwells have to be installed if groundwater is to be tapped for irrigation purpose - here and there some bore holes, which are considered as tubewells in local parlance, have indeed come up, but far more for meeting low-level drinking water rather than irrigation needs. The extent of unutilised capacity in the case of dugwells averaged 23-28 per cent, quite comparable to that of small-scale surface water based irrigation works (28-32 per cent in the case of flow works, and 18-31 per cent in the case of lift irrigation).

Tehri dam project is in doldrums. The rub of the Tehri dam issue is identified in chapter 11, entitled 'What is Wrong with Tehri Dam'? The critical matter here is one of seismic hazard on which, unfortunately, expert opinion is sharply divided. A possible way out is suggested for the decision makers at the highest level.

In the case of the Sardar Sarovar Project, the danger of waterlogging developing within its command has been widely expressed by anti-big dam lobby. How the innovative measure of conjunctive use of ground and surface waters is likely to keep waterlogging at abeyance is dwelt upon in chapter 12, the last chapter of part I.

Reviews of books pertaining to the subject of water resource development for irrigation constitute a useful source material on irrigation literature. The author, who has done many reviews of studies and reports for various journals, picks up some of these, with a view to providing a critical appreciation of his own of such works which tend to be quoted widely. We begin with the short report by the late Mrs. Krishna Bharadwaj who was invited by the Indian Council of Social Science Research (ICSSR) to carry out the second survey of research on irrigation economics in India.

The weaknesses of this survey report are highlighted in chapter 13. There is little merit in the survey report as its author was not well-equipped to do justice to the task entrusted to her by the ICSSR.

The Centre for Science and Environment, New Delhi, brings out periodically Citizens' Report on the State of India's Environment. In its third report released in 1992, the CSE picked up the theme of floods in India and brought out its investigative document entitled *Floods, Flood Plains and Environmental Myths.* This author's critique of this rather controversial report is presented in chapter 14. The flood proofing in the Himalayan basin cannot be achieved on the same surer footing as that of drought proofing of drought prone regions with the aid of irrigation works. Yet, some misgivings loosely expressed in this report about the role of big dams in containing flood damage need to be taken with due caution. Why big dams fail to eliminate the flood menace needs to be understood more fully than the way it is analysed in this report.

INTACH, another Delhi-based organisation, has evinced keen interest in the big dam issue, and carried out two book-length evaluative studies on Tehri and Narmada dams. Our reactions to these studies are presented in chapters 15 and 16.

In chapter 15 first is examined Vijay Paranjpye's cost-benefit computations of Tehri project, duly underlining his grave errors in this area. Next some observations are made on the use of rate of return criterion employed by Indian Planning Commission in judging the desirability of power projects. It is suggested that time is now ripe for abandoning this narrow criterion and use instead the wider cost-benefit approach, as is used for clearing irrigation projects. The vital issue of seismic hazard posed by this project is already taken up for comment in chapter 11.

The INTACH evaluation study of the Narmada dams, prepared by a team of investigators under the overall leadership of Vijay Paranjpye, has been widely noted and commented upon. In chapter 16 a comprehensive review of the study is offered. Among other things it is brought out that surface lift irrigation, suggested as one of several alternatives to the SSP, has its own weaknesses which are brought home by looking at the success stories in this regard from the

Panchmahals district of Gujarat state. Why the INTACH study did not dwell on the issue of optimum height of the Narmada dams is touched upon. This issue, alongwith the question of volume of flow in the Narmada river, is touched upon in chapter 20, whose section I is an attempt at looking afresh at the reminiscences of late Kanwar Sain, the doyen of irrigation planners in the post-Independence period.

Benefit-cost analysis of investment projects is a fascinating subject. Despite there being great refinements in its methodology over the last two decades or so, faith in the veracity of BC ratios has dimmed over the years. That project promoters should overproject the BC ratio for their pet projects is not as disturbing as when independent project evaluators indulge in subtle manipulations, either with a view to killing an otherwise viable project, or making its BC ratio too rosy. In chapter 17 we look into two such contrary evaluations of the controversial Narmada dam (Sardar Sarovar Project) by the Tata Economic Consultancy and Vijay Pranajpye.

On the whole, the water bounty of India is good, more so in comparison to very many countries of the world. The principal drawback with our water bounty is its acute spatial (as well as temporal) unevenness. In chapter 18 we look at the problems of water resource management in north western India, a low rainfall region of the country. No wonder, there is great wrangling on water sharing of common rivers among the states of this region, notably between Punjab and Haryana both of which have witnessed green revolution. The bitterness between these two states has been accentuated by the phenomenal rise in rice cultivation for which great quantities of irrigation water are needed.

Water, being a complex resource, is well suited for multidisciplinary approach, calls for which are invariably made at congregations of water experts. It is now thus widely perceived that economists and other social scientists can play a useful role - alongwith engineers, geologists, soil physicists, hydrologists, agronomists, etc. in water planning and development.

In the first section of chapter 19 we report on a multi-disciplinary study from the Punjab Agricultural University. The study focusses on the demand and supply sides of irrigation water in the state of Punjab. Water imbalances for various agro-climatic regions of the state are computed. How much groundwater depletion occurs as a result of these imbalances is worked out, and the estimates checked with ground reality. An interesting contribution of this study is to draw attention to gross and net groundwater withdrawals. In the case of paddy the authors claim that the gap between gross and net irrigation (withdrawal) is high, with as much as two-thirds of tubewell water percolating back to groundwater table.

In the second section of this chapter we offer some glimpses from a well-documented book on water resources on a global canvass. This should serve as a good backdrop to our own problems in water resources development. For example, flood control is quite an intractable problem all over the world. Likewise, that afforestation of river catchments adds to water flows is shown to be of questionable veracity.

In the concluding chapter 20, entitled 'Two Great Stories', we first review the book of reminiscences written by India's most distinguished engineer of the post-Independence era. His views on ideal height of a dam like Sardar Sarovar Project merit attention and high praise. In the second section we review a book on the giant Hoover Dam of the United States which metamorphosed the Californian economy. The challenging task of taming a wild river in inhospitable environs is poignantly brought alive in this highly readable book by Joseph E. Stevens.

CHAPTER 2

TALL OR SMALL DAMS: THEIR STRENGTHS AND WEAKNESSES*

Irrigation and power development through the construction of big dams has been strongly questioned during the recent years. Looking at their demerits, the critics have been urging the Indian planners not to go in for such dams and instead explore alternative schemes for meeting the nation's pressing needs of irrigation and power. To generate power from our water resources, run-of-the-river schemes and micro hydel projects have been commended to the planners. Likewise, for meeting irrigation needs, construction of small dams, farm ponds, and small-scale lift irrigation schemes based on both surface water bodies and groundwater aquifers, have been fervently offered as alternatives.[1]

The suggested alternatives have not really appealed to our water planners. Initially, engineers in the upper echelons of water planning process were quite dismissive in their attitude, and to some extent this could be justified or defended on the plea that some of the very vocal critics lacked adequate understanding of the extremely complex nature of water resource. To illustrate this point with a concrete example, one known votary of groundwater irrigation cause has had the erroneous perception that India has enough groundwater

---

* Originally prepared for Economic and Political Weekly. Owing to delay in publication by EPW, it was published in *Facts For You*, February, 1992, without notes and Appendix.

to sustain a thriving irrigated farming, without any need for huge investments in canals and big dams.[2] No wonder, he did not carry any conviction with water planners, notwithstanding his signal contribution in drawing attention of the nation to the numerous ills of canal irrigation in India. Mercifully, well irrigation versus canal irrigation is no more a live issue, except for some controversy about the comparative cost-effectiveness of these two modes of irrigation from the larger social angle. The central issue is now one of tapping our river waters through large or small dams. It was primarily to sort out this issue that a symposium on 'Large Dams vs. Small Dams: Socio-Environmental and Techno-economic Assessment' was held in New Delhi on December 2, 1991 under the auspices of the Central Board of Irrigation and Power (CBIP) and the Sardar Sarovar Narmada Nigam Limited (SSNN).[3]

It was purportedly the first of a series of such symposia aimed at informing or educating the big dam critics about why the option of small dams (below 15 metre height) is actually no alternative but a complement to large dams in any integrated water planning for a river basin as a whole. This grand aim was little fulfilled because few of the critics turned up at the meeting, and one does not find even a single paper by any one of them among the two volumes of papers made available to the participants at the venue of the symposium. This absence was perfunctorily regretted by the organisers in the opening remarks. One could not readily ascertain why the critics predominantly stayed away. One of them, present in the hall, took the podium to inform us how he received the intimation only three days earlier.[4]

The proceedings became essentially one-sided, with an occasional counterpoint from the rostrum. While one was impressed by the humble postures in the defence of big dams, the onesidedness was marred by the overhang of the SSNN on the entire symposium. The engineers associated with it accounted for 12 out of the 26 papers read at the symposium, with the Theme Paper also from a consultant engineer to the SSNN whose chairman presided also over the opening, non-technical session. Since the rest of the papers were also largely from Gujarat state, it appeared at times as if the SSNN had hijacked the symposium forum to project its own case on the controversial Sardar Sarovar Project. In point of fact, the cited examples in rebuttal of critics' contentions or suggestions were mainly drawn from the state of Gujarat.

There is no intention to give here a complete account of what transpired at the symposium. Readers interested in the papers (see Appendix) should procure these from the CBIP. These are in two volumes : Volume I is the Theme Paper by J.F. Mistry and Volume II carries the 25 contributed papers.[5] What follows is a short account of some salient points that struck this writer, who too has been concerned with the big dam controversy.

Seismic Hazard

Dr. Jai Krishna, the eminent earthquake engineer, made four main points. First, a tall dam attracts smaller forces due to earthquakes than a small dam. Dr. T. Ramamurthy of IIT, Delhi, endorsed this point with an eloquent analogy of an adult vis-a-vis a 4-year child better withstanding a given blow. Second, an earthquake is an oscillating force, not unidirectional, and a rock fill dam can better cope with it, through the phenomenon of slumping. Three, the reservoir-induced seismicity (RIS) is seldom more than 4 on the Richter scale. One speaker informed the house that of the 11,000 big dams in the world (out of at least 36,000 such dams existing in the world) for which seismic records are available, less than one per cent report RIS. Fourth, ground acceleration, a coefficient of earth's gravity 'g', tends to taper off after an earthquake on the Richter scale rises above 7. So, one should not 'extrapolate peak ground acceleration on an exponential basis from the values for earthquakes of magnitude less than 7, as is being erroneously done by critics of the Tehri dam, Dr. Jai Krishna said.

Sunil K. Roy, an environmental critic of big dams (especially the Tehri dam), pointed out he never cast any doubts on the engineers' ability to build earthquake-proof dams. His apprehension was on another count, namely, toppling over of the fragile Himalayan hillsides into the reservoir due to an earthquake, leading to a dam break.[6] K.N. Srivastava of the Geological Survey of India, argued, at the fag end of the symposium, that the Himalayan rivers keep on cutting through their beds, leading to continuous slips from the highly slopy hillsides so formed. Whereas afforestation of such hillsides would aggravate the phenomenon of slips (due to extra load of the trees), the major dams would help in mitigating such phenomenon, the reservoir offering a sort of "toe support" to the hillsides.

Siltation of Reservoirs

Mr. Srivastava, while discussing the problem of siltation of reservoirs, made following observations, based mainly on investigations in the Bhakra reservoir area. First, the formation of a lake running into miles along the river (58 km. in the case of Bhakra's Govind Sagar lake) slows down the inflow of silt into the main dam area, and thus fears of reservoirs becoming ultimately inoperational are highly exaggerated. This reduction in inflow of silt is because of the following two reasons : (1) As a result of the above-mentioned "toe support", the number of slips is greatly reduced (from 150 in 1956 to 40 in 1977-78 in the Bhakra case), and (2) there is added formation of deltaic buildup or "check dams" on the confluence points of the tributaries into the reservoir. The Central Water Commission (CWC) studies published recently, pointed out some speakers, also underscore that high siltation rates observed during the first 15-20 years of a dam get reduced later on. But the imperative of catchment treatment, through watershed management programmes, was not denied.[7]

Large vs. Small Dams

On the much-exciting issue of large versus small dams, speaker after speaker (and all the paper writers) at the symposium took the harmonious standpoint, namely, both kinds of dams have their due place in fuller exploitation of our water resources, irrespective of their comparative merits and demerits. There was only one writer, J.S.R. Mohan Rao (retired chief engineer), who pleaded, albeit mildly in his oral presentation, for not so mega or giant dams as are being currently conceived or planned in the country.[8] "Wherever two or more relatively less larger dams are feasible at reasonable costs in place of one much larger dam, construction of such unduly and unnecessarily large dams shall be avoided, sacrificing facilities and economies involved in such single giant dams to certain extents for the sake of reducing or minimising the environmental impacts." It may be clarified here that in Mohan Rao's scheme of things the environmental impacts include the "submergence of precious lands and failure consequences" but possibly not the very serious and intractable relocation and rehabilitation (R & R) problems of dam oustees. Anyway, some scaling down of the height of a mega dam does substantially reduce, by implication, the magnitude of these problems of rehabilitation and relocation of the dam affected persons.[9] The proponents of the big dams at the symposium did not reveal any deep felt appreciation of these two aspects of dam building in today's situation, unlike 100 years ago, of submerged areas being well-settled ones.

Three following perceptions or propositions emerged from the symposium :

(1) Large dams, which impound large river flows, cannot be technically replaced by a series of small dams. At such points or dam sites the river flows become too large for impoundment by small dams which are feasible on small rivulets and streams, mainly encountered in small tributaries and in the upper reaches of big rivers. In a way, small dams in the upper reaches and big dams and barrages elsewhere in a river basin are feasible.[10]

(2) Dams in a river basin cannot be raised everywhere. In other words, the dam sites are limited by nature, and particularly scarce for building very large dams. That is why

on the few good dam sites available in a river basin with monsoonal flows big reservoir-based storage of such flows (for use later in the year) becomes necessary. Even when enough storage sites do exist, both the construction costs and the implied costs of land and forest submergence from a number of less large or medium or small dams (of equivalent storage to one given big dam storage) would inherently be substantially more. (Theoretically, according to Dr. Jai Krishna, submerged area rises as a square of the height of a dam. So, 64 dams of 1/8 H height are needed to replace one dam of height H, so as to keep the submergence at the same level).[11] Two concrete evidences were cited on this matter. One pertains to a CWC investigation in the Mahanadi basin (Orissa), which revealed that replacing the proposed big Girna dam (storage = 603 million m^3) by a scaled down or smaller Girna dam (storage = 185 Mm^3) and 8 other smaller storage works (combined capacity = 603-185 = 418 Mm^3) would prove, on the *rough reckoning,* 150 per cent costlier in capital cost and 60 per cent more land submerging (not to mention greater losses incurred in evaporation (50-60 per cent more) from larger waterspread and lower power generation because of reduced 'head' of the same storage of water). The second example is about the investigative effort to replace one big Heran (Haran) dam in the lower reaches of a river in Saurashtra (Gujarat state) by six smaller dams (not of exactly comparable storage) to be built in the upper reaches (inhabited by tribals) revealed the following comparative picture of these two options :

S.No.	*Item*	*Single dam option*	*Six small dams option*
1.	Gross storage (Mm^3)	380	230(0.61)
2.	Utilisable storage (Mm^3)	296	215(0.73)
3.	Irrigation capacity (ha)	39,500	28,700(0.73)
4.	Submergence:		
	(a) gross area (ha)	3,503	3,650(1.04)
	(b) culturable area (ha)	2,860	2,640(0.92)

(c) complete villages (nos)	12	5(0.42)
(d) partially submerged villages (nos)	8	16(2.00)
(e) affected population (nos)	8,270	10,300(1.25)
5. Capital cost (Rs. crores)	19.70	25.48(1.29)

Source : Prepared from data in J.F. Mistry's Theme Paper.
Note : Figures in parentheses indicate small dams as a multiple of single dam.

(3) Irrigation capacity of small dams during drought years is highly suspect in comparison to that of big dams, a point that was underlined by several paper writers/speakers at the symposium.[12] The vulnerability of a small dam during drought can be illustrated with data from one symposium paper by P.K. Jindal *et.al.*, on one small earthen dam at village Karoran in the Kandi area of Punjab, constructed by the Punjab Agricultural University under its 'Operational Research Programme'. This dam received during the drought of 1987 (rainfall fell steeply from the normal level of 935 mm to 314 mm) an inflow of only 181.5 ha.-cm. (*i.e.*, acre-inches), which was about 68 per cent below the gross storage of 570 ha.-cm. of the dam reservoir — the corresponding reduction in irrigated area is not indicated in the paper.

In years of heavy rainfall (or when a rainstorm occurs), the probability of breaching of a small dam (normally not having adequate investment in its surplussing or spillway system) is high, thereby damaging fields and farm assets in the command area — when the tanks are located in a series on a given stream, there is a 'cascading effect', *i.e.*, tanks breach one after the other. To restore such breaches entails substantial capital costs which are not fully reckoned with by those who view small dams as a low cost option *vis-a-vis* large dams.

On Development Model

Sunil Roy, while enumerating a number of points of criticism about large dams policy (some totally misplaced or misperceived, *e.g.*, new canal capacity created every year is offset wholly by new areas lost due to waterlogging-salinity),[13] underlined the urgent need for developmental work on the upstream side of a dam, a hitherto undoubtedly neglected thing in Indian developmental planning which is geared to meeting the rising needs of towns and plains on the downstream side of a dam. In a related comment Ramaswamy Iyer, who earlier offered a balanced view on the dam controversy in *EPW* (September 1989 Review of Agriculture) once again drew attention of the participants that the criticism of big dams is part of a larger criticism of the ongoing developmental planning and should not be narrowly viewed simply as an issue between large and small dams. Here I would like to recall how Sundar Lal Bahuguna, the veteran opposer of the Tehri dam, reacted excitedly when in a seminar on large dams for hydel power I suggested that a part of such power be earmarked exclusively for use of the upstream people who mainly bear the social costs of dam building. He said he would withdraw his opposition to the dam if one-fifth of power generated from the Tehri dam is given free to upstream residents (for use in waterlifting for irrigation from the Tehri reservoir, operating cableways across the reservoir, etc.) This reaction signifies the urgent need for development activity for the benefit of people on the upstream side of the proposed big dams in India. Certainly, this is not to be done by the dam builders but by the Yojana Bhavan and the planning departments of the state governments.[14]

Concluding Remarks

One hopes that next time the CBIP (or CWC or any other agency) organises a symposium (a workshop would be better) on dams it must ensure adequate participation by the dam critics also. Besides timely notices, some of the known critics ought to be coaxed and cajoled into writing papers and also come to the meet. There is no doubt that the big dam lobby is very belatedly offering to inform us in an open forum their side of the story. Still, the opportunity should be grabbed. Among other things, such a get-together may make the promoters of mega dams realise how these are ill-suited in the present socio-political environs and why somewhat less tall dams should be considered on the precious few dams sites available in our river basins. At the same time, the other side might show a better appreciation of the harsh limits of the alternatives being suggested by them. While the promoters are being overdriven by the compulsions of expanding the irrigation base of the Indian agriculture and the electricity supply for the economy as a whole,[15] the opposers are overrating the potentiality of the alternatives contemplated by them to achieve the same twin-goal. Both sides badly need education about the rival's standpoint in open fora across the table (not in the press where one cannot conveniently retract and recant).

NOTES

1. The need for expanding irrigation at the secular rate of around three per cent per annum is also questioned on the ground that dryland technologies too can play an ample role in meeting our growing needs of food, fibre and fodder.
2. For one, he could not distinguish between stock and flow dimensions of groundwater availability. For another, he could neither realise that a good deal of groundwater is itself of canal origin in the first place, nor appreciate duly the imperative of conjunctive water use in water planning.
3. While the CBIP was listed as the organisers of this symposium, the SSNN was billed as the co-sponsorer in the official papers. The writer gathered that a major part of the symposium costs on account of food and convention hall charges was borne by the SSNN.
4. While cataloguing the criticism of the ongoing planning emphasis on big dams, he urged the organisers to circulate to the participants his own paper, which was duly done. At a later stage in the day, we were informed by that one environmentalist had urged the organisers to hold one next meet where a single case history of one large dam was probed holistically in all its plus and minus aspects.
5. The General Reports of the three reporteurs on the papers for the three Technical Sessions, alongwith a List of Delegates

with adresses, all available in printed form, may also be sought. But the reader should beware of very many printing goofs, especially in the excellent Theme Paper. Hopefully, the CBIP would bring out before long some account based on the oral presentations made at the symposium, as also an errata sheet.

6. This concern was expressed to me during coffee break by Prof. Subhash Chander of IIT, Delhi, a renowned real-time, flood forecaster - he said this was how the recent dam burst in Italy occurred. He thinks that leaving a couple of feet unfilled in a reservoir could prevent a dam burst resulting from hillside toppling into a reservoir.
7. Soil conservation experts sometimes insist here upon two rather unrealistic points. First "no dam should be built till the catchment has been treated with soil conservation including grass land and forestry till it yields no more than 5 hectare metres of silt per 100 square km per year (that is to say, 5 mm of soil erosion per year from each hectare of catchment area). Till then, even if a site is good from geology point of view, it should remain a taboo". (Personal communication from Dr. J.S. Bali, the leading soil conservation expert of the country; within parenthesis amplification added by this writer). Second, the entire cost for this treatment ought to be debited to the dam account.
8. His short paper merits attention for many other sensible points.
9. How a 10 per cent reduction in dam height reduces the extent of submerged area (as well as storage capacity) for selected dams is shown by K.C. Thomas in his paper included in this writer's edited books on big dams (1990).
10. A barrage is more a device for impeding than for impounding a river flow so as to raise the surface water level in a river for establishing a diversion canal, or for pumping water for civic uses.
11. He also maintains: "for every site on a river there is only one optimum height of a dam for maximum benefits and minimum environmental changes. Therefore, there is no point in this controversy".
12. This arises because of the low probability of simultaneous occurrence of severe drought in all the tributaries feeding a reservoir behind a large dam.
13, Such exaggerations are also found in the writings of votaries of large dams who deliberately understate the ratio of submerged area of benefitted command area for large irrigation dams and

simultaneously overplay the same ratio for small dams — one speaker mentioned a ratio of one in the latter case. (In the first Kanwar Sain Memorial Lecture of 1990, the distinguished speaker mentioned a ratio of 200 times of that for large dams. When I objected to it afterwards, he said he was visualising farm ponds as the alternative as per the suggestions put forth by the Narmada Bachao Andolan. For small dams and rural ponds together, he still places the submergence ratio "10 to 15 times larger"). In this connection Ramaswamy Iyer put us wise as follows. "Let us not be content with making debating points. Those who argue against big dams may be wrong on some counts, and some of them may be polemical in their approach. The engineers may be equally polemical in their defence of large projects. What is important is to recognise the depth of the environmentalists' and the human rights activists' concerns; at least some of them are driven by a moral fervour. We must respect their concerns and address the issues involved".

14. At present, 12 per cent of the hydel power from central schemes is earmarked free for the state in which the scheme is located. The host state should in turn give this power share free to upstream areas.
15. The option of small dams alone drastically curtails the hydel power potential of our water resources, as this potential is directly proportional to height of a dam (and volume of live storage).

APPENDIX

LISTOFSYMPOSIUMPAPERS

S.No.	Title	Author
1.	Optimisation of Water Development and Management.	C.C.Patel
2.	Adequate and Timely Funding for Large Dam Projects.	Ashok Chawla
3.	Planning of Large Dams and Small Dams—Costs and Benefits and Techno-Economic Viability.	C.G.Desai
4.	Principles and Special Aspects of River Basin Planning.	I.M.Shah
5.	Approaches to Balanced Planning of Water Resources Projects-Large and Small Dams	J.S.R. Mohan
6.	Water Resources Planning & Development.	M.G.Raichur
7.	Environmental Planning in Relation to a Large Dam Project in India.	A.V.Gururaja
8.	Sustainable Development-Alternatives in Water Resources & Energy Sectors.	K.R.Datye
9.	Developing a Model for Resettlement and Rehabilitation.	Bhagyesh Jha
10.	Role of Major Dams in Water Resources Development.	R.B.Shah
11.	Large Dams-An Overview.	C.R.S. Pillai & K. Srinivasa Raju
12.	Role of Small Dams, not Alternative but Supplement to Large Dams.	N.B.Desai & N.K. Sonetha
13.	Large Dams Vs Small Dams-Is it really so?	D.J. Baxi
14.	Planning through Appraisal for Small Dams in Saurashtra Region.	U.D. Datir & P.K. Majumdar
15.	Narmada Valley Projects : What & Why?	P.A. Raj
16.	Effect of Siltation - Life of Reservior.	N. Ramaswamy B.J. Parmar
17.	Environmental Impact of Some Large Dams of Gujarat.	M.U. Purohit N.K.Sonetha K.G. Rathod
18.	Special Features of Sardar Sarovar Dam.	B.J. Parmar G.L. Java
19.	Performance Evaluation Parameters and Economy in Large anad Small Dams.	Piyush Parikh A.V. Shroff D.L. Shah

20.	Economic Necessity vis-a-vis Enviornmental Impact of Large Dams-A Case Study of Kangsabati Project, West Bengal.	N.R. Panda K. Chatterjee
21.	Geotechnical and Seismic Considerations in the Design of Large Dam.	D.M. Pancholi U.D. Datir
22.	Large Dam-Reservoir Induced Seismicity.	G.L. Java
23.	Performance Evaluation of Mini Dams in the Kandi Area of Punjab State-A Case Study.	P.K. Jindal B.N. Rao N.S. Sur
24.	Large Dams vs Small Dams.	D.V. Varshney
25.	Evaluation of Intangible Benefits of Water Resources Projects.	M.K. Sharma
26.	Theme Paper.	J.F. Mistry
27.	Environmental Impact Assessment for River Valley Projects.	Sunil K. Roy

CHAPTER 3

ISSUES IN INDIAN WATER RESOURCE DEVELOPMENT*

This writeup is an attempt to recapitulate some of the salient points emerging from the four-day congregation on water held at Nagpur last year. The recapitulation is largely on the basis of notes taken by the author when the paper writers, rapporteurs, chairmen of several sessions, and chief guests made their presentations from the rostrum. As the two volumes containing the papers were not made available to the author in advance, these could be hardly read amidst a very tight schedule of sessions. Furthermore, the recapitulation is partial, and in this the author touches on points that struck him.

The first two days of the meet, namely, 5 and 6 February 1992, were earmarked for the Third National Water Convention, sponsored by the National Water Development Agency (NWDA) and co-organised by the Nagpur Centre of the Indian Water Resources Society (IWRS). The last two days, 7th and 8th February 1992, were devoted to the National Seminar on Large Reservoirs - Net Environmental Gain or Loss? organised solely by the IWRS (Nagpur).

1. Waterlogging/Salinity Issue

The problem of waterlogged, salinised and alkalinised lands in India figured in many presentations. The avowed critics of major irrigation works in general and big dams in particular presented high estimates of areas under such lands.

---

* First published in *Facts For You,* September, 1992.

More importantly, they tried, overtly or covertly, to link such land degradation, to the development of canal irrigation, without ever referring to other factors behind such degradation, namely, (1) the establishment of railways, roads, protective bunds along rivers, etc., (2) naturally waterlogged areas in high rainfall alluvial plains (including deltaic coastal regions), and (3) naturally salinised areas in the arid western India and the 'usar' lands of Central and East Uttar Pradesh - over a million ha. area in U.P. is naturally 'usar'.

For example, Kisan Mehta (who said he had earlier helped in stalling the Silent Valley Hydel Project of Kerala) mentioned that the degraded lands of the above two categories in India presently account for an area somewhere in the range of 18-25 million ha. Taking the figure of total irrigated area in the country to be in the range of 48-58 million ha., he observed that over two-fifths of the land benefitted by irrigation has been degraded. In view of the widely-held view that only big canal irrigation, and not minor irrigation, can cause land degradation, Mehta could not see the absurdity of the numbers he chose for presentation. As nearly two-fifths of Indian irrigation is from canals, what he was trying to drive at, consciously or unconsciously, was that canals do as much damage to land resource as to raising their productivity. (A variety of this proposition, aired occasionally in India in environmental circles, is that no net expansion in irrigated acreage occurs because land getting waterlogged/salinised every year matches new land area brought under irrigation every year through newer canals, a phenomenon of the Middle East irrigated agriculture).

Pro-dam speakers, mainly Indian irrigation engineers, tried to underscore two points on the issue under discussion. One, the land degradation in question arises also from several factors other than canal irrigation development. Two, statistics of waterlogged/salinised land within selected canal commands, on the whole, do not, reveal any alarming picture, more so when such areas are viewed in proportion to the irrigation potential of the canals. M.V Bhave, a chief engineer of Maharashtra, pointed out that a study of 21 major canal commands, having an aggregate command area of over 1.1. million ha. in the state, revealed waterlogging/salinity in less than 2 per cent of the total command area. Likewise, on the Tawa Project in Madhya Pradesh, widely berated as having badly waterlogged command by the critics of the Narmada dams, more than one engineer (notably Mahodhaya, a retired SE of M.P., and Debnath, Executive Member, Narmada Control Authority) reported that now the problem has disappeared for all practical purposes: barely 400 ha. area was waterlogged as against an irrigated command area of over 1.5 lakh ha. (A like claim is made by the Irrigation Department of U.P. for the other badly criticised canal system, namely, the Sarda Sahayak - but not at this meet).

The aforesaid contrariness in the revelations underlies the imperative of unearthing two things: (a) the reliability of the agency/agent doling out the estimates about waterlogging/salinity, and (b) the definitional aspects of the phenomenon. More importantly, we have to distinguish between areas *visibly* waterlogged and areas waterlogged *in the crop root zone only*, as also between areas (i) *wholly* waterlogged, (ii) *partially* waterlogged (i.e., when water table has intruded into the lower parts of the crop root zone), (iii) *seasonally* waterlogged (say, in the main wet season of the year but fit for cultivation in the dry season), and (iv) *likely to be waterlogged in the near future.* Otherwise, we can get an erroneous picture of land degradation due to waterlogging. Let me concretise this point with an example. The widely quoted first Citizen's Report on Environment, released by the Centre for Science and Environment, New Delhi, expressed an apprehension that half the canal-irrigated area was waterlogged/salinised. But a check with the cited statistics reveals that the affected area in question is *inclusive of area likely to adversely affected in the near future.* Likewise, the question of additivity between waterlogged and salinised areas is of doubtful veracity, as the same area tends to figure both as salinised as well as waterlogged.

2. Risk of Earthquake Disaster

Reservoir-induced seismicity (RIS) was discussed by many speakers. Three noteworthy points in this regard need be mentioned here. First, RIS phenomenon is not inevitable in the case of every reservoir. Guha (School of Environmental Sciences, Pune) reported that there were only 120 cases of RIS for the whole world. M.V. Bhave said that RIS in India was reported from only five out of 3634 reservoirs. At the global level, Tandale recalled that Murty reported 0.67 per cent cases of RIS for 14,000 lakes in the world. Such low percentages of RIS are somewhat misleading. If only truly large reservoirs are kept in the reckoning, the percentage incidence of RIS would be much higher than that portrayed by the speakers.

Second, Guha said it is not very meaningful to talk of RIS threat in the case of the Himalayan dams where natural seismicity of a high order (above 8 on the Richter scale) can occur - RIS is usually of intensity less than 4 on the Richter scale.

Third, one earth scientist (geologist in plain language) was of the view that underlying tectonic disturbances (sliding movements of the earth's plates) are the basic cause of natural earthquakes. As and when these occur in the neighbourhood of a big reservoir, these tend to get inappropriately dubbed as RIS. (There was one speaker who took the unusual view that the Koyna quake, of intensity above 5 on the Richter scale, was not of the RIS category). He gave two amusing analogies to convey his particular viewpoint. One was about the firing of a gun: the simple act of pressing the trigger of a gun cannot be deemed to be the basic cause of the havoc wrought by the resultant gunfire. The second one was about the crashing of a tree branch, already broken from inside due to some other cause, when a flying crow alights on it for a perch: crow's perching *per se* cannot be deemed to be the cause of the falling down of the branch.

3. Relevance of International Norms

Z. Hasan, Director General, NWDA, argued for major reservoirs, citing cases in the USA where the storage capacity was three times the mean annual flow in a river, while we are not attempting storage of even 50 per cent of the flow in a river. He was weakly countered by a delegate, that let us not bring in what another country like the USA does.

Dr. Dabholkar (Sri Ram Institute of Industrial Research)

made some pertinent observations, especially for the consideration of our environmentalists who interact with their western counterparts. The core of his presentation concerned the issue of norms or standards relevant for our society in the realm of environment, medicine, public health, etc. He first took the example of municipal water supply in India, say, in Delhi whose quality is way below that in the west, say, in Berlin. Though it is surely not safe drinking water for the western visitor to the capital who therefore does not imbibe it, Dr. Dabholkar wanted that even such lower quality water need to be made available first in all the countryside before we should invest in its quality improvement in municipal areas to the safe limits prescribed in the west. Another issue of standards is the case of withdrawal a decade ago of Maxoform, an effective and cheap anti-dysentry drug, from the Indian market because it was found to cause death one in a million cases in the USA. He said he is informed by his socially concerned physician friends in India that the non-availability of such a low-cost drug has raised mortality from dysentry in India.

4. Environmental Degradation in Narmada Basin

Dr. Afroz Ahmad, formerly a scientist with G.B. Pant Institute of Himalayan Environment and presently with the NCA, highlighted the adverse state of environment in the Narmada Basin and stressed the need for sustainable basin development. He informed that impacts of human activities on the environments have caused imbalance in the equilibrium of environmentally sensitive Narmada Basin. He pointed out important factors like population pressure, migration and settlements, unplanned land uses, agricultural expansion, timber, fuel and fodder demand, and overgrazing which have accelerated ecological degradation. He emphasized that the Narmada basin with its high biodiversity and rich genetic resources (thick tropical forests of moist to dry deciduous trees) two decades ago is now severely degraded, having slopes with bare looks and no soil to sustain plant growth.

He underlined the desertification in various districts of Jhabua, Dhar, Khargone and Khandwa of the Narmada Basin, mainly because of combined pressure of both human and livestock population. He informed that shortage of fuel, fodder and drinking water in several tribal villages compels the women to walk long distances (10-12 km.) in difficult terrain to fetch water, collection of fuelwood and fodder. On the basis of existing state of the environment, he stressed the need for Sardar Sarovar Project and the development of other water resources projects in the basin for ensuring sustainability. He felt that the afforestation programme using ecological concept and sustainable development of irrigation would go a long way in reversing this desertification process through restoration of degraded lands in the basin. (He became the butt of bitter criticism from the anti-big dam proponents in the hall).

5. Questionable Perceptions About Irrigation

Dr. B.M. Bhatia, known for his economic researches on Indian famines, while chairing the first technical session on 5 February, caused a flutter in the hall by questioning the beneficial role of irrigation. Why? He did not discern any positive association between it and land productivity across districts of east India. Though he mildly reiterated this view on the concluding day also, adding that no positive association existed also between land productivity and fertiliser use—he still made a categorical plea in favour of major reservoirs. (He told me later that his observations on lack of relationship between irrigation/fertilisers and land productivity was based on an *impressionistic reading of districtwise data in Bhalla and Tyagi's book).*

Dr. Y.C. Arya, a scientist with the Water Technology Centre, IARI, Delhi, presented, as is his wont, some facts running counter to intuition and conventional wisdom. Three of his points were as follows. One, though irrigation sector absorbed 87 per cent of all the water consumed annually in India — rice alone accounting for two-fifths of total water use in agriculture — the "efficiency of water use" in agriculture is only one per cent. Two, though 0.08 ha.m. (800 m^3) of water is used, on the average, to produce one ton of agricultural produce, for sugarcane (fruits and vegetables included) this is far lower (0.02 ha.m.) than for foodgrains (0.16 ham). He argued for raising overall water productivity in agriculture through a shift in irrigated area allocation away from foodgrains to fruits and vegetables. Participants from Maharashtra, where attempts are being made to shift area away from sugarcane, expressed misgivings to me. Three, another shift he recommended was use of irrigation storage for dry season instead of kharif season cropping.

One can only conjecture where the rub of the matter is. For one, he may not be distinguishing appropriately between a ton of rice and a ton of sugarcane / vegetable / fruit. This is suggested by Purohit's paper, whereby he overblows the impact of irrigation development on agricultural output in the command of Ukai and Mahi projects in Gujarat (He is CE, SSP, and presented the same faulty tables earlier in the Delhi symposium on Large and Small Dams).

If due distinction is made, say, by referring to energy equivalents, sugarcane would no more be less water consuming *vis-a-vis* non-rice foodgrains. For another, his concept of efficiency is irrelevant if he is counting the water contained in the final plant body (before drying it) as an indicator of real use of applied water — he confirms this in a communication to me. Thirdly, his switchover from kharif to dry season irrigated farming needs further investigation — such a shift was first suggested by Shukla in the late sixties for M.P. agriculture.

6. Role of Afforestation

On the first day, during the first technical session, Mr. Mehrotra, a proponent of soil and water conservation, rightly lamented that only 3 per cent of the public sector outlay for Indian agriculture has been allotted to soil / water conservation. He presented evidence from some micro case studies of the tremendous benefits of afforestation in India, giving rise to so much of water conservation *in situ* that 79 per cent reduction in peak flow was observed. This huge attenuation in peak flow was contested by Mr. Padhye, retired CWC Chief and former Secretary of the Ministry of Water Resources, who said that if such high moderation in peak flow could be realised by having forests in the catchments, then there should not have been any flood in the Ganges in ancient times when the Himalayas did have dense forest cover. He wisely cautioned that one should not generalise from research experiences based on small streams onto large rivers. Mr. Mehrotra said that flood attenuating role of forests is much more valid for temperate than for tropical rainfall regions.

7. Losses and Leakages in Drinking Water

K.G. Dave, President, Indian Water Works Association and an authority on municipal water supply, said 25 to 45 per cent loss in municipal water conveyance (average 33%) is observed in India. He cautioned, while later presenting the paper by Vasavada, that statistics of municipal water consumption per capita are inclusive of losses in conveyance and, therefore, one should beware of using them in juxtaposition with norms of water requirements. This loss includes pilferage and unpaid supply but not significant losses on leakage from pipes / taps at the consumer end. He pleaded for (a) water metering , (b) less of public water standpoints, (c) a comprehensive water law (to prevent farmers unauthorisedly taking surface reservoir water meant for drinking purposes), and (d) toning up of the local bodies management skills.

8. Smaller Versus Bigger Dams

Z. Hasan concluded, on the basis of alternative options for diverting 664 m cm. of Kerala water to irrigate 87,500 ha. area in Tamil Nadu (plus incidental power generation), that. a combination of six smaller storages is inferior to a single large storage in terms of submergence and capital cost. By including one site (no. 4 of Aramputodu) having exceptionally high cost (Rs. 318 crores for a live storage of only 27 m cm.), the authors have tried to overblow the case against smaller dams. Incidentally, this paper shows that the rise in total submergence in smaller reservoirs is not all that high (much less than 60 per cent adumbrated by some CWC engineers on the basis of another, much quoted, hypothetical study from Hirakund basin in Orissa).

9. Sedimentation of Reservoirs

H.C. Bhatia, Irrigation Research Institute, Roorkee, presented a post-project appraisal of sedimentation of big reservoirs of India. On the basis of Ichari, Ram Ganga and Mata Tila reservoirs (all in U.P.), he found (a) the empirical formula for estimating the rate of sedimentation grossly understating the actual, observed rates during construction and after construction of reservoirs, and (b) the rate becomes constant after some time.

10. Native Methods of Water Management

Kisan Mehta, the veteran opponent of big dams, said that with indigenous methods of water management and farming rice yields of the order of 10 tons per ha have been documented for Tamil Nadu for the 18th century on lands under the control of temples. He wanted the revival of such practices, as an alternative to big dams, to meet India's pressing needs of foodgrains, to which this author had drawn attention in his keynote paper (reproduced here as chapter 5).

11. Micro Hydel Power

Kisan Mehta, as also Mohan Dharia (former Deputy Chairman, Planning Commission), wondered why we in India cannot go in for hydel power generation based on micro and run-of-the river schemes as has been achieved in Sweden and Japan. Dharia, of course, admitted that rainfall in Japan does occur throughout the year. From such evidence one may infer that snow caps might be serving the role of storages for the run-of-the-river schemes in the Scandinavian country.

12. Population Pressure and Poverty

Protecting our growing population from shortages of foodgrains by developing irrigation in general and major storages in particular was emphasized by more than one speaker, thus justifying environmental loss, if any. K. Mehta put forth the plea that poor people's lack of access to foodgrains today does not stem from food shortages but from other causes. Poverty as a pollutant/threat to environment was underlined by some speakers, to press home the imperative of development in India.

Concluding Remarks

Some concluding observations would be in order. First, the pro-bigdam participants outnumbered others by a big margin, though the difference was not as stark as in the Delhi symposium on dams three months earlier. The travel costs, as also lodging and boarding tab, were to be borne by the participants. This was not much of a hurdle for the engineers who could get their participation sponsored by their respective departments. This means that for ensuring less unequal participation by those who are opposed to big dam idea ways and means must be found by the organisers to defray their participation costs.

Second, I would like to comment on the need for modifying the seasonal pattern of our rivers through afforestation and various soil conservation works. While I accept this need for modifying the hydrograph of a river—whereby the peakedness is reduced and the degree of perenniality rises to cater to our summer-time water needs — we need to be realistic here in our expectations. Because of the monsoonal character of our precipitation (unlike the gentler rain of summer and snow precipitation of winter in Europe and North America), there are limits to flattening an Indian river's hydrograph. While we can certainly make a big river somewhat less big through afforestation and conservation works, we cannot make them run like a canal with uniform flow throughout the year, however effective be the attempt to detain peak flows in the upper hilly reaches of a big river. Therefore, man-made storage works on rivers are unavoidable if we do not wish the waters to flow down to the seas.

Third, besides a conjunctive use of river and groundwater, we need far more of conjunctive use of micro, mini, medium and major dams in our river valley projects. Small dams and check dams upstream of a big dam enhance the life of the big dam by containing the siltation process in the latter.

Fourth, I would like to end on a note of observations sent by Dr. Maria Saleth, an upcoming ecology economist (but not present at Nagpur), on the big dam debates in the country. He writes to me as follows:

"The development of a correct perspective essential for policy formulation is seriously hampered by an emotionally charged partisan tendency, not just between the groups on both sides of the issue but also between the partisan groups and those who try to bring some sanity by advancing a middle-way path. Since the issue has been deliberately graduated from economics to politics and economic facts and figures are used only to make a political point, any attempt to provide a rational approach to find a reasonable solution to the issue is viewed with suspicion and met with criticism from both groups. A case in point here is your suggestion of 'appropriately scaling down the dam height' to accommodate the genuine concerns of both the proponents and opponents of big dams".

Acknowledgements

I am truly grateful to those participants who were kind enough to react to the draft version of this write-up. In particular, I am grateful to Dr. Afroz Ahmad, Dr. Z. Hasan, Dr. B.M. Bhatia, Dr. Dabholkar, and Dr. Arya. Readers are cautioned, once again, not to treat it as a complete record of the proceedings of the four day meet at Nagpur.

CHAPTER 4

IRRIGATION IN THE EIGHTH PLAN — A CRITIQUE*

The final version of the Eighth Five Year Plan is now available. So, one can closely look over its contents pertaining to Indian irrigation. The proposed programme for this segment is of as much interest as is the planners' own progress report therein on the state of affairs in this vital segment of Indian agriculture sector. Let us begin first with a quick glance at the agenda for this segment for the next five years, 1992-93 to 1996-97.

Plan Programme

Investments in four categories of works, namely: (1) major and medium irrigation, (2) minor irrigation, (3) command area development (CAD), and (4) flood control and drainage works, constitute the irrigation segment of a Five Year Plan. At 1990-91 price level, the proposed investment outlay for these four categories amounts to about Rs. 32,500 crores.

This hefty sum would become still bigger if one reckons with (a) supporting investments (for operating electric pumpsets) of the order of Rs. 4,000 crores earmarked for rural electrification programme under the energy sector, and (b) huge investments in minor irrigation works, especially in wells, which take place on farmers' private account — the precise estimate is unknown, but it could be as high as the

---

* Abridged version published in *Facts For You*, November, 1992.

public sector outlay (about Rs. 6,000 crores) set aside* for minor irrigation. These investment statistics should reassure us that irrigation development continues to be the kingpin in planners'strategy for agricultural growth. These exceed the contemplated allocations for agriculture and allied activities (Rs. 22 thousand crores), and compare well with the corresponding allocations for rural development head (Rs. 34 thousand crores).[1]

As usual, major irrigation works account for a lion's share of the public sector investment cake set aside for irrigation segment whose breakup is as given below :

I. Major and medium irrigation	Rs. 22,414 crores
II Minor irrigation	Rs. 5,977* crores
III. Command area development	Rs. 2,510 crores
IV. Flood control	Rs. 1,623 crores
Total	Rs. 32,525 crores

* Excludes private and supporting investments on public account.

The principal outcome of the above investments would be expansion of irrigation capacity of the nation. While by definition no increase in irrigation capacity can occur from investments meant for flood control and the CAD programme, some of the investments on irrigation proper also, especially under major and medium irrigation head, would be of replacement type (euphemistically called 'stabilisation' or 'modernisation' works in the plan parlance), without any resultant increase in irrigation potential as such. No less importantly, some of the capacity in major and medium irrigation works will materialize beyond the Eighth Plan time horizon.

In all, new irrigation capacity addition of the order of 15 million hectares (m.ha.) is anticipated by the end of the Plan. Over two-thirds of this additional capacity would be from minor irrigation works, for which a good deal of the investment funds have to come from farmers' own account. More specifically, irrigation capacity for 10.71 mha of crop area is envisaged from minor irrigation works, largely from dugwells and tubewells, though separate breakup of minor irrigation capacity is not given in the Plan document. The anticipated contribution from major and medium irrigation works is placed at about 5.09 m.ha.

New irrigation capacity takes some time before it is fully utilised. Therefore, actual expansion in irrigated area tends to lag behind the creation of new capacity. In view of this, the Plan anticipation is that actual utilisation of new capacity would be of the order of 13.6 million ha: 9.36 m.ha. from minor irrigation, and 4.25 m.ha. from major and medium irrigation. Thus irrigation capacity worth two m.ha. of crop area would remain unutilised at the end of the 8th Plan period. This underutilisation will be witnessed in both categories of irrigation works: 0.84 million ha. in major and medium irrigation works, and about 1.35 m.ha. in minor irrigation works.

Adequacy and Realism

Among many pertinent questions, two pertain to the adequacy and the realism of targets of the proposed programme for irrigation. The central objective of irrigation development is one of steady expansion in farm output, especially of foodgrains, so as to meet the rising requirements of a growing population. Elasticity of foodgrains output w.r.t. expansion in irrigated area being unity, let us see how much per cent expansion in irrigated area is being planned for during the 8th Plan. An addition of 13.60 million ha., over a level of 75.60 m.ha. *supposedly* achieved by the beginning of the 8th Plan (70.89 m.ha. achieved by the end of 7th Plan plus 4.81 m.ha. achieved during two years, 1990-91 and 1991-92, which have elapsed between the end of 7th and the beginning of 8th plan), means almost 18 percent expansion in irrigated area over the 8th Plan period. If grain output expansion of the same percentage order materialises, it should suffice for meeting our domestic demand, which may grow by about 10 to 11 percent on account of simple population growth and by another 6 percent or so on account of per capita income growth.

As for realism, it is not possible to offer any categorical answer to that question. What is likely to be achieved of the proposed targets of irrigation expansion depends on several factors. Here, past achievements in achieving targets, especially in the most recent years, are of considerable relevance, though past need not repeat itself in its entirety in the future. It is here that the planners have made our task somewhat more difficult. For some unknown reason, the achievements in the Seventh Plan are not appraised in the context of original or even revised targets. All we are informed in this Plan document is the following, namely, past addition to irrigation potential from the major and medium works has "been between two to three million hectares per five year plan with the exception of Second Plan (1.05 m.ha.) and Fifth Plan (4.02 m.ha.)". Even such a meagre but comparable assessment has not been made in the Plan report about minor irrigation.

Large Scale Irrigation

Two observations on the above quote from the Eighth Plan report are necessary. First, it is not correct to state that potential created from major and medium irrigation works during the Second Five Year Plan was of the order of one mha only. The correct figure is double this level, that is, about 2.14 m.ha. (14.33 - 12.19 vide Table 2 on p. 57 of Volume II). Second, the corresponding achievement during the last Five Year Plan (1985-90) was quite low, namely, 1.51 m.ha. only as per the Planning Commission's own data in respect of created irrigation potential for the end of the Sixth and Seventh Plan periods. In view of this dismal performance against a target figure of 2.9 m.ha., one may be tempted to take not a very sanguine view of the proposed target of over 5 mha for major and medium irrigation for the Eighth Plan.

This target, however, appears not all that incredible

when we go by the Commission's own statistics of achievements during the last two years when 1.28 m.ha. of major and medium irrigation potential was added. And if we go by statistics of actual utilisation instead of potential created, the picture does become much less unrosy. From this angle, the achievements of the recent years appear to have been *in excess* of the created potential, as is brought out by the following data set:

Period	Major and medium irrigation (mha)	
	Created potential	Actual utilisation
7th Plan	1.51	2.44
1990-91	0.675	0.759
1991-92	0.604	0.686

The source of this excess performance, so to speak, needs to be understood. It is a sort of lag or spillover effect. That is to say, a part of the achievement in utilisation is nothing but the unutilised irrigation potential of the earlier period. As this factor would operate in ongoing Eighth Plan, one should be prepared to show realism in judging the feasibility of an additional utilisation target of 4.25 m.ha. (i.e., 0.85 m.ha. per year). After all, an utilised potential of 3.75 m.ha. did exist in major and medium irrigation at the end of the Seventh Five Year Plan. As some of it got utilised in two subsequent years prior to the beginning of the Eighth Plan, the reported figures of utilisation for these two years came to exceed the new capacity additions of these two years.

The proposed investments on major and medium irrigation works during the Eighth Plan are earmarked for ongoing schemes. As the planners had allowed fresh starts on too many new projects in the earlier plans, notably in the Fifth Five Year Plan (1974-78), the nation would now have some benefit of this lapse of the past, with investments yielding capacity benefits within the 8th Plan period on a much greater scale than has been the case hitherto. The pertinent question now is one of planned investments for major and medium irrigation works taking place in practice. The misgiving here is that state governments are finding it now increasingly difficult to find investment funds.

It is not our purpose here to analyse the factors and forces behind lack of investment funds with the state Governments, as also with Centre albeit on a less stringent scale. For our limited purpose it would suffice to mention about the massive burden of subsidies (including hidden subsidies such as on rural power tariff). These subsidies have gradually shrunk the investment cake, resulting in stagnation if not outright decline in fresh investments in real capital formation in Indian agriculture sector. Admittedly, governmental failure to keep price inflation under control has itself accentuated the paucity of funds with the state governments.

Unfortunately, the Eighth Plan report does not record the erosion of investments in irrigation segment on account of price inflation in recent years. In point of fact, there is a covert attempt to duck the issue, committing in the process some grave errors. For instance, there is this atrocious statement that the average cost per hectare of potential created from major and medium irrigation works "has risen steeply from around Rs. 1,060 during the First Plan to over Rs. 42,700 in the Seventh Plan." This forty-fold rise in unit investment cost of large-scale irrigation works is gravely misleading because it is not derived from investment Rupees of comparable purchasing power over time. Had the Commission take pains to record irrigation outlays at constant prices also, say, of 1970-71, the correct picture of rise in unit investment cost between the First and Seventh Plan period would be probably nearer four times, not forty times. It is for this reduced magnitude of rise in unit investment cost that the Commission's identification of numerous factors contributing to cost rise in irrigation is relevant.

For the first time, it is refreshing to find some harsh realities of Indian planning being stated forthrightly, if not bluntly, in the Plan document. For example, look at the following denunciation of large-scale irrigation planning in the country :

> "The biggest single malady in the major and medium irrigation sector right from the First Plan has been the continued tendency to start more and more new projects resulting in wanton proliferation of projects, thin spreading of resources and consequent time and cost overruns. Though all the Plans, without exception, declared their intention to give priority to complete the ongoing schemes, the addition of new schemes continued unabated". (p. 58).

Is this simply an instance of self flagellation by the supreme planning body of the country? Or, is the ire covertly directed at politicians for interfering in an overriding manner in our water planning? Another possible interpretation could be that the Centre is now openly castigating the states for not abiding by plan guidelines in the matter of fresh project starts. If so, one is at a loss why the Centre did not discipline the states much earlier albeit in some indirect manner.[2]

While the Commission is very eloquent in divulging details about the number of new project starts in different Plans, it is not so forthcoming in respect of ongoing (*i.e.*, incomplete) ones. Thus it does not inform us for how long these projects have been lingering on. So, in the absence of a Plan-wise frequency distribution of projects we have no way of rejecting the much-aired criticism that some of these projects (major as well as medium ones) are of the First Plan vintage![3] The Commission's lack of interest (or forthcomingness in case it has compiled such a breakup for its own official record) in this vital matter is a puzzle. All that it has to say on the matter is reproduced below:[4]

> "At the end of the Seventh Plan, there were as many as 182 major... and 312 medium ongoing irrigation projects requiring... a huge amount of Rs. 39,044 crores (at the 1990-91 price level) to complete them. A list of ongoing major and medium irrigation projects is at Statement

3.2. The frequency distribution of expenditure incurred upto the end of Seventh Plan on such ongoing major and medium projects is as given in Table 4" (p.58).

Small Scale Irrigation

The past performance of minor irrigation has been very encouraging, with achievements often crossing Plan targets. The planners, however, do not give any such account in the Eighth Plan report. Anyway, the target of an additional minor irrigation capacity of the order of 10.7 m.ha. during 1992-97 appears quite reachable once we realise that the achievement in this regard during the Seventh Plan was of the order of 9 m.ha. as per the assessment of the Planning Commission. And the pace of progress during the subsequent two years, 1990-91 and 1991-92, has not slackened in any way, registering yearly additions of 1.8 m.ha. and 1.9 m.ha., respectively.

A look at the statewise progress in minor irrigation development reveals the pre-eminent place of Uttar Pradesh. This state's share in national total at the end of the Seventh Plan stood at over 16 m.ha., which constituted over 35 per cent of the corresponding national total of over 46 m.ha. During the last two years this percentage share had been still higher, well over 60 per cent. In a way, this regional imbalance in minor irrigation development is sought to be maintained during the Eighth Plan, as Uttar Pradesh is allotted half the target for new minor irrigation capacity for the period 1992-97.

It is true that U.P. is a very large state, and its endowment of water resources for minor irrigation development is higher than those of very many other states, especially in southern and western India. Yet doubts persist about according such high primacy to this state in developing minor irrigation potential in the coming years. Two of these may be stated here. First, the state suffers from chronic power shortages.[5] Its power sector has lagged far behind the national power sector which itself has failed to expand *pari passu* with our growing power needs. As a result, available power supplies in this state are getting thinly spread among growing multitudes of electric pumpsets used in tubewell irrigation, the principal mode of small-scale irrigation of the state. In the absence of requisite step-up in outlays for power generation and rural electrification, the process of decline in running hours per tubewell per year would continue unabated. Attention is being drawn here to this missing link of supporting investments in power sector on public account because the imperative of such investments in not realised by those who erroneously subscribe to the view that minor irrigation is a low-cost option for the Indian economy.

Second, there is a question mark as to whether so much of minor irrigation development in U.P. is a sustainable proposition. The statistics of *ultimate* minor irrigation potential, duly mentioned in the Plan document, suggest an irrigation capability of only 13.20 m.ha. against this state. By the beginning of the Eighth Plan a minor irrigation potential of the order of 18.75 m.ha. had already come into being in this state as per the data with the Planning Commission. If the 8th Plan target of 5.44 m.ha. is added to this already big figure, we get a massive minor irrigation potential of 22.20 m.ha. by the end of Eighth Plan. We thus reach a number that is exactly 9 m.ha. above the ultimate minor irrigation potential of the State.

The Five Year Plan reports never give separate data for groundwater and surface water components of minor irrigation. But we do know this breakup from other reliable sources, especially from the reports of the working groups constituted by the Planning Commission for doing the spade work for formulating Plan proposals on minor irrigation. Thus we find that bulk of the ultimate minor irrigation potential of U.P. is from groundwater sources. Small-scale surface water based schemes account for barely 1.20 m.ha. out of 13.20 m.ha. of its ultimate minor irrigation potential.

It is true that this estimated 12 m.ha. ultimate potential from groundwater is admittedly underassessed. One revised estimate for the state, as per the new procedures suggested by the Central Groundwater Board, is placed at 18 m.ha. Even if we go by this revised estimate, the proposed programme for minor irrigation for U.P. appears excessive in groundwater realm. This would give rise to the envisaged minor irrigation capacity markedly overshooting the sustainable level in U.P. Specifically, the minor irrigation potential by the end of Eighth Plan could be about 3 m.ha. in excess of even the upwardly revised estimate of 19.2 m.ha. for the state's ultimate minor irrigation capacity. Thus the Eighth Plan unwittingly provides for overexploitation of -tate's groundwater resources by a sizable margin of one-sixth (one-fourth on the basis of unrevised or present estimate of 12 m.ha.).[6]

This issue of sustainability of groundwater based farming emerges at the national level also, though in a much less attenuated form. The anticipated minor irrigation capacity of 61 m.ha. in 1996-97 turns out to be 6 m.ha. more than the current estimate of 55 m.ha. for ultimate minor irrigation potential. The resultant excess would be in the form of over development of groundwater irrigation. At the aggregate level, the Yojana Bhavan is not yet prepared to face the logic of its own numbers. Why? The conjecture here is two-fold. On the one hand, the Commission is convinced that the estimate of 55 m.ha. for ultimate irrigation potential that it has hitherto employed in its water planning for nearly two decades is seriously understated. On the other, such statistics of achievements in minor irrigation capacity as have been used by it so far in its Plan preparations are most probably overstated. An inkling about this second presumption comes from some remarks one comes across in the Eighth Plan document itself, especially in paras 3.6.4, 3.8.1 and 3.8.2. As an illustration, the following remark is noteworthy:

> "The Plan estimates of potential created by minor works, computed form reports of State Governments, are at variance with data compiled by the Minor Irrigation Census from the village records" (para 3.6.4, p. 62, Volume II).

The direction and the extent of the difference between two sources of data, namely, (1) progress reports of state governments submitted to the Planning Commission at the time of seeking Plan approvals/funds, and (2) the Census of Minor Irrigation commissioned by the Centre in 1986-87, are discreetly held back from the public. As this census report is not yet officially released, we have no option but to go by unofficially published/released information in this regard, however partial or preliminary in character this may be. In what follows this comparison is undertaken for two states, U.P. and Gujarat, for both of which alone we find the odd situation of minor irrigation development even today exceeding ultimate minor irrigation potential. There does exist a substantial difference between the two sets of data. However, we have mixed results as regards the direction of this difference.

According to the census, the created minor irrigation potential in U.P. in 1986-87 was of the order of only 9.21 m.ha. The corresponding estimate from the background Plan documents can be derived by adding to Sixth Plan end (1984-85) achievement figure viz. 12.131 m.ha., the *actual achievements* during 1985-86 and 1986-87, namely, 0.844 m.ha. and 0.872 m.ha., respectively. So we end up with a Plan estimate of about 13.85 m.ha. which turns out to be about 4.6 m.ha. *higher* than the census figure. In contrast, the Plan figure in the case of Gujarat state is much *below* the census one. Here, the census figure stands at about 3.854 m.ha., well above the corresponding Plan figure of 1.728 m.ha. These revelations caution us not to conclude (a) that the census estimate would always be less than the Plan estimate, and (b) that the census statistics should invariably be treated with greater confidence. We must not forget that, so far as the estimate of irrigation potential as such is concerned, one cannot assert that in adopting *unit* norms of irrigation capacity the administrators of one source, say, the census of minor irrigation, would necessarily be doing a more credible job. The task of assessing irrigation potential is far more ticklish in the case of minor than major irrigation works. This observation has been necessitated because of a streak of fascination for census of minor irrigation detected by the author in the Eighth Plan write-up on minor irrigation.

It does not speak well of Indian water planning that the planners have not yet taken a view on the new estimates of our ultimate irrigation potential from groundwater resources. Their observations on the matter in para 3.11.2 (p. 64) do not add anything worthwhile on the subject. For one, they drift into side or subsidiary issues. For another, one important sentence is badly drafted: instead of mentioning the revised crop delta figure of 0.48 ha-metres (inappropriately abbreviated as m.ha. in the para), it states the revised ultimate irrigation potential of 80 m.ha.

It may be pointed out here the revised estimates found favour with the Working Group for Minor Irrigation for the Eighth Plan (1990-95), whose report was submitted in July 1989. If the Commission has reservations on the same, it should say so explicitly, and not obliquely through a persistence with the earlier estimates. The task of revision has admittedly not been accomplished satisfactorily for some states, notably West Bengal and states underlain with hard rocks (Gujarat, Maharashtra, Andhra Pradesh, Karnataka, Tamil Nadu and Madhya Pradesh). For a water abundant state such as West Bengal, the ultimate potential from groundwater has been revised, strangely, *downwards* on the questionable basis that net irrigation needs of crops here are 0.94 metres/ha., twice the national level. And in the case of groundwater scarce hard rock states the estimates have been *jacked up*. While the case for upward revision exists for all states, the occasion to do so has been misused to obtain motivated estimates for many states.

Before concluding this section on minor irrigation, it is necessary to point out one error about shallow tubewells in the Plan report. Their number is incorrectly reported as 4.75 lakhs (it should read 47.5 lakhs or 4.75 millions) in the following para on the composition of minor irrigation works in the country:

> "As per 1986-87 Minor Irrigation Census, 95 lakh wells, 0.64 lakh deep tubewells and 4.75 lakh shallow tubewells have been dug; 4.22 lakh surface works completed and

the number of pumpsets energised rose from 0.2 million in 1950-51 to 11.2 million by 1989-90" (p. 61).

Command Area Development

Many well-meaning people strongly feel that instead of concentrating on developing new irrigation capacity it is more sensible now to concentrate resources and attention on getting full production benefits from already established projects with performance much below par. To some extent, the CAD programme has been added to Indian water planning in the mid-seventies precisely with this consideration in mind. Since this too is a resource intensive job, resource allocation for this purpose poses the dilemma of growth versus maintaining spatial equity in development. In other words, further allocation of developmental resources to tracts which have already benefitted in the first instance from simple conversion from rainfed to irrigated farming, means deprivation of other rainfed tracts from benefits of a simple switchover from rainfed to irrigated farming. While production gains arise in both cases, spatial inequity in farm income and wealth increases under the first alternative, that is, the CAD programme.

In a country of continental dimensions and diversity, pressure for spatial spread in developmental planning is quite acute.[7] The concept of CAD has been so modified that the central objective has become one of utilisation of unutilised capacity of major irrigation projects. In other words, the focus is on converting rainfed fields into irrigated ones by utilising the unutilised capacity through measures like construction of field channels, land levelling and land shaping. To a large extent, this overcomes the dilemma mentioned earlier.

Though this author is not in favour of a full-blooded CAD programmes[8] at the present stage of our development, he certainly would like the programme as it is to be implemented in a much more effective manner.

Other Comments

1. *Additivity Problem*

This problem in additivity of irrigation potentials has two facets. One is about whether irrigation potential created through major and medium schemes over a given plan period is wholly additive to that created through minor irrigation schemes over the corresponding period. The other is about these new capacities being fully additive to those already established at the beginning of that plan period. Evidently, some of the new capacity may be of the replacement genre, whereby a newer type of irrigation becomes a substitute for an older mode of irrigation (say, a new tubewell replaces a dugwell) or the same type which has outlived its utility. In such a case, net addition to total irrigation capacity is found to be less than that implied by the new capacity numbers.

Leaving aside the replacement aspect for the moment,[9] let us address ourselves to the other aspect, namely, additivity of irrigation capacities of two principal categories of irrigation. Attention to this has been drawn for the first time in the Eighth Plan document, albeit in an indirect manner. The issue has been , so to speak, forced on the planners by the results of the Census of Minor Irrigation, 1986-87, which revealed that one-tenth of capacity utilisation in the case of a minor irrigation work is in a supplementary or supporting role with another source of irrigation. This is mentioned in the Plan document in the context of past progress in groundwater irrigation in the following words:

> ".....The Plan estimates of potential created do not distinguish between the gross area irrigated by groundwater as a sole source and as a supplement to surface works. The Minor Irrigation Census has estimated the extent of supplementary irrigation by works at nearly 2.9 million hectares, representing nearly 10 per cent of the estimated potential of groundwater works at that time. This distinction between sole and supplementary irrigation by the wells is unfortunately not observed by most states. To that extent, the estimates

of potential reported in the Plan documents are not strictly comparable with those compiled under land use and cropping statistics" (para 3.8.2, p. 63).

The problem of jointness or conjunctiveness in irrigation sources is typically a phenomenon of canal commands. In the case of protective canals like those of northern India, canal supplies are inherently inadequate for practicing intensive farming based on fully meeting irrigation needs of crops right upto the recommended or optimum level for a crop. In order to (a) raise water-intensive crops like paddy and sugarcane, and (b) practice intensive farming upto the full profit margin, farmers in such canal commands maintain their own sources of irrigation, generally wells, from which the needed water supplies are met. To a large extent, the tailend reaches of a non-protective canal system are no better than the protective canal commands, with canal supplies being poor both in quantum and timeliness. So, such tailend farmers too have found it worthwhile to invest in their own wells.[10]

The data format of colonial days still in use does not allow village functionaries to record irrigated area statistics on a highly differentiated basis. While principal sources of irrigation are well distinguished, there is no provision for recording cases of multiple use of sources of irrigation for a given irrigated crop. In the even of joint irrigation from two or more sources, the functionary is expected to go by the single dominant source of irrigation. But the classification task becomes too problematic if village fields/plots as such, and not crop areas, are to be classified by type of irrigation status, as is the whole import of compiling statistics of net irrigated area by type of irrigation. Under the current outmoded classification, one is at a loss while categorising an irrigated *plot* of a farmer to which he mainly applied tank water in the wet season and depended primarily on his own well water in the subsequent dry season.[11]

The need of the hour is to know how much of total (gross) cropped area under irrigation in a given year is under solo or single source of irrigation by type (canal, tank, tubewell, dugwell, etc.), and how much under multiple irrigation (canal-cum-well, or tank-cum-well). This will throw some useful light on the rise of conjunctive irrigation in the country. And this a manageable task. On the other hand, gathering information on number of waterings per crop and by season, however interesting such information might be, is altogether an infeasible task. Such information is best gathered through periodic sample surveys, not through total enumeration year after year (as is recommended in the Plan document while dealing with needed improvements in data base of India irrigation).

It is partly because of conjunctive use of two sources of irrigation that statistics of gross irrigated area as per the land utilisation data can well exceed the corresponding figures of the Planning Commission based on reports from the States. The difference as of today is unknown, thanks to the great lag (almost 5 years) in the publication of land utilisation statistics. So, we do not know how much gross irrigated area for 1991-92 was there corresponding to the Planning Commission's estimated figure of 75.70 m.ha. (as per capacity utilisation). The latest statistics from both the sources are for the end of the Sixth Plan (1984-85), for which the estimates of the Planning Commission stood about 6 mha above the corresponding figure of 60.58 m.ha. from the land utilisation records. In point of fact, this kind of difference is noticeable since 1960-61.

	Gross irrigated area (mha)	
	Plan documents	Land records
Second Plan end	28.05	27.98
Third Plan end	32.20	30.90
1968-69	35.80	35.43
Fourth Plan end	42.20	40.28
Fifth Plan end	48.50	46.08
1979-80	52.70	49.21
Sixth Plan end	60.58	54.67

It needs to be pointed out that the problem of lack of additivity is not confined to that between major and minor works only. When wells happen to be used as a supplementary source within tank commands, the non-additivity arises between two minor irrigation works.

2. *State of Finances*

The financial state of public irrigation works in India has been worsening since the early sixties. Things are bad not just in respect of large-scale irrigation schemes; these are equally dismal in the case of medium surface irrigation schemes, and minor lift irrigation schemes, especially public tubewells (operated departmentally or through public tubewell corporations). In the case of lift irrigation schemes, the dismal financial picture becomes still graver when one takes into account the substantial hidden subsidy in electric power supplied by the public electricity boards. The following extract from the Eighth Plan report's write-up under the head 'Pricing of Water' gives the impression as if the financial mess is *solely* due to gross underpricing of public irrigation service:

> "It is well known that the water charges collected do not cover even working expenses, not to speak of depreciation charges and contributing even a moderate return on investments. It is worth noting that just prior to Independence (1945-46) public irrigation schemes showed a surplus of Rs. 7.92 crores after meeting working expenses, interest charges and setting off losses on unproductive works. (This author may clarify that the "unproductive" irrigation schemes were those which could not pass the financial productivity criterion of earning a stipulated rate of return to cover the interest cost of capital funds. In a way, these were the so-called protective irrigation schemes for famine-prone areas). After Independence the position has deteriorated rapidly. According to estimates for 1987-88, the annual loss of irrigation systems amounts to a staggering Rs. 1,705 crores. The same estimate shows that the gap between

the annual working expense and the gross receipts from water rates stood at over Rs. 400 crores. There has also been reluctance on the part.of State Governments to adjust water rates at least in states with rising costs. Similar problems exist in the case of groundwater irrigation where water rates reflect only about 1/6th of economic water rates. Electric charges for agriculture purposes including pumping of water are also highly subsidised" (pp. 67-68).

Irrigation is quite a capital intensive activity, more so in the case of large-scale irrigation works. Recovery of this capital cost through water tariff that is inclusive of depreciation charge is beyond debate.[12] The rub of the matter in pricing public irrigation is the issue of recovering opportunity cost of capital resources used in establishing such irrigation. The Planning Commission seems to favour recovering much less than the full opportunity cost of capital when it laments about irrigation investments 'not contributing even a moderate return'. The argument for such recovery is spelt out in the following terms of spatial equity and tenability:

> "This situation, in which the State is investing enormous amounts of public money, largely borrowed, without recouping any part of it, is both inequitable and untenable — inequitable in as much as irrigation increases the productivity of the users and enables them to enjoy, without bearing a reasonable part of the costs, a benefit not available to majority of cultivators and untenable in as much as the failure to recover costs increases the burden on the already severely strained budget and is bound, in course of time, to adversely affect the ability of the State to maintain or to continue expanding or improving irrigation in new areas" (p. 68).

The above rationale is admittedly one-sided, somewhat overlaced with the economists' efficiency principle that a user should pay for the cost of the public service he receives.

In applying this principle to public irrigation, one has to contend with the following counter points:

1. An individual farmer alone does not capture all the benefits which accrue to the economy at large by extending irrigation cover to rainfed farming.
2. To the extent irrigation in India is a prior requirement for agricultural development and rural transformation —just as education/literacy is a prior requirement of a well-functioning participatory democracy—, the state has to bear the brunt of resources needed for the same, whether these are raised through taxation or public borrowings.
3. The cost plus basis of water tariff should be applied after deducting (a) costs of inefficiencies of project implementation and operation, and (b) fictitious or inflated costs on account of bribery and corruption.[13]
4. Some of the costs are recovered indirectly when irrigation availability enables the expansion of crops, such as sugarcane and tobacco, which are principal raw materials of industries carrying excise and other taxes.

Lately, we have been investing about Rs. 3,000 crores annually in our public irrigation works. Even if the deficit of the order of Rs. 500 crores in annual operational costs of public irrigation had not been allowed to occur, the irrigation sector would have had an additional investment outlay available for its expansion and improvement. Needless to say, the fund paucity for the sector would pratically vanish if annual interest and depreciation cost of the order of Rs. 1,500 crores or so (as per the planners' idea of a moderate rate of return) had also been recouped from the farmers. While the case for upward revision of prices for water is valid, the occasion should not be used to jack these up on simplistic consideration of users must bear full resource cost.

Finally, we have to contend with externalities or linkages in price fixation. On the one hand, water tariff fixation on high cost public lift schemes is constrained by the prices charged for public surface irrigation: if the latter happen to be low, the fomer cannot be pegged much out of alignment with them. This is one reason why users pay a fraction of the resource cost of lift irrigation schemes run by public corporations, because their beneficiary farmers validly seek some parity with public canal rates paid by the canal irrigators in the same state/tract. On the other hand, this very parity principle works across state boundaries, preventing states with higher costs of irrigation development to charge rates higher than those prevailing in nearby states.[14] Harsh realities like these have to be reckoned with. Also, there is need more for hard and appropriate thinking on the matter, without indulging in inanities or wishful and wishy-washy thoughts like the following ones:

> "The general principle should be to establish an implicit coalition between the interests of the farmer and the irrigation authorities. To the extent it succeeds, it offers substantial returns to both. In the long run a stable and efficient irrigation system would ensure an adequate water price which the farmer would willingly pay... They (i.e., farmers) simply view it as another tax, not a fee for a service." (p. 68)

3. Environmental Degradation

Development of man-made resources like irrigation is seldom without loss in natural resources in quantity or quality. In the case of irrigation development in India, such loss has been primarily in the shape of (i) decrement in forest cover due to the construction of big dams,[15] (ii) damage to farm land due to rise of waterlogging-salinity within canal commands (and along big feeder canals), and (iii) depletion of, or damage[16] to, groundwater stock due to overdevelopment of groundwater-based farming. These and related issues like siltation of reservoirs are very briefly touched upon in the Plan document under three separate sections: (a) Environmental Aspect, (b) Waterlogging and Salinity, and

(c) Regulations and Development of Groundwater.

In recent years, environmental critics of Indian canal irrigation have put forth tremendous losses in environment from such irrigation development. Unfortunately, on this score the planners merely try to reassure the nation— and with out-of date statistics in the case of waterlogging-salinity. After parading, state by state, the conjectural estimates in this regard from the Report of the National Commission on Agriculture (1976) the following assurances on the problem are held forth:

> "It is reported that the spread of conjunctive use of groundwater with that of surface water, especially in Punjab, Haryana and parts of U.P., has substantially lowered the water table and helped contain waterlogging/salinity. But there has been no systematic or comprehensive survey so far". (p. 64)

This absence of information on a point of great criticism of Indian canal irrigation is regrettable. This is possibly indicative of insensibility within planning circles to the issues of environmental degradation. Whatever be the factors behind such a failure, the author endorses the Plan suggestion that there should be a systematic survey to assess the extent, nature and location of waterlogged and saline/alkaline lands in existing project commands. While such a survey requires cooperation and assistance from canal project staff, the findings would lack credibility if the assessment is totally done as an in-house job by canal authorities. This caution is being sounded because at some recent national meetings (e.g., Third National Water Convention at Nagpur) participants from state irrigation departments put forth incredibly low figures of waterlogged areas in selected canal commands of their states. For example, a presentation from Maharashtra, based on in-house information for twenty two major projects, showed the incidence of waterlogging to be confined to about one per cent of the total command area only. The figure for Tawa project in Madhya Pradesh and Sarda

Sahayak project in Uttar Pradesh were, likewise, showing still lower incidence of waterlogging for these two projects for which critics' figures of high incidence of waterlogging, mentioned in media writings, stood unchallenged for many years.

On groundwater depletion, the Plan document has nothing solid to tell us. One cannot gauge the seriousness of this problem from an observation like "there are complaints of over-exploitation of groundwater in several parts of the country." And one does not find any realism in their assessment that "over-exploitation of groundwater should be discouraged by (i) legislative measures and their implementation, and (ii) suitable water and power tariffs." It is not that the states have predominantly not enacted any groundwater regulation laws ever since 1971 when a model bill in this regard was sent to them by the Centre. Legislative regulation of groundwater use is an unworkable proposition in the Indian conditions of small and fragmented land holdings. That is why both Gujarat and Tamil Nadu states, having enacted the necessary legislation, have achieved little on implementation side.

To think of monitoring groundwater withdrawals at an individual well owner level in this country shows terrible ignorance of the sad state of general administration in the countryside. Lack of administration enforcement has forced state electricity boards to give up collecting electricity bills from farmers on the basis of electric meters and adopt instead the pernicious flat power tariff based on horse power of the electric motor installed at the time of giving electricity connection. This harsh reality of the countryside is not realised by those who, in season and out of season, keep on urging the State: (a) to price canal water on volumetric basis, and (b) to regulate groundwater withdrawals by farmers. In the Indian conditions, the key to preventing groundwater depletion is via development of surface water-based irrigation to the hilt. Such development, whether through large-scale or small-scale works, not only lowers the need for groundwater irrigation but also adds to groundwater recharge in a big way — two-thirds of groundwater in Punjab is of canal origin.

4. Flood Control

The task of flood control has not been tackled as vigorously as the one relating to drought proofing, though the flood-prone and the drought-prone areas are of almost equal areal extent of about 40 m.ha. each. For one, the very need for flood protection in the east Gangetic plains, the most flood-prone region of the Indian sub-continent, has not been felt that intensely as has been the case for protective irrigation in drought-prone regions of western and southern parts of the Indian sub-continent. This may be, due to Gangetic farmer's awareness of two sides of the coin: while floods might destroy crops, livestock and property, these also renew soil vigour and moisture. For another, there is a good deal of ineffectuality in the flood protection measures adopted so far. And the latest report of the Centre for Science and Environment on floods of the Indo-Gangetic plains has further added a bolt from the blue with its harsh assessment *a la* Arrow's Impossibility Theorem of Welfare Function: since the Himalayan floods are uncontrollable because of the futility of afforestation programme and engineering structures (embankments, dams, etc.), the people in these plains must reconcile to living with the flood hazard.

In the immediate future, conventional works, such as embankments, drainage channels, and flood zoning would continue, though the Plan document admits "there is scope to improve the effectiveness of these investments both from the technical and economic viewpoint". Evaluation studies for such works constructured in the past are envisaged in the Eighth Plan. So far, about 15,600 km. of embankments and 33,100 km. of drainage channels have been constructed. One hopes that the benefit-cost ratio tool is applied in low gear but appropriately in expost evaluative exercises of such works, lest real problems of lack of maintenance, or shoddy construction job, should be sidetracked in evaluation. Finally, while preparing master plans for flood control and drainage for major rivers and expanding the flood forecasting network, the imperative of flood forecasting *in real time* has become all the more urgent if living with floods is unavoidable. Such flood forecasting-cum- warning is so necessary for avoiding human toll during the actual flood calamity.

Concluding Observations

The highly adverse Morse-Berger report on the Sardar Sarover Project, which is slated to add about 1.8 mha of irrigation capacity by the end of the Eighth Plan, has cast a cloud on newly started but controversial dams. But there is no dearth of other ongoing projects for putting our investments in and still achieve the overall target of new capacity creation in the Plan. So, the crucial question is one of requisite investments forthcoming for the irrigation sector (including rural power supply system) during the plan.

There is no denying that a latent sense of complacency prevailed at the Centre about the state of development in Indian agriculture during much of the eighties. Fortunately, the Centre has lately become alive to the dangers ahead. This augurs well for agricultural development in general and irrigation development in particular in the coming years. Time alone will tell whether this concern at the Centre would help the fund-starved states find the requisite money for projected investments in irrigation and rural power supply.

NOTES

1. Sharp price inflation in the economy since 1990-91 has already eroded the real value of these projected investments.
2. The Centre cannot absolve itself of its failure here, because it did nothing to prevent Karnataka for starting half a dozen new irrigation schemes on an inter-state river without prior approval of the Planning Commission which could do no more than simply keep on listing them as *unapproved* projects in its own files and plan documents. The result of this lapse is the extreme postures today adopted by states on the Cauvery dispute. Now that the total water requirements of all major

irrigation works in the Cauvery basin well exceed the quantum of water flow of this river, the task of resolving the dispute through the usual principles of water sharing of common rivers has become very ticklish.

3. A couple of years ago, one engineer from Maharashtra told this author that one medium project in his state dates prior to the First Plan.
4. As the entire outlay for large-scale irrigation is now earmarked for the ongoing major and medium irrigation schemes only, the problem of spillover projects would be much less pressing during the subsequent Plan. However, such projects would still require a lion's share of the anticipated allocations for major and medium projects of the Ninth Plan. After all, the financial provisions for Eighth Plan for such works constitute just 57 per cent of the total funds required to complete the existing ongoing schemes.
5. Availability of electricity for pumpsets, according to the Census of Minor Irrigation, was for a duration of just 5 hours per day for private wells in U.P. during 1986-87. The duration was an hour more for public tubewells which are expected to run round the clock at peak season to meet water needs of about 80 ha. area per public tubewell — this duration averaged two hours per day for surface lift irrigation schemes like river pumped canals. In contrast, rural power supply in the states of Punjab, Haryana and Karnataka was for 8 hours daily — 10 hours in Gujarat.
6. Actual overexploitation of groundwater may, however, be averted because of actual withdrawals being less than those indicated by capacity data. Among other reasons, this lower withdrawal is due to (a) less than the recommended level of irrigation for crops, and (b) actual irrigated area being less than the capacity level.
7. It is this pressure which possibly forces state politicians to make too many fresh starts on irrigation schemes, knowing that the needed investments would not be forthcoming in requisite amount over the planned gestation period.
8. A well-conceived CAD programme is, acre for acre, no less expensive than irrigation development itself.
9. Replacement needs of Indian irrigation are steadily rising. The same is true for many other public sector activities like railway tracks, rail and road bridges, urban sewerage and water supply piping.
10. Considerable private well irrigation has developed also within tank commands of southern India, mainly for coping with

large year-to-year fluctuations in tank supplies to which paddy crop is very sensitive.

11. Evidently, the phenomenon of multiplicity in irrigation sources poses greater hazard of misclassification under net area basis than on crop area basis.
12. The need for indexing this charge with rising nominal unit cost of irrigation due to price inflation is obviated to the extent the collected amount of depreciation charge is put in an account that yields interest rate comparable to that of price inflation.
13. Why should beneficiary farmers pay for these unwarranted costs of public irrigation, which might today account for half the nominal resource cost of establishing public irrigation?
14. This attempt to seek spatial parity in canal water tariff can extend to other spheres. For instance, the farmers body, BKU, is urging Haryana farmers not to pay the recently upward revised power rates because these are now much above the corresponding rates charged from their brethren in U.P. and Punjab: while the rate is Rs. 22.50/hp in U.P and Rs. 18/hp in Punjab, the new Haryana rate is Rs. 39/hp.
15. According to some big dam supporters, big dams are not a major factor in the loss of forest cover in the country, because one to two mha so lost constitutes barely 5-10 per cent of the total loss of forest area.
16. Damage to groundwater resource arises when nearby saline or brackish waters intrude into voids created by excessive pumpage, as has been reported in the villages close to Saurashtra coast. If pumping continues without monitoring of salt content of the pumped water, soil salinity builds up, damaging eventually the land resource.

CHAPTER 5

POPULATION PRESSURE, IRRIGATION IMPERATIVE AND ENVIRONMENT*

Introductory Remarks

Though I feel a sense of privilege in being called upon to present my paper at this national seminar, I am doing so with a tinge of unease. This uneasiness stems from an apprehension that an irrigation economist cannot have much say on matters of net environmental impact of building big reservoirs for irrigation, power generation and flood control. And if he has indeed something to say, it might consist of commonplace observations, and possibly not so germane to the central question before the participants here. Still, I am venturing to address you, hoping I would get away with it the way distinguished American faculty, especially in Economics, sometimes gets away in handling graduate teaching load-he doles out what he knows, what he has researched on, and what he feels concerned with on a particular day in a class, without bothering much about the course requirements. What follows is mainly a look back exercise, with forward looking glances in passing. Kindly

---

* Invited keynote paper for the National Seminar on Large Reservoirs—Environmental Loss or Gain?, 7-8 February, 1992, Nagpur, under the auspices of Indian Water Resources Society, Nagpur Centre. Appeared in *Facts For You*, April 1992, without notes and bibliography.

bear with its personal tenor, a bit of plain speaking, and, of course, with its tangencies, if any.

We live in an age of too much questioning of everything, from values, customs and traditions to the basic sciences and the very basis of our knowledge. Therefore, today nothing would be taken for granted. In the public domain, one has to make timely and well-prepared responses to criticism, without being dismissive simply because much of the criticism appears in the first place to be either misplaced or factually wrong. Afterall, to draw out a stonewalling or dithering individual/ institution by grossly overstating the points of criticism or grievance is not an unfair ploy or stratagem.

Heightened environmental/ecological consciousness has added a potent, new dimension to the questioning process. It has undoubtedly enlivened the development debate, posing a considerable challenge to development planners, including the promoters of major irrigation works — even foreign donors of development funds to developing nations have begun paying heed to the environmental question.

Imperative of Irrigated Farming

When around 1985 I finished writing my research study, *Irrigation in India's Agricultural Development*, I hardly noticed any serious opposition to the idea of developing irrigation in the country. Because of the capricious character of Indian monsoons, the case for such development was taken for granted. In point of fact, delays in the execution of irrigation works, whether major, medium or minor, caused anxiety and concern all round. As major irrigation works backed by huge reservoirs have long gestation period and serious time overruns also occurred in their execution, the need for developing such works indeed began to be questioned right in the middle of the Indian planning effort. The thrust of this questioning was to suggest to the central planners some diversion of plan resources away from major to minor irrigation schemes, which were portrayed as idealized investments: extremely low gestation period, low unit cost of development, free from the problem of underutilisation of capacity; no adverse development of-waterlogging, salinity and alkalinity within their commands; no submergence of forest or fertile valley lands; no intractable problems of relocating and satisfactorily rehabilitating dam oustees; no seismic hazard, or malarial and other waterborne diseases to cope with, etc.

The planners never did any perceptible diversion of allocations away from major irrigation. But they did a lot to ensure much greater minor irrigation development under farmers' individual ownership, especially of well irrigation, through two instruments, namely, long-term institutional finance for farmers and a programme of rural electrification aimed primarily at pumpset energisation instead of village habitation lighting. As a result, farm growth commensurate with enhanced population growth could be maintained.[1] Without this planned expansion in irrigation base of Indian agriculture, the spectre of latter outstripping the former might have haunted us, thereby jeopardising the very planning effort itself. Here, two weighty considerations need to be underlined.

First, the very development effort, especially in the area of social services (public health, education, mass communication, etc.) tends to enhance the population growth by causing one sided disequilibrium between birth and death rates. That is to say, in the initial stages of planned economic development mortality rate gets moving down without any corresponding dent in fertility rate which tends to stayput - even evincing a bit of rising tendency for a little while. It is only when the level of development (especially in living standards, literacy and women's status) crosses a threshold value that birth rates begin climbing down from their high pitch observed in subsistence, stagnating economies characterised by high mortality. Development, eulogised by some Indian demographers as the best contraceptive, begins impacting fertility rate after this threshold is crossed, which does not happen over a couple of five year plans but over a couple of generations. In the meantime, population pressure mounts instead of easing,[2] adding to the woes of the planners.[3]

Second, agricultural transformation through non-irrigation instruments in non-temperate regions like ours is not all that an attractive option. Two such instruments are: (1) offering incentive prices to Indian farmers, and (2) investing in dryland technology. At the commencement of planning in 1951, there were misgivings if our subsistence farmers would respond to price incentives and thus expand food supplies sufficiently. These were times when conventional wisdom was suffused with perceptions such as: (i) Indian farmer's behaviour towards farm product prices borders on irrationality, and (ii) farming is a way of life, not a business proposition in our country. It was much afterwards (early sixties) that some reassurances about Indian farmer's rationality emerged, notably from the pioneering research work of Dharm Narain and Raj Krishna.

Farmers' responsiveness to price signals was thus established but at micro or individual crop level. Evidence at macro or aggregate crop output level was still lacking. That is to say, farmers do reveal resource allocative efficiency, putting more acreage, manures, human and animal labour to the growing of more remunerative crops, but the price elasticity for total crop output is feared to be approaching zero (though positive). Thus they could be depended upon to shift resources out of non-foodgrains to foodgrain crops in response to price stimuli for achieving greater production of foodgrains, but with a questionmark as to the resultant rate of agricultural growth. For agricultural growth to materialise, we need strengthening of the production base, for which requisite investments, both in fixed and working capital, have to take place.

Irrigated vis-a-vis Dryland Agriculture

The question now boils down to one of backing to the hilt the development of irrigated or dryland farming. Agricultural research economists have decomposed agricultural growth into three distinct components or sources: (1) increase in total crop area, (2) improvement in crop yield, and (3) change in crop mix in favour of more valued crops. In making quick and sizable impact on these three components of growth dryland techniques, especially soil and water conservation measures, are not of much avail, though these do need promotion on grounds of environmental considerations lest we should pass to the coming generations a degraded production base. Besides this angle of inter-generation equity (which is core of the new concept of sustainable development), case for investment in dryland technology rests on the political imperative of maintaining spatial equity in growth in a federal polity. Surely, these two equity considerations could not be accorded primacy over the productivity objective arising out of the compulsions of feeding a large, growing population.

Soil and water conservation measures, without the development of wells and tanks which now constitute an integral core of new watershed management concept in dryland technology, help the agricultural growth process mainly through one component only, namely, improvement in crop yield, though both in level and stability terms. Irrigation, on the other hand, gives larger impetus to this process as it works via all three components of growth (with considerable positive interaction, i.e., the component improvements occur in a reinforcing manner). Even though the irrigated yields have certainly not risen in India by a factor of three to four following the introduction of irrigation in rainfed areas, yet the impact has been considerable, especially in low and medium rainfall regions, as per innumerable micro level studies based on survey data.

I would like to dispel here any misgivings still entertained about the impact of irrigation on intensity of cropping (i.e., crop area effect of irrigation). Such misgivings were very much in the air following the Panse Memorial Lecture of venerable V.K.R.V. Rao in 1974. Among others, Dharm Narain's work once again removed these misgivings. Still, some murmurs are heard now and then. So, I invite interested readers' attention to my own study (Dhawan 1993) on the matter, wherein I have shown that national expansion of gross irrigated area by one hectare increases total crop area by somewhere between 0.46 and 0.66 hectare — there is sharp variation in impact from state to state.

Given the climatic conditions in our country, dryland farmers are rightly disinclined to intensify the use of yield-raising farm inputs, notably of the leading input of chemical fertilisers which have been very successfully used by their counterparts in Europe and North America who have undoubtedly far greater risk-taking capacity and simultaneously face much lower production risk from rainfall failure. This perception about disinclination is amply borne out when we segregate agriculture sector into its two segments, rainfed and irrigated, and study the comparative yield behaviour of the two segments. For the period 1970-83, yield of foodgrains produced in the rainfed segment rose at the annual incremental level of 12 kg. per hectare. No less importantly, its rise was far from steady (CV = 9.2 per cent). In contrast, the yield of irrigated foodgrains reveals a much stronger uptrend (42 kg/ha per year) along a less unstable path (CV = 5.3 per cent.) This comparative picture is even somewhat more favourably tilted towards irrigated farming when we look at the two segments in totality (foodgrains plus non-foodgrains).

	Irrigated farming	Rainfed farming
1. Overall crop yield rise per annum	41 kg/ha	11 kg/ha
2. Coefficient of variation (CV) of overall crop yield	4.3 per cent	9.3 per cent

The stability gain from development of irrigated agriculture is of importance from several angles: food security of the nation, the scale of buffer stock of foodgrains, stability of farm prices, farm incomes, etc. One vital facet of this stability gain is in the shape of substantial drought proofing of agriculture. This is borne by the comparative rates of contraction in foodgrains production observed during drought years as per the following statistics for the two segments:

	1972-73	1974-75	1979-80
1. Percent reduction in irrigated foodgrains production	8	10	6
2. Per cent reduction in foodgrains produced from the rainfed segment	18	14	22

Large-Scale Vis-a-Vis Small-Scale Works

The foregoing evidence of irrigation's impact is for all irrigation sources taken together, and so is quite pertinent for rebutting those dryland technology protagonists who have been lately putting forth their case by passing some wholly unwarranted observations on our irrigated agriculture.[4] But this evidence is not appropriate for warding off widespread criticism directed at major irrigation works as such. For that, one would need a further break-up of the irrigated segment into its component sub-segments and then pinpoint the productivity and stability roles of major irrigation works. This is admittedly no easy task in measurement but is not all that formidable as it may appear at first thought. We must recognise that the onus of proof (about major irrigation works having delivered the goods in the area of productivity and stability) is on the promoters of such works.[5]

Protagonists of minor irrigation in India have revealed a remarkable asymmetry in critical appreciation. They are long on their adverse critique of major irrigation, and too short on their critique of minor irrigation. In fact, it is mainly their 'romance of minor irrigation' that makes them shy away from looking at some of the harsh ground realities of minor irrigation in India, especially in respect of small-scale surface water based irrigation works and shallow dugwells. They are unduly carried away by the success stories of private tubewell irrigation development in northern India, without realising two things. One, tubewells cannot be installed in all regions or everywhere in India, as over two-thirds of our land mass is underlain by hard rocks ill suited for the introduction of tubewell technology.

Second, this technology has its own inherent environmental dangers. If waterlogging is an ever present danger in major irrigation works, so is its reverse process, namely, groundwater depletion, in the case of groundwater-based agriculture in general and tubewell-based agriculture in particular. Just as waterlogging produces soil salinity in semi-arid regions before long, so does groundwater depletion in the coastal tracts and in arid areas. The void created by such depletion gets surreptitiously filled up due to intrusion of sea/saline water lying nearby. Afterwards such intruded waters get pumped up for irrigation activity, and their dissolved salts begin the cumulative process of soil toxity. It is sheer naivette to plead for prevention of such groundwater depletion through legislative measures and groundwater regulations in the Indian conditions of small land holdings and too many farmers. The real preventive remedy lies in conjunctive irrigation, which helps in containing waterlogging as well.[6] Such linkages in environmental benefits have been little appreciated by groundwater protagonists in India. A like beneficial linkage between watershed management programme and major irrigation works needs to be duly appreciated by the promoters of such works which do tend to crowd out the needed investments in watershed programmes. It is time to strike balances in plan allocations. For a country of continental diversity it does not make much sense to pursue a uniform policy everywhere, or to accord primacy to one option to the total exclusion of other options.

Adverse environmental/ecological implications of major irrigation have been far more noted than the few beneficial ones. Thus greening of deserts and semi-arid lands with such irrigation has not merited due attention. Nor due credit is being given to large dams for substantially augmenting groundwater regime in low and medium rainfall regions of the country, thereby sustaining a thriving groundwater-based farming in such regions. For instance, two-thirds of the groundwater recharge in Punjab originates from canals fed by waters of Bhakra and Pong reservoirs. Without such recharge, groundwater-based farming in this state would be a fraction of what it is today. These gains should not be ignored while bemoaning the development of waterlogging in the cotton belt of the state. (The evidence about the overdevelopment of groundwater irrigation in the rest of Punjab should not be taken at face value).

What is irksome about this imbalanced evaluation of the environmental impact is that little serious attempt is made to catalogue all aggravating factors behind a given adverse effect, say, increase in waterlogged area. As a result, the entire adverse effect gets ascribed unfairly to irrigation factor.[7] By not reckoning with the multiple causes, one can possibly miss how the very development of irrigated agriculture can mitigate the adverse effect ensuing from non-irrigation factors. This is aptly illustrated by the case of ruinous deforestation in India, behind which lies the rising pressure of population as one major basic cause. By augmenting the production of biomass from our limited resources of arable land, irrigated agriculture does help containing, albeit indirectly, the mounting pressure of man and domestic animals on our already degraded forest land.[8]

Concluding Observations

Some concluding remarks need to be made here. First, the foregoing presentation should not lull us into a false sense that all is well with Indian irrigation development. I have no doubt that irrigation would continue to be the kingpin in India's agricultural planning in the foreseeable future.[9] Still, one cannot ignore very many ills afflicting Indian irrigation sector that need to be rectified urgently and effectively.[10] There is no doubt that some of these ills have arisen because of the decision to expand irrigation capacity in an accelerated manner after 1971, whereby pre-investment investigative work in connection with projects got neglected. But the unsatisfactory quality of many a construction work and managerial/supervisory neglect in completed works cannot be attributed to forced pace of irrigation development for reasons of compulsions of population pressure or political exigency arising out of the Indo-Pak war of 1971. While it is patently unwarranted to expect a production impact performance of the magnitude of a demand-determined irrigation system from a supply-determined one, this limitation should not be indiscriminately offered as defense for covering up the rectifiable deficiencies in our large canal systems.

Second, financial unviability of public irrigation can be put up with so long as the economic viability from larger social angle remains sound, But it needs to be recognised that deterioration in the former beyond a point tells upon the latter when there is paucity of investment funds. As such funds get increasingly absorbed in bridging the growing financial hiatus due to increasing scale of the completed segment of public irrigation system, the fund paucity becomes still more acute, to the detriment of both the ongoing and the proposed new irrigation works on the one hand and the completed works on the other. Given politicians' proclivity for making more fresh starts on new irrigation schemes rather than on (a) completing the ongoing ones first, and (b) funding adequately the preventive repair and maintenance costs of the completed ones, huge time and cost overruns in project completion and diminished benefits from completed works become *ceteris paribus* inevitable.

It is time to resist (rather than assist) such proclivities so as to counter the critics who allege that such proclivities suit the irrigation engineers' own game plans. Otherwise, boons can become curses in the end.

Finally, the insidious growth of *population needs arresting.* The lurking dangers here need far wider recognition. Instead of sounding merely alarm bells some imaginative handling of the family planning message is required. Population bomb is not to the good of environment, developmental planning, and people themselves.

NOTES

1. A one-to-one correspondence between irrigation development and foodgrains production is found in India. Though the elasticity of foodgrains production w.r.t. actual gross area irrigated for the period 1965-85 is 1.03 (± 0.09) at the national level, it varies across regions, being as low as 0.49 for Central India as compared to 1.25 for northern India (0.75 for western Indian and 0.82 for eastern India — the estimated value of 2.07 for southern India is to be interpreted with great caution). For more details, see Dhawan (1993).
2. Though some dent has been made in the birth rate during the course of four decades of Indian economic planning (including some weak measures of family planning), the reduction in fertility rate has been not enough to offset the dip in mortality rate during the same period, with the result that growth of population continues at the stepped-up rate of over 2 per cent per annum (compared to a rate of 1.2 per cent prior to the planning period).
3. The oppressive character of our population pressure is not effectively brought home by the rate of rise in our population. The rate of

growth of 2.11 per cent per annum, recorded during 1981-91, has meant an addition of 161 million persons, equivalent to thrice the population of the United Kingdom and about two-thirds of that of the United States of America. *Source*: Antony (1992). It is this population pressure which is putting everything under siege, including the environment.

4. See, for example, Ramanna's keynote paper at last year's Annual Conference of the Agricultural Economists at Hyderabad, and the combined Report of the US Dryland Farming Team released by the Indo-US Sub-Commission on Agriculture in 1987. In this connection, see Dhawan (1992) and Dhawan (1988) — the later one is a critique of the above report.
5. It is unwarranted to insist on a 'reverse' proof (about alleged failure of such works) from their critics who usually make their case with the help of few telling examples like the Tawa project from central India and the Sarda Sahayak project from northern India. The need of the hour is for economy-wide evidence, and not some counter citation of striking success stories like the Bhakra Nangal.
6. Appropriate pricing of electric power for pumpsets is another useful preventive measure against the danger of groundwater depletion in low rainfall regions, as also in coastal plains.
7. Occasionally, the author has seen such exaggerated estimates of waterlogged / salinised area within canal commands that he has to suggest to the concerned persons for a check-up with the area of a canal project. One factor in this exaggeration is non-realisation that there is lack of additivity in areas suffering from waterlogging and areas suffering from salinity. Another factor is to club together areas/fully affected, partially or seasonally affected, and likely to be affected at a later date.
8. Here is another instance of a positive linkage between development of irrigated farming and the indirect protection it affords to preserve the forest cover. It is not widely realised that in some wonderful stories about dryland farming without recourse to chemical inputs, biomass of the adjacent forests becomes an input of no mean significance.
9. Even after all our ultimate irrigation potential is developed, say, in the next two decades, Indian irrigation sector may still absorb a large chunk of our investible resources for agriculture. For one, replacement investments of public irrigation works are to take place. For another, in the absence of (a) any breakthrough in dryland technology for HYV crops, and (b) sharp reduction in the rate of growth of population, modernisation of irrigation works for better water management would require funds.

10. Who would or should do this rectification? Irrigation planners at the Centre and at state capitals? State irrigation administrators and state legislators? Foreign donors like the World Bank? The IMF? The Prime Minister? There is need for concerted, conjunctive action here.

BIBLIOGRAPHY

Antony, T.V. (1992). The Family Planning Programme.— A Different Strategy, Symposium on India's Development in the 1990's held in New Delhi, 28-29 January,1992 under Ford Foundation auspices.

Dharm Narain and Shyamal Roy (1980). Impact of Irrigation and Labour Availability on Multiple Cropping, IFPRI Research Report No. 20, Washington, D.C.

Dhawan, B.D. (1988). Dryland Versus Irrigated Farming, *Economic and Political Weekly*, 19 March, pp. 575-76.

__________ (1991). Role of Irrigation in Raising Intensity of Cropping, *Journal of Indian School of Political Economy*, Vol. 3, No. 4, October -December.

__________ (1992). Dryland or Irrigation Technology? (typescript).

__________ (1993). Trends and New Tendencies in Indian Irrigated Agriculture. Commonwealth, New Delhi.

Indo-US Sub-Commission on Agriculture (1987). Combined Report of the US Dryland Farming Team and the Economics Team Visits to India, March/April and June 1987.

Ramanna, R., (1991). Watershed Approach to Dryland Agricultural Development, *Indian Journal of Agricultural Economics*, Conference Number, Vol. 46, No. 3, July-September.

Rao, V.K.R.V. (1974). New Challenges before Indian Agriculture, *Journal of the Indian Society of Agricultural Statistics*, Vol. 26, No. 1.

CHAPTER 6

CANAL VERSUS WELL IRRIGATION : MYTHS AND REALITIES*

Not very long ago, any irrigation was considered right for Indian agriculture. But since the advent of high yielding varieties (HYV) of wheat and paddy, a sea-change has occurred in this perception. Now, the rate of growth of the agriculture sector, as also its ability to cope with a drought, has come to be associated with groundwater development. Surface irrigation is now deemed inferior to groundwater irrigation, and our planners are being called upon to accord higher priority to groundwater development. Groundwater has come to possess the following virtues:

(1) Groundwater resource is much more bountiful than surface water.
(2) In comparison to big dams, groundwater irrigation is a low-cost option for our economy.
(3) Groundwater-based farming has much higher land productivity.
(4) Environmental degradation, forest submergence, population dislocation and rehabilitation problems of dam oustees are absent in groundwater irrigation.
(5) Unlike substantial underutilisation of irrigation capacity

---

* This paper is an abridged version of the paper presented to the Seminar on the Economics of Land and Water Resources in India, held on 22-24 July 1989 at NSS Wadia College of Commerce, Pune. It appeared in *Facts for You*, August, 1992.

observed in the case of big dams, there is almost full utilisation in the case of wells and tubewells.

(6) Time lag between investment and returns is low in groundwater case, whereas construction of big projects lingers on for decades.

As a groundwater economist, my primary concern is with restoring correct perspectives on the economics of groundwater irrigation. In this paper, I propose to focus mainly on the following three aspects:

(i) the beneficial role of seeped-in canal waters;
(ii) the cost advantage of groundwater irrigation;
(iii) the unutilised capacity and its nature.

Water in general and groundwater in particular is a complex resource. There is ample room for misunderstandings, more so when any one generalises from limited regional experiences for this country of continental dimensions. Furthermore, one has to be very circumspect in interpretation of facts of costs and returns relating to groundwater, and in drawing policy implications from these.

I. Beneficial Role of Canal Seepage

An unconventional view of economic development is one of converting adversities of Nature to mankind's advantage. From this standpoint, the deleterious canal seepage from major irrigation works can now be looked upon benignly as it is a wonderful source of artificial groundwater replenishment in groundwater-short areas. In fact, the long-run sustainability of much-acclaimed groundwater-based agriculture of low rainfall regions of northern, western and southern India now hinges on the seeped-in waters from surface irrigation development works like canals and tanks.

A canal system is inherently very leaky, in the sense that a large part of the conveyed water is lost to groundwater table. In a completely unlined system serving farmers using conventional methods of water application to their fields, as much as 70% of the canal water can be lost, mostly to the groundwater table.

This cumulation of seeped-in canal waters, if unchecked, tends to raise the water table, leading before long to problems of waterlogging and soil salinity. No wonder, then, the fear of waterlogging from canal irrigation has been haunting irrigation engineers/administrators in India since the turn of the last century.

To contain the canal seepage via suitable canal lining and to prevent waterlogging-salinity through an extensive network of drains is a very costly proposition. Extra capital costs needed for canal lining and drainage are too high to be recouped from farmers practicing traditional subsistence farming in which the economic value of irrigation is much less than that in modern, market-oriented farming based on intensive use of bio-chemical inputs. This is what made waterlogging in canal commands an inevitable consequence during the British rule in the Indian subcontinent. But this need not be so now because intensive irrigated agriculture today can yield enough extra output/farm income to cover the added costs of canal lining and drainage. The question is whether the drainage of seeped-in waters be achieved through conventional horizontal drains or via vertical drainage through establishment of wells within canal commands. The recent thinking has been favouring vertical over horizontal drainage. This is for two powerful reasons. Firstly, the vertically drained waters are put to good economic use by the farmers in a number of ways enumerated below. Secondly, it leads towards the development of conjunctive use of groundwater and surface water resources, an avowed objective of irrigation planning these days.

The value of groundwater to a canal farmer hinges on the type of canal. Evidently, it will be higher if the canal supplies are restrictive in some respect. In a one-seasonal canal supplying water mostly for cropping in the main wet season, groundwater can be used to obtain an extra crop during the dry season when land lies fallow in much of our country. Even if a low yielding pulse crop is being grown in the dry season, the well water can enable a farmer to shift onto a more remunerative crop. Also, access to well water can also enable him to either advance the sowing of his main crop of the wet season or prepare rice nurseries early enough in case canal releases are contingent on the onset of the monsoons.

Groundwater becomes a substantial source of augmenting the meagre canal supplies in northern India where the protective principle ensures that hardly one-third area of a farmer can be fully irrigated with canal supplies. As the canal system here is somewhat of a perennial nature, investment in groundwater irrigation strengthens irrigated agriculture in a major way. Farmers are able not only to complete their irrigation operations in time and on most of their land, but also go in for crops that cannot be easily matured on canal supplies alone. Thus private tubewells in Punjab and Haryana have enabled farmers to grow paddy which needs copious watering in a somewhat continuous manner—rotational irrigation system in vogue here is not conducive for paddy cultivation. Likewise, installation of private tubewells within the Ganga-Yamuna canal system of western Uttar Pradesh has enabled farmers to grow much more sugarcane than would be warranted by this protective canal system.

Even in a non-protective canal (loosely described as productive' canal) of the type existing in southern India, one's own well could be much more than a mere standby arrangement against canal deficiencies during drought. Here, the tail reaches are not well served because farmers in upper reaches appropriate more than their due share of canal supplies. In clear violation of the canal regulation these farmers grow more of heavily - irrigated crops like paddy and sugarcane. In such a circumstance, the tail-end farmers cannot practice intensive farming without the aid of well irrigation. Incidentally, this brings home an important truth: canal farmers are not going to invest in their own wells if they do not experience shortages of canal water.

The key idea behind conjunctive irrigation is one of enhancing the magnitude of irrigation benefits from the given volume of water resources. In other words, the benefits attained under conjunctive irrigation are considered much more than the sum total of separate benefits to be realised from developing the two water bodies in isolation. As the concept of conjunctive irrigation is not yet worked through for implementation purpose, some pertinent — and a bit uneasy — questions do arise. Will the extra resource cost of developing conjunctive system be justified by the extra benefits? In such a system, will every farmer be required to meet his water needs from both groundwater and surface water? When used conjunctively, does any positive interaction (in the sense of complementarity) between two water sources occur in the crop production activity?

It is not my purpose to pursue here these questions. It would suffice to give here some quantitative idea about the magnitude of beneficial effects of surface irrigation development on the groundwater-based farming of some groundwater short regions of India. It is hoped that this quantitative assessment would go a long way in sobering up the zealous proponents of groundwater irrigation, as also the crusaders against major irrigation works — both do not appreciate the harsh realities of irrigation in water scarce or low rainfall regions.

The seeped-in waters are found to quadruple the rate of return of investment in well irrigation in Ahmednagar district of western Maharashtra. In a specific case of the Mula canal in this very district, these waters have boosted the groundwater-based farming, both in terms of number of sustainable wells and crop output per well. The eightfold increase in output from wells is an indirect output contribution of the Mula project, and is no less than the direct output resulting from the canal-irrigated acreage of this project. No less striking are the empirical results for the Punjab. Here, at least half of the state output from private tubewell irrigation can be confidently attributed to groundwater that is of canal origin. A similar result is true for private tubewells in Muzaffarnagar district of western U.P.

In Tamil Nadu state, both canal and tanks together make a substantial augmentation to its natural groundwater availability. Somewhere between one-fourth and two-fifths of the total output of the order of 7 million tons from wells established in the state may be traced to seeped-in waters of canal/tank origin. Whatever be this fraction, bulk of the seepage into groundwater table is from the state canal network. These findings should set at rest the controversy about surface versus groundwater irrigation for low and medium rainfall regions.

II. Pitfalls of Cost Comparisons

For any productive activity, two types of costs arise. One is the capital cost, and the other is the operational cost. Capital costs arise in the construction phase, whereas operational costs are incurred after the construction phase is over. Evidently, it is inappropriate to compare two irrigation projects on the basis of unit capital cost alone if their cost structures substantially differ. It is a well known fact that operational costs *vis-a-vis* capital costs are of far greater significance for wells than for canals (and tanks). Given this structural difference in costs, cost comparison based on capital costs alone can put well irrigation in an undue advantage over canal irrigation.

Nowhere in the Five Year Plan Reports one comes across concrete figures of unit capital requirements for different types of irrigation works. Therefore, one must be wary of any such estimates. The cited figures are usually the handiwork of analysts who try to grind them out from the following two sets of statistics listed in the plan documents:

(1) Actual or anticipated outlays for major, medium and minor irrigation works for each plan period;

(2) Planners' own estimates of irrigation potential created, or anticipated to be created, in each plan period for each category of irrigation.

Faulty estimates of unit capital cost can be generated when plan outlays are divided by corresponding estimates of irrigation potential. To begin with, the plan statistics on outlays for minor irrigation do not give a full picture of capital resources required for developing minor irrigation capacity in the country. The reported outlays are for the public sector only. Thus the plan outlays for minor irrigation works are not inclusive of farmers' own investments in tubewells, dugwells, pumpsets, etc. Since the plan statistics on minor irrigation potential are for the entire minor irrigation segment (public and private account), the collation of the area and outlays data given in the plan documents gives rise to seriously understated estimates of unit capital requirements of minor irrigation. Needless to say, a similar collation for major and medium irrigation works yields an estimate of unit capital cost which is free from the element of underestimation as the major and medium irrigation schemes are envisaged entirely for the public sector.

Secondly, there is lack of compatibility between outlays on irrigation in a given plan period and the resultant addition to irrigation capacity in the same plan period. It is well known that the gestation period for a major irrigation project is about 10 to 12 years under efficient conditions of implementation. As irrigation capacity of an ongoing project is not created in direct proportion to investment expenditure in a given plan, a lack of correspondence between plan outlays and created irrigation potential can exist for a given plan period. This can distort the estimate of unit capital cost, the distortion being more serious in the case of major than minor irrigation works like wells which can be usually constructed within a single year.

The third limitation of the plan outlays on irrigation arises from the fact that some of those are not meant to result in any addition to irrigation capacity. For instance, outlays on (1) research and investigation organisations like the Central Water Commission and the Central Groundwater Board, (2) remodelling of headworks, lining of channels and strengthening of drainage in old irrigation works, and (3) replacement of old works that have outlived their useful lives, are not envisaged to enhance irrigation capacity as such. Instead, these are meant more to improve the productivity of the irrigation system as such. Evidently, such outlays unduly raise the derived figures of unit capital costs, the rise being obviously higher for major works.

The foregoing exposition of the principal drawbacks of the plan data on irrigation sector clearly brings out that the estimates of unit capital cost for irrigation works, when derived from such data, can be quite erroneous. Such derived estimates, as we shall demonstrate presently, could be grossly understated in respect of minor irrigation works — especially for wells and tubewells — and considerably overstated for major and medium irrigation works. Evidently inferences based on a comparative analysis of such unit capital cost estimates for various irrigation works cannot be accepted without reservation.

In a capital-short economy like ours it is a very appealing thing to commend to planners options which appear least capital using. In this context, we must reckon with two things, namely, (1) the supporting investments required for each option, and (2) the replacement time after which fresh investment is required for each option. Let us, therefore, look at these aspects of major and minor irrigation options, so as to ascertain which option may strain our capital resources less in the long run. In my assessment, the capital saving argument, contrary to the general impression, is more tilted in favour of major than minor irrigation.

Generally speaking, the useful life of major irrigation works is reckoned at 100 years, after which the civil structures of the canal network need to be reconstructed. As far as the dam is concerned, its life is governed mainly by the number of years it would take to get the 'dead' storage of the reservoir to fill up with silt and debris brought by water inflowing into the reservoir. It is widely agreed that the rate at which reservoir siltation is occurring in India is much higher than the rate assumed by dam designers. Even then, reservoirs are expected to serve useful purpose for 100 years or thereabouts. So, the need for replacement investment in the case of major irrigation works is anticipated to materialise after 100 years. This is far in excess of the corresponding period for minor irrigation works, especially tubewells which are expected to last for 20 years or so under good maintenance conditions. Likewise, pumpsets fitted on open wells need replacement investment in 15-20 years time. It is only the investment embedded in dugwell proper that requires replacement after a much longer time, say, about 50 years in the case of masonary wells located in alluvial soils and 100 years or more for dugwells in hard rock regions.

Major and medium works use the natural force of gravity in their operation, while (groundwater and surface waterlift schemes) need energy for countering the pull of gravity. Thus supporting investments in the energy sector are minimal for canals but quite substantial for minor irrigation. In particular, electric pumpsets / tubewells need requisite investment in power generation equipment and rural electrification system. An average pumpset in India required about 4 KW of power during the mid seventies when each KW of generating capacity cost nearly Rs. 3,000 in capital outlay alone. Today, energisation of a pumpset costs Rs. 20,000 (this is exclusive of investment in power generation).

This author's attempt to compare correctly unit capital costs of major and minor irrigation during the Fifth Plan period (1974-78) reveals the following. The plan statistics yield an estimate of Rs. 6,110 per ha. of irrigation potential created in major and medium irrigation segment during the Fifth Plan period. On the same basis, the estimate for minor irrigation for the same plan averages about Rs. 3,710 per ha. Reckoning with (a) supporting investments, and (b) investments on farmers' own account, this estimate rises to above Rs. 10,000 per ha., which is about two-thirds more than that for major irrigation works. Likewise, the advantage in operating costs is in favour of major irrigation.

The operating cost for canal irrigation in India averaged about Rs. 60 per ha. during 1980-81. This is almost one-tenth of the corresponding cost for groundwater. It is very likely that this differential varies over time and Indian space. Here, two observations would suffice for a discerning reader. First, the operational costs are strictly recurring costs, thereby excluding both the depreciation charge as well as the interest charge on investment cost. Second, an attempt has been made to work out the recurring cost in resource use terms. While we have tried to keep out the elements of taxes and subsidies, no attempt has been made to shadow price the inputs. Thus, the cost of electricity used in wells equipped with electric pumpsets (now the most prevalent mode of groundwater irrigation in the country) is reckoned at the resource cost of supplying it to rural areas. That is, we value electricity neither at its opportunity cost elsewhere in the economy, nor at the highly-subsidised rates actually paid by farmers.

III. Phenomenon of Underutilisation

Capacity utilisation is quite a fascinating subject. But simplistic analysis here can be misleading. Let me give an example. Till the beginning of the eighties one came across the assertion that, while there was full utilisation of capacity in the case of minor irrigation works, there was underutilisation in the case of major irrigation works. There were few discerning readers who knew that full utilisation in respect of minor irrigation works was simply a working assumption of the planners in the Yojana Bhavan. As this assumption was given up from Sixth Plan onwards, the problem of underutilisation of created irrigation potential appeared in the case of minor irrigation works also. It is mainly because of this change in basis for computing capacity utilisation that one now finds that overall level of utilisation of total irrigation potential has now become lower than before. Is this decline a myth or reality?

I must admit I have not carried out any sustained research work on this ticklish question of capacity utilisation. In what follows I would like to share my thoughts on the subject, so as to minimise scope for misgivings in this area.

Capacity utilisation is a fascinating area for industrial economists. In the case of irrigation activity, it is a tricky thing that needs to be handled with extreme caution. It is imperative to appreciate the true nature of our much-talked about problem of underutilisation of water resource. Its two distinct aspects need to be distinguished, namely, the problem of exploitation of water resources as against the problem of full utilisation of the exploited resources. In either case, the picture that may emerge from analysis is affected by the units of measurement, namely, whether the progress is viewed in terms of area statistics or volume of water. In terms of area statistics, it would appear that over three-fourths of the national groundwater potential is already tapped. But the volumetric approach, that is usually adopted by the Central Groundwater Board, would yield an entirely different picture, namely, nearly three-fourths of the groundwater potential is yet to be tapped. What is the ground reality in this area? Mercifully, both the approaches yield similar results in respect of surface irrigation development, that is, six-tenths of the exploitable potential has so far been developed. Here, however, the picture of utilisation of the created potential is sensitive to the approach chosen for analysis. Generally, the area approach, which is normally used by scholars, yield lower rate of utilisation than does the other approach by volume of water. This may be attributed to two reasons. Firstly, while translating volume of water available in reservoirs/streams into their area irrigable counterpart, there creeps in overoptimism with regard to (a) water losses in conveyance, (b) curbing the cultivation of water intensive crops like sugarcane and paddy in canal commands in low rainfall areas, and (c) kharif demand for irrigation in high rainfall areas. As the conveyance losses turn out to be higher and the farmers get away with greater proportion of their crop area under water intensive crops, the utilisation in terms of area statistics becomes lower than that indicated in project reports. The important thing to realise about this unutilised potential is that the water may neither be remaining in the reservoir nor wholly flowing to the sea.

Secondly, the very basis for computing created irrigation potential has been somewhat questionable, Potential is said to be established when the canal network owned and maintained by the irrigation department is completed. Field channels, the last bit of the canal system, are supposed to be set up by farmers. Evidently, farmers' failure to do so would give rise to underutilisation of created potential. Lately, attempt is being made, mainly through the Command Area Development programme, to construct field channels as part of the project.

Irrigation being a capital intensive activity, periodic reports of gross underutilisation of capacity of new irrigation projects become a source of dismay. Such estimates of underutilisation of irrigation capacity, derived as these are from a simple juxtaposition of actual area irrigated (A) against area potentially irrigable (P), need to be interpreted with caution last erroneous inferences should arise. A low value of this utilisation ratio (A/P. 100) does not necessarily mean that lot of costly water is flowing to the sea. For the ratio tends to recede below 100 as the actual crop pattern tends to tilt in favour of heavily-irrigated crops (like sugarcane and paddy). Since Indian farmers have shown much stronger preference for paddy and sugarcane than what has been contemplated in irrigation project reports, this imparts an inherent downward bias to the utilisation ratio. Likewise, a high value of this ratio does not imply a near-capacity utilisation situation if each irrigated hectare receives much less irrigation water than what is contemplated in the capacity estimate 'P'. Since Indian irrigation system is believed to be delivering to farmers water much less than the provision made while designing the system, some perceptive scholars have rightly perceived an element of upward bias in the utilisation ratio on this count.

To what extent this upward bias is counterbalanced by the downward bias due to the deviation in crop pattern is not possible to figure out. Given these limitations, one cannot conclude much about the true extent of underutilisation of irrigation in India by a simple recourse to the utilisation ratio. Apparently, for the irrigation sector as a whole the official statistics of irrigation potential and benefitted area reveal a picture of 'good utilisation' that compares favourably with the level attained in the Indian Industry sector, that is, above 85 percent. Some observers have discerned a downward tendency in the ratio. This tendency has partly emerged because of a change in procedure, in the sense that in recent years statistics of utilisation are no more computed on the assumption of full utilisation of minor irrigation potential. Anyway, much of this 'unutilised capacity' is in the surface irrigation works.

Given the pitfalls of the utilisation ratio as a measure of performance, some critics have taken recourse to alternative ways of judging the extent of underutilisation in Indian irrigation. Since the principal objective of irrigation is to augment agricultural production, they appraise the performance of Indian irrigation by comparing the crop yields of irrigated lands with some normative levels. These normative values are seldom drawn from the expected values used in the irrigation project reports (while computing the ex-ante benefit-cost ratio for a project) but are derived from two data sources namely, (1) crop yields observed prevailing on well-managed irrigation systems elsewhere, and (2) yields realised on national demonstration plots. In terms of foodgrains, Indian yield on irrigated lands averages about 20 quintals/ha., which is far below the level of 50 to 60 quintals/ha. in the Far East, and also substantially below the level of 35 to 40 quintals/ha. obtaining on the demonstration plots. Evidently, in such reckonings the performance of Indian irrigation emerges in poor light. But one may question the relevance of such an approach to the problem of underutilisation of capacity on two counts. Firstly, irrigation by itself is expected to enhance rainfed or unirrigated crop yield (varying from 4 to 8 quintals/ha.) by 3 to 5 quintals/ha. only. The high crop yields in the Far East, as also on the demonstration plots, are based on very intensive application of bio-chemical inputs. Thus the lower yields may be partly traceable to the less intensive application of fertilisers and pesticides. The question is : what are the determinants of input intensification in agriculture?

Secondly, much of the Indian public irrigation is deliberately designed not to encourage very intensive farming but to promote irrigated farming in as much areal extent as possible. In other words, canal water is rather thinly deployed by fixing large command area in relation to availability of irrigation water. (In technical terms, 'water allowance' is kept low, or 'water duty' per unit volume of water is kept high). What ever be the motives behind such 'under-irrigated' farming, in which irrigation needs of plants are not met upto the point at which maximum yield potential of a crop is attained, such farming effectively brings about maximisation of crop output per unit of irrigation water. Then, why judge its performance in terms of crop output per unit of area?

IV. Summary View

(1) Groundwater is naturally much less bountiful than surface water. In low rainfall regions, hardly one fourth of the irrigation potential can be tapped from natural groundwater sources. Here, man-made efforts in developing canals (and tanks) provide a key to the development of a productive, stable and sustainable groundwater-based agriculture. For, these surface water works act as powerful instruments of artificial ground water replenishment.

(2) Irrespective of the type of irrigation, its development is a very costly proposition. Any one talking of developing groundwater irrigation at a fraction of the high cost of major irrigation works is taking a partial view of costs incurred by the nation in developing groundwater irrigation in India. The true

cost advantage may be in developing canal, and not well irrigation.

(3) The issue of developing this or that irrigation resource is, by and large, a non-issue in the Indian context of scarcity of water resources and their close interlinkage. If at all any special emphasis on developing one particular source of irrigation is needed, we may pursue the following policy for different regions. Since much of the unexploited groundwater potential of the nation is presently located in the high rainfall areas of the east Gangetic plains and Madhya Pradesh, groundwater irrigation may be promoted here. Elsewhere, promotional efforts should be much more directed at surface water exploitation.

(4) Since the basis for adjudging underutilisation of irrigation capacity is admittedly of a questionable merit, one should beware of such estimates. Much of utilised irrigation potential of major irrigation works of the nation is of a fictitious nature. This is especially true for works located in low and medium rainfall regions of southern and western India. To some extent, the illusion of underutilisation of irrigation potential is heightened by the following two factors: (1) Deliberate overassessment of the irrigation capability of an irrigation work being promoted for clearance from the Centre, and (ii) the incompletion of distribution network because of resource paucity.

(5) The sustainability of canal-based agriculture is threatened from two sides, namely, excessive siltation of reservoirs, and the twin problem of waterlogging and salinity development in the canal command. Both are very vexitious problems, much less amenable to technical solutions than to organisational solutions in the realm of preventive action. There is no alternative to commensurate investment in programmes of soil conservation in the catchments of the reservoirs, so as to keep the siltation rate within tolerable limits. Drainage is likewise an answer to waterlogging. But it is better to achieve this in a vertical instead of horizontal manner, that is, through wells and tubewells. Towards this end, a policy of extensive canal irrigation may induce farmers to invest in their own wells/tubewells, which would serve the twin purpose of supplementary irrigation and vertical drainage of the seeped-in canal waters.

REFERENCES

Chawla, A.S. and Sharma, H.D. (1984). Conjunctive Use Components — A Comparative Study. National Seminar on Modernisation of Canal Irrigation at Lucknow, Indian Water Resources Society, Roorkee.

Dhawan, B.D.(1989a). Studies in Irrigation and Water Management, Commonwealth Publishers, New Delhi.

Dhawan, B.D. (1989b). Mounting Antagonism towards Big Dams, Economic and Political Weekly, Vol 24, No. 20, May 20.

Dhawan, B.D. (1988). Irrigation in India's Agricultural Development, Sage Publications, New Delhi.

Dhawan, B.D. (1986). Economics of Groundwater Irrigation in Hard Rock Regions, with special reference to Maharashtra, Agricole Publishing Academy, New Delhi.

CHAPTER 7

REPLENISHING GROUNDWATER RESOURCE*

Introduction

It is now a widely accepted principle of irrigation development that groundwater and surface water be better exploited in a balanced manner. This balanced development, which is nothing but simultaneous development of irrigation from both these sources of water of a region, is called conjunctive irrigation. This preoccupation with a single water source is no more looked upon with favour in irrigation planning circles.

Whereas too much attention to development of-canal irrigation gives rise to problems of waterlogging and salinity before long, exclusive reliance on well irrigation can deplete- and sometimes damage also- groundwater resource. Such depletion has occurred all over the world, thanks partly to the advent of two technologies of power pumps and ground boring. In India, the depletion has occurred in some pockets of groundwater-short northern, southern and western regions of the country.

This has led to two demands. On the one hand, state legislatures are being vociferously urged upon to enact suitable groundwater regulation laws. On the other hand, the Indian water planners are being called upon to invest in

---

* Published in the *Financial Express*, 10 April, 1990.

measures aimed at replenishing groundwater resource through artificial means.

Both these demands are of an alien origin, in the sense that the idea behind them is picked up from elsewhere, notably the United States. Little wonder, then, their workability in Indian conditions of small land holdings and scarcity of land resource is of doubtful value. In what follows the focus is on artificial groundwater recharge. To comprehend the mechanics of artificial groundwater recharge, we must first understand what is natural groundwater recharge.

What is Groundwater Resource

Natural groundwater recharge occurs every year, the source of recharge being rainfall. This happens in two principal ways: (1) infiltration of rain drops directly into the ground, and (2) soaking of fields with flood waters of a river in great spate. Usually, the component (1) is much bigger than the component (2). However, if the floods are pervasive and the flood waters are held back in the fields for considerable duration, the component (2) can become quite substantial *vis-a-vis* the other component. If groundwater resource in a tract is already depleted, ample 'empty' or porous space in the voids of ground underneath exists for absorbing flood waters.

Whatever has seeped through the ground, whether directly from rainfall or via flood waters, the whole of it is not deemed as groundwater resource which can be tapped for irrigation (or industrial/civic use) purpose. The tappable part is the one which has managed to reach, through the downward pull of earth's force of gravity, the level of groundwater table. The rest of it is retained in the crop root zone from where crops meet their needs of water (for evapo-transpiration as well as for metabolic purpose). This crop root zone is generally taken as the top 5 to 6 feet of the soil depth, that being the normal length of the roots of a field crop. (In-between the crop root zone and the water table is the so-called 'capillary' zone). The moisture of this root zone is not counted as part of groundwater resource.

Artificial Recharge

Soil-climatic factors of a tract play a dominant role in natural groundwater recharge. More the rainfall, the higher would be the recharge. Likewise, the harder the ground geology, the less would be the recharge from a given rainfall. Both rainfall and geological factors being given in nature, there emerges a fixedness in proportion of rainfall that becomes groundwater resource for each given tract.

Usually, about one-fifth of the rainfall precipitation becomes groundwater recharge in tracts underlain with deep alluvial soils such as those found in the vast Indo-Gangetic alluvium of northern parts of the Indian sub-continent. To illustrate, if Punjab receives 600mm of rain in a normal year, about 120 mm will become groundwater resource of the state. The same fraction for hard rock regions of southern Indian peninsula varies between one-tenth and one-twentieth; for arid or desert areas like western Rajasthan the fraction is nearly one-hundredth. Whatever be the natural level of the fraction for a tract, the quantum of volume of groundwater recharge varies considerably from year to year as the level of annual rainfall in a year fluctuates as per the rainfall cycle of the tract. That is to say, the volume of groundwater recharge tends to diminish during drought years, but rises perceptibly during above-normal rainfall years. It is the mean value of this recharge over several years that is reckoned as the groundwater potential of a tract.

A rain drop splits into three portions after touching the land surface: run-off water, water infiltrating into the land, and instantly evaporated water. By artificial recharge the connotation is one of enhancing, through man-made interventions, the magnitude of the fraction of rainfall infiltrating to the groundwater table. In other words, the human action is such as leads to a decrease in the run-off water, which reaches streams and rivers, and an increase in the infiltrated water. For instance, erection of bunds in paddy fields may sharply raise the fraction of the rain water seeping to water table. Some of this gain, however, may be eroded as fine clay begins to settle down below the paddy fields, forming a sort of impermeable crust that impedes the process of downward movement of the infiltrated water. A similar improvement occurs when small farm ponds are excavated by farmers with a view to providing "life saving" irrigation to their crops during a break in the monsoon spell. Likewise, advent of social forestry can enhance groundwater recharge in that area. Since trees have very deep root system and have large water requirements to meet the evapo-transpiration needs of their massive foliage, they tend to utilise most of the added groundwater recharge.

A percolation tank is an apt example of human endeavour to improve groundwater availability through artificial groundwater recharge. Such tanks are to be distinguished from conventional irrigation tanks. They are constructed with the sole purpose of enhancing rainfall infiltration into the ground. This objective is achieved by bunding a small stream at a point where the bed rock is porous ('murum'). The porosity of the rock allows much of the ponded water to infiltrate to the groundwater table. This improves groundwater availability in wells established on the downstream side of such a tank. Unlike in an irrigation tank, there is no provision made for water sluices in the bund of a percolation tank. As the effectiveness of a percolation tank hinges on the porosity of the rock under the tank spread, some prior investment in geological investigation is needed in identifying suitable tank sites. Otherwise a percolation tank can become merely an 'evaporation' tank when constructed in haste on an impermeable tank site. The possibility of such infructuous investment in tanks is high during drought years when crash relief works are constructed with a view to providing some gainful employment to the people.

An irrigation tank, which is characterised as a minor surface irrigation work in Indian irrigation parlance, does also improve groundwater recharge, but incidentally. As the tank water is allowed to move in earthen channels issuing forth from tank outlets or sluices to fields in the tank command, a small fraction out of it seeps through to the groundwater table during the course of conveyance. Likewise, some percolation of groundwater table occurs in the tank spread area, depending upon the porosity of rock material underlying the tank bed. But the most substantive addition to groundwater resource comes from field percolation. That is to say, tank water applied to a crop tends to seep well below the crop root zone down to the groundwater table. This could be as much as one-fifth of the tank water applied in most crops, but could be almost one-third if the irrigated crop happens to be paddy. Since paddy occupies more than nine-tenths of the total crop area in the South Indian tanks, such tanks become a marvellous source of groundwater recharge. The gradual decline in tank irrigation in India means that an important source of man-made groundwater recharge has been weakened. Whatever be the seepage rate, the point to note is how the very development of surface water-based irrigation *incidentally* improves groundwater availability.

What happens on a small-scale in the case of a single tank occurs on a massive scale in the case of major canal system. A canal system is inherently very leaky: a large part of the water released from the headworks of the canal system is lost to groundwater table. While the loss in conveyance can be substantially cut by investing in canal lining, precious little can be done about loss due to field percolation. Typically, 50 to 60 per cent of the water released in a totally unlined canal system ends up as groundwater resource. Even in a lined system, this percentage is quite substantial, 35 to 40 per cent. Thus, developing canal irrigation is a marvellous but incidental way of artificial groundwater recharge. Therefore, those who are concerned about groundwater depletion in groundwater-short areas should commend to the water planners surface water based irrigation works, especially canal networks.

Today, north-western wheat belt of India, comprising Punjab, West U.P. and parts of Haryana, is said to be very bountiful in groundwater endowment. This bounty is mainly due to the extensive development of canal irrigation in this area. As no worthwhile investment was undertaken here either in canal lining or in a horizontal drainage system, the seeped-in canal water gradually built up the water table. The intensive development of private tubewell irrigation in this region is being sustained by these seeped in canal waters. As the canals here are protective in character and meet only about one-third of the irrigation needs of farmers, this induces the farmers to invest in tubewell irrigation. (Incidentally, the rise of private tubewell irrigation has ensured vertical drainage of the canal tracts).

Punjab Experience

Let us look at the Punjab experience more closely. Today, this state is deemed well endowed in groundwater. But this is not a natural occurrence. By nature, the state cannot be rated high in groundwater availability. Prior to the development of canal irrigation, good availability of groundwater was confined to narrow strips in the vicinity of its perennial rivers. Elsewhere, groundwater was found deep below the land surface. In quantitative terms, groundwater availability was not good because the total rainfall of the state is low (about 60 cm.). Even if one was to adopt the norms for rainfall infiltration for the alluvial areas as per the Groundwater Estimation Committee (1984), the groundwater recharge amounts to somewhere between 12 and 15 cm. per unit of land area. The gross inadequacy of this amount for providing irrigation in the state may be judged from the fact that for wheat crop during the rabi season a farmer requires about 45 cm. of irrigation water as recommended by the Punjab Agricultural University. In fact, for the common paddy-wheat sequence the recommended (net) irrigation applications would amount to at least eight times the above level of groundwater availability.

But for canal seepage, much of the groundwater would be encountered far below the ground surface as the sandy soils of the state fail to impede the downward pull of gravity on the infiltrated water. No wonder, then, that much of the groundwater-based farming in the state in the pre-canal era (i.e., Mughal times) was confined predominantly to tracts adjoining perennial rivers of the state which kept the groundwater table high enough for animal-operated persian wheels (rahats) that could not cope with water table deeper than 35 feet below the ground surface. In such a groundwater regime, the establishment of a state-wide network of canals is akin to perennial rivers keeping the ground-water table high all over the state. Despite over-exploitation of groundwater (partly due to rainfall deficiency since 1979-80) and the resultant lowering of water table, the lowered water table is still far above the pre-canal level of 50 to 100 feet observed during the Mughal days. For example, the depth to water table in Patiala district, known for recession in water table by about 5 metres since 1973, is still about 30 feet only.

Let us see how much of the crop output of the state's groundwater-based agriculture can be attributed to the seeped-in canal waters withdrawn through nearly 0.7 million shallow tubewells established by the state farmers by the mid-eighties. The total crop output from 0.7 million tubewells may be placed at 14 million tons in foodgrains equivalent units. This is worked out as follows. The land productivity under wells during the mid-eighties stood around 6.5 tons per net hectare. (It is a projected estimate based on the following past bench-mark estimates : 1.75 tons for 1950-51, 3.06 tons for the mid-sixties, and 5.46 tons for the late seventies). Its multiplication with the reported area of 2.21 million hectares under well irrigation in the state during 1984-85 gives rise to an output figure of about 14 million tons — the corresponding estimate for output originating from nearly 1.4 million ha. of canal-irrigated area may be placed at 4.9 million tons.

Assuming for the moment that the groundwater resource was in a state of full exploitation in the mid-eighties, the task of assessing how much of the groundwater-based output (of 14 million tons) is to be ascribed to the seeped-in canal waters becomes really one of finding how much of the groundwater recharge of the state can be attributed to artificial groundwater recharge as distinguished from natural recharge. The available evidence, though not very firm, indicates that canal waters account for at least half of the total groundwater recharge of the state — the upper limit to this fraction could be as high as seven-tenths.

Thus anywhere between 7 and 10 million tons (foodgrain equivalents) in the mid-eighties in the state were raised with the help of percolated water from the main and minor canals, from water courses below the final outlet (turnout), and from canal-irrigated fields. When this is reckoned alongwith the direct output from canal-irrigated fields the total output augmentation from the establishment of major surface irrigation works in the state becomes much more impressive. For, in the mid-eighties the net canal-irrigated area of the state is estimated to have yielded about 5 million tons in foodgrain equivalents. Thus, the ultimate contribution of canals is 2.4 - 3.0 times the directly reported output from canal irrigation.

Tamil Nadu Experience

Let us look at estimates for Tamil nadu in the South, where both canals and tanks are together very important man-made instruments for incidental groundwater recharge. The natural availability of groundwater in this state is modestly good, except in the low rainfall districts like Coimbatore and Dharmapuri. For one, it is a state with medium rainfall conditions. Secondly, its normal rainfall of the order of 1000 mm is rather well distributed over both the south-west and the north-east monsoon periods of the year, thereby enhancing scope for groundwater replenishment through a greater fraction of rainfall infiltrating into the ground. Thirdly, though much of the state is underlain with rocky geology, the rocks here are not that impervious as of the basaltic areas of Karnataka and Maharashtra in the Deccan plateau — their lack of compactness and crystalline character at places provides more porous space for water storage underneath the ground.

The goundwater regime of the state has further improved because of extensive development of surface irrigation works. The state is well known for its long recorded history of both small-scale and large-scale irrigation works based on surface water flows. Half the state area is presently under irrigation. Now, further development of irrigated agriculture is getting hampered because the irrigation potential of the state is now almost fully exploited. Eversince the full development of surface irrigation potential was attained towards the beginning of the Fourth Five Year Plan, more and more attention got focussed on groundwater development. In terms of number of wells/pumpsets per unit area, the state ranks at the top among the Indian states. But for the seepage from canals and tanks, the level of development of well irrigation in the lower rainfall tracts of the state would have been seriously hindered, as also creating problem of pressure on groundwater resource. The portion of field percolation in total canal/tank seepage here is relatively high because of the mono culture of paddy under surface irrigation works in the state. Anyway, now well irrigation is the single most important source of irrigation. It is estimated that gross cropped area under state wells during 1978-79 was about 1.7 million hectares as compared to about 1.2 million hectares under canal irrigation and about 0.9 million hectares under tank irrigation. When one reckons with the higher land productivity under well irrigation, nearly two-thirds of the state agricultural output turns out to be from groundwater-irrigated lands.

Towards the end of the seventies, each net hectare area under well irrigation produced about 6.50 tons in foodgrains equivalent units. Thus, the total production from lands under well irrigation amounted to about 6.95 million tons. Somewhere between one-fourth and two-fifths of this production may be attributed to the seeped-in canal and tank waters.

Concluding Remarks

Hydrologists invariably emphasise hydrological linkages of water bodies, but without a precise quantification of their economic implications. Our limited attempt to quantify these reveals interesting results with regard to the beneficial role of canal waters in improving groundwater regime and groundwater-based agriculture in water-short regions. These waters have boosted the groundwater-based farming both in terms of number of sustainable wells and crop output per well. At least half of the state output from private tubewell irrigation in Punjab can be confidently attributed to groundwater that is of canal origin. In Tamil Nadu state, both canals and tanks together make a substantial augmentation to its natural groundwater availability. Somewhere between one-fourth and two-fifths of the total output of the wells established in the state may be traced to seeped-in waters of canal/tank origin. These findings should set at rest the controversy about surface versus groundwater irrigation for low and medium rainfall regions.

CHAPTER 8

HIGH CAPITAL NEEDS OF MINOR IRRIGATION DEVELOPMENT*

Introduction

That huge capital funds are required for developing minor irrigation facilities is not well appreciated even in quite knowledgeable circles. This lack of appreciation rekindles memories from early Indian planning experience. The First and the Second Five Year Plans were drawn up on a tacit assumption that capital needs of the agriculture sector in a developing economy are low. That capital needs of a modern agriculture sector can be quite high was brought home during the course of Third Plan. This realisation deepened as it was discovered that the unit cost of major irrigation for each hectare of crop area benefitted was substantial (it is now in the neighbourhood of Rs. 45,000/ha.).

But the erstwhile charming view of minor irrigation being a low cost proposition still persists in popular mind, as also in non-engineering circles in which big dam idea has become an unwelcome proposition. The central objective of this article is to dispel this 'romantic' view or myth.

Basis for the Myth

Let us first explore how the view that minor irrigation is a low cost option in India might have originated in the first

---

* Abridged version published in the *Financial Express*, 16 January, 1993.

place. I can think of two possible reasons. The first pertains to the scale or size of an irrigation work, which can get mentally ignored in mind's calculus. A single minor irrigation work (a tank or a tubewell or a dugwell) does indeed require a tiny amount of investment in comparison to a single major irrigation scheme. Without relating the investment to the crop area to be benefitted from a single minor irrigation work and not looking at the (derived) estimate of unit cost per irrigated hectare for that work, one cannot say whether in a capital-short economy this work is really a low cost option *vis-a-vis* another work of much larger size (in terms of investment as well as benefitted area). If readers come across comparative investment data for one major and one minor irrigation work only, in the absence of corresponding statistics on crop areas to be benefitted from the two many of them can hastily form the loose impression of minor irrigation development being a low cost proposition.

The second factor, quite related to the first one, arises out of the history of public irrigation development in India under the British rule. Till the thirties of this century (when public lift irrigation through big tubewells was undertaken for the first time in Uttar Pradesh), public irrigation has been based on surface water sources, without recourse to any water lifting. That is to say, 'flow' irrigation has been in vogue, in which the force of the earth's gravity is harnessed to move water from the tapping point, say, a barrage or a weir on a river, to farmers' fields. In the case of small surface irrigation works like tanks and 'kuhls' in hilly areas, the resultant financial demand on the budgets of the state administration is obviously small. But for major public irrigation works the investment needs were found to be too high to be accommodated within the limited revenue resources from taxes and non-tax sources of those days, thereby necessitating their financing from capital budget. Such works came to be labelled as major irrigation schemes in official parlance. Likewise, schemes individually making little demand on the revenue budgets came to be described as minor ones, thereby possibly creating an erroneous impression as if their construction entails low capital outlay per unit area brought under irrigation. Whereas the costs of major irrigation were envisaged to be recovered from the beneficiary farmers — so as to repay the borrowed funds used in their establishment — no such cost recovery was visualised in the case of minor irrigation works (recovery was limited to their recurring costs, i.e., maintenance and operational costs). Before long, a financial norm was evolved to categorise public irrigation works into minor, medium and major schemes. While this three-way, somewhat unique to India, categorisation still continues, its basis since 1977-78 is no more financial outlay but area to be benefitted by a scheme: CCA to be less than 2000 ha. for a minor work; 2,000-10,000 ha. for a medium work, and above 10,000 ha. for a major work.

Totality of Development Costs

In adjudging the costliness of any man-made activity one must take a total view of costs incurred in establishing and in maintaining that activity. This totality has two distinct dimensions. On the one side, we must reckon with both the one-shot and the recurring costs. On the other, all development outlays, irrespective of who incurs these, must be taken into account. In other words, the capital costs have to be viewed from the angle of the economy as a whole. Thus, costs on private as well as public account have to be duly counted. Also, any crucial supporting outlays without which an activity is inoperable have to be duly reckoned with.

For instance, in the development of minor irrigation involving the use of electric power the requisite capital cost of establishing the electricity supply system for meeting the power needs of electric pumpsets has to be kept in mind. Without such supporting investments in power generation, in transmission system and in rural electrification, installation of more electric pumpsets could only result in overburdening the existing electric supply system.

This overburden may manifest itself through either (a) less availability of power for pumpset operation both in quantity and in quality terms, or (b) diversion of power away from non-agricultural sectors by the government so as to maintain intact power supply to agricultural pumps. In the situation (a), the crop output-augmenting role of minor irrigation development gets substantially eroded when farm output does not expand commensurately with increase in irrigation capacity. In the situation (b), the society obtains the benefit of additional farm production from new capacity in minor irrigation at the hidden cost of output foregone from industry and other productive sectors from where electricity diversion takes place. In practice, a mix of these two situations has prevailed in India because expansion in power supply system has lagged behind demand for power from all sectors taken together.

For a number of reasons I am not going to probe here into the topical but highly complex issue of comparative costliness of minor and major irrigation options in India. For one, this issue loses significance once one duly appreciates two compulsions: (i) the imperative of balanced or conjunctive development of both major and minor irrigation, and (ii) the obligation to develop all sources of irrigation because of poorer endowment of our water *vis-a-vis* land resources on the one hand, and our huge and growing needs of food on the other. For another, requisite and firm data for settling the issue beyond the pale of doubt are not yet available. The recourse by some investigators to statistics on irrigated areas and financial outlays given in Five Year Plan documents generates unit cost estimates of dubious reliability for two reasons. One is the non-mention of private investment on minor irrigation on farmers' own account in Plan documents. Because of this omission, the derived estimates of unit capital cost of minor irrigation development come out on the low side. The other is the long gestation period of major irrigation schemes which tends to overstate, in a scenario of accelerated development of irrigation, the unit capital cost for major irrigation.

Therefore, we better focus here on the limited question of the sheer costliness of minor irrigation as such. After all, the aim of this article is to underline this very aspect of modern minor irrigation, for which we propose to take a total view of capital costs of developing this mode of irrigation with the aid of electric pumpsets. Electric pumpset is an efficient waterlifting mechanism. The number of such pumpsets has increased phenomenally over the period of planning in India. Of the existing total number of minor irrigation works of the order of 15 million, over nine million are equipped with electric pumpsets. In contrast, such pumpsets accounted for hardly 2 per cent of all minor works in 1951 when planning commenced in the country.

Typical Capital Cost Estimates

Electric pumpsets in use in India are typically of 5 HP capacity, each costing about Rs. 8,000. According to the statistics periodically released by the Central Electricity Authority (CEA) in its document *All India Statistics: General Review*, there were nearly 7.6 million connections given for agricultural pumping purpose by the end of 1988-89. Their combined 'connected load' amounted to nearly 28,000 MW in the total 'connected load' of the order of 106,000 MW for the nation as a whole. Thus the average 'connected load' per agricultural connection works out to nearly 3.64 MW (4.88 HP). Some regional variation in this average capacity per connection/ pumpset is discernible as per the following figures :

1. Northern Region	4.06 KW
2. Western Region	3.87 KW
3. Southern Region	3.24 KW
4. Eastern Region	3.33 KW
5. NE Region	9.64 KW

Obviously, the rated pumpset capacity in a region would be higher if large capacity tubewells and community surface lift irrigation schemes are relatively more in the total number of agricultural connections. Thus, the average capacity for U.P. turns out to be nearly one-fourth higher than that for

Punjab (3.45 KW) because U.P. has more of large capacity state tubewells in total number of tubewells as revealed by the following data derived from the Census of Minor Irrigation (1986-87).

	Punjab	*U.P.*
1. No. of shallow electric tubewells (000)	485	359
2. No. of deep electric tubewells (000)	1	28
3. Total	486	387

Though the capital cost of an electric pumpset rises with its horse power, the rise is much less than proportionate. While analysing the scale economies in tubewell irrigation in India it is found by this author that for pumpsets in the capacity range of 5 to 75 HP the elasticity of pumpset price w.r.t. horse power or capacity is about 0.42. Generally, this cost component does not account for a major share of total capital cost of a minor irrigation work. More importantly, its share in total cost tends to diminish with increase in the size of a minor irrigation work. In the case of deep tubewells set up under public aegis in U.P. it is found that this share is anticipated to decline from 17.4 to 11.5 per cent of total tubewell installation cost when the tubewell discharge capacity is raised 12 times (from 0.014 cubic m/second to 0.168 cubic m/second).

Typically, capital cost of installing a dugwell/tubewell today varies as follows: about Rs. 20,000 per dugwell, Rs.7,000 per shallow tubewell, and Rs. 600,000 per deep tubewell (under public aegis) — these costs are exclusive of electric pumpset cost in the case of dugwells and shallow tubewells. These costs vary across regions of the country, partly for reasons of differences in dimensions of wells and partly because of differences in ground geology. Thus a dugwell in hard rock region would cost possibly twice as much as a dugwell in alluvial areas. Likewise, this cost rises with increase in either depth of the well or depth to water table.

Anyway, an idea about regional variations in construction costs of dugwells can be gathered from the estimates given in column 4 of Table 1. These statistics once again show that the share of electric pumpset cost in total cost of a composite dugwell is lower in comparison to the cost of civil works of a dugwell.

TABLE 1

STATEWISE CONSTRUCTION COSTS OF WELLS UNDER JAWAHAR ROZGAR YOJANA DURING 1988-89 TO 1991-92

S.No.	*State*	*No. of wells*	*Total cost (Rs. lakh)*	*Cost per well (Rs. 000)*
1.	Andhra Pradesh	14,521	4,807	33
2.	Bihar	109,739	16,313	15
3.	Gujarat	14,972	3,779	25
4.	Karnataka	7,437	2,111	28
5.	Madhya Pradesh	46,207	6,912	15
6.	Maharashtra	21,843	6,150	28
7.	Orissa	33,380	3,868	12
8.	Rajasthan	22,602	4,830	21
9.	Tamil Nadu	8,286	2,060	25
10.	W. Bengal	15,450	4,709	31
	All India	304,760	63,481	21

Source: Annual Report, Ministry of Rural Development, 1991-92.

Irrigation Capacity Norms

Measurement of irrigation capacity of any irrigation work is a ticklish task, more so in the case of a minor irrigation work. It is not our purpose here to dwell on the myriad difficulties one encounters in such measurement. This explicit mention is being made here so as to underscore that such estimates, needed badly as these are, be better taken with due circumspection. Without such capacity estimates for electrically operated minor irrigation works, one cannot derive unit capital cost for each hectare of crop area brought under such irrigation.

We have two sources on such capacity norms. According to the Groundwater Estimates Committee (1984), a dugwell equipped with a pumpset could irrigate about two crop ha. area per year in the states of Andhra Pradesh, Bihar and Maharashtra. Likewise, a shallow tubewell could irrigate following areas in different states.

1.	West Bengal	3 ha.
2.	Andhra Pradesh, Bihar, Haryana, Tripura and Rajasthan	4 ha.
3.	Punjab and U.P.	5 ha.
4.	M.P.	7 ha.
5.	Tamil Nadu	8 ha.

Capacity norms can also be derived from the data on total estimated irrigation potential and the number of minor irrigation works gathered through the Census of Minor Irrigation. Such data are distinguished by five categories of minor irrigation works: (1) dugwells, (2) shallow tubewells, (3) deep tubewells, (4) surface flow irrigation works, and (5) surface lift irrigation works. In the case of dugwells the derived estimate of irrigation capacity per dugwell turns out to be on the low side because many of these dugwells are still equipped with traditional water lifts operated with animal or human power. It is well known that such traditional wells have much less irrigation capability than modern dugwells equipped with pumpsets. According to the Groundwater Estimates Committee, the following order of differential in irrigation capacity between these two types of dugwells could exist in various regions of the country:

	Irrigated area (ha)
1. *Andhra Pradesh*	
Dugwell with 'mhot'	0.5
Dugwell with pumpset	2.0
2. *Bihar*	
Dugwell without pump	
(i) upto 3 metres diameter	0.6
(ii) 3-6 metres diameter	1.0
3. *Maharashtra*	
Dugwell with 'mhot'	0.5
Dugwell with pumpset	2.0
4. *U.P.*	
Masonry dugwell with persian wheel	1.5

In view of the non-availability of separate statistics for dugwells equipped with electric pumpsets, we have adopted the following procedure to get at the needed estimates. We have identified those states where dugwells are predominantly equipped with power pumps. Assuming that diesel-powered and electric-powered pumpset are identical in irrigable area capacity, we give in Table 2 the derived capacity norms for such identified states. We find the capacity estimate for modern dugwell in Gujarat, namely, 3.6 ha. per dugwell, to be comparatively high. For Tamil Nadu and Andhra Pradesh, this very estimate is marginally above one hectare, and it is in the neighbourhood of 1.5 ha. in hard rock states of Karnataka, Maharashtra and Madhya Pradesh. Thus it is only in Haryana that one comes across the estimate to be nearer the two ha. norm typically mentioned for a dugwell with electric pumpset in groundwater circles.

The estimates of irrigation potential per tubewell and per surface water lift are also listed in Table 2. There is much more variation across states in these two categories of works than observed in the case of dugwells. This is indicative of two things. First, there is much more scope for varying the scale or size of a tubewell or lift irrigation scheme than is possible with a dugwell. In point of fact, water yield from a dugwell is not as elastic with respect to its dimensions, especially w.r.t. its diameter, as is the case with a tubewell. Second, aquifer variations across states in the case of tubewells might be quite pronounced, especially outside the Indo-Gangetic plains.

Supporting Investment Per Pumpset

Investments in urban electricity supply system arise on three counts: power generation, power transmission, and power distribution. While extending the electricity supply system to rural areas with a view to energising pumpsets in farmers' fields, a fourth type of investment, namely, rural electrification, becomes necessary in Indian conditions.

TABLE 2

STATEWISE IRRIGATION POTENTIAL PER MINOR IRRIGATION WORK WITH PUMPSET

S.No.	*State*	*Dugwells*	*Shallow tube-wells*	*Deep tube-wells*	*Surface lift irrigation*
1.	Andhra Pradesh	1.2	2.5	10.1	7.4
2.	Gujarat	3.6	11.0	24.0	21.3
3.	Haryana	2.2	5.0	14.4	78.9
4.	Karnataka	1.5	2.2	2.5	7.2
5.	Madhya Pradesh	1.4	4.0	8.8	3.6
6.	Maharashtra	1.6	2.0	2.0	5.1
7.	Orissa	NA	8.2	30.0	21.8
8.	Punjab	NA	6.4	81.6	10.0
9.	Tamil Nadu	1.1	1.7	2.7	3.5
10.	Uttar Pradesh	NA	4.1	65.0	NA
11.	West Bengal	NA	2.6	63.5	NA

All these investments on four counts must take place in a balanced manner for creating an efficient electricity supply system, though investment in power generation is of a prior character. The thumb rule for this balanced investment is that for every four Rupees of investment in power generation segment, two Rupees be put in transmission segment, one Rupee each in distribution segment and rural electrification. One of the weaknesses of investments in Indian power sector during the course of planning has been under-investment in transmission and distribution system (a like deficiency has been noted in the case of major irrigation works also where conveyance and distribution network is underfunded *vis-a-vis* headworks or dam building).

We have to find answers to two following questions before we can figure out the supporting capital investment required for energising one electric pumpset. First, what is the magnitude of the cumulative investments that have taken place so far in the Indian electricity supply system as a whole? Second, what portion of this capital has to be attributed to the electric pumpsets?

Taking up the second question first, the proportion of total electricity used by agriculture sector could be a worthwhile basis for apportioning joint capital costs. According to the CEA statistics, Indian agriculture utilised about 24 per cent of the total electricity sold during 1987-88 as well 1988-89 when the number of electric pumpsets was around 8 million. Bur from the point of view of connected load Indian agriculture accounted for nearly 27 percent of the total system load. These percentages suggest that one-fourth of the capital cost of electric power system in India can be fairly allocated to the electric pumpsets.

The capital locked in Indian electricity supply system can be estimated in two ways: either as a summation of Plan-wise outlays for the power sector, or as sum total of capital shown in the books of the various electricity boards, private power companies, and central power corporations like the National Thermal Power Corporation and the National Hydro Power Corporation. In either case, one encounters the problem of capital being at book or historical values. In view of the price inflation prevailing since the Second Five Year Plan, capital estimate so obtained through cumulation requires upward price adjustments so as to reflect investment costs of today. Such adjustments cannot be carried out without information on the time path of this capital accumulation in the past, something which is not readily available.

Our purpose being quite limited, we have chosen the following indirect route to get at the order of capital locked in Indian electricity supply system. At 1990-91 prices, the 8th Plan outlay for power sector is placed at about Rs. 80,000 crores. As a result of this investment, about 21,401 MW of new installed generating capacity would be added during the 8th Plan. The installed capacity existing at the end of 1989-90 is found to be about twice this proposed new capacity. Thus, one may say that about Rs. 160,000 crores (at 1990-91 prices) stood invested in our electricity supply system as on 31st March, 1990.

Of this investment, one-fourth or about Rs. 40,000 crores may be attributed to 8 million electric pumpsets. Thus we get an estimate of Rs. 50,000 for supporting investment per pumpset. So, to energise a pumpset worth Rs. 8,000 the supporting investment for the nation today is in the neighbourhood of Rs. 50,000. Once we reckon with this figure we at once realise that modern minor irrigation based on electric pumpsets is a highly capital using activity. If the area to be irrigated is only two hectares, this cost averages Rs. 25,000/ha. While this would be relevant for dugwell irrigation, for a tubewell, with almost twice the area benefited, the supporting investment would be half as much. Thus the private and the resource cost of developing minor irrigation with the aid of electric power could typically be taken as given below:

	Total capital cost		*Cost per ha.*	
	Private Rs.	*Resource Rs.*	*Private Rs.*	*Resource Rs.*
1. Dugwell with electric pumpset	28,000	78,000	14,000	39,000
2. Shallow tubewell	20,000	70,000	5,000	17,500

Concluding Remarks

The above mentioned unit capital cost per ha. for minor irrigation development could vary from region to region. Anyway, these do show that in the case of tubewell irrigation one might assert categorically its less costliness *vis-a-vis* major irrigation whose typical cost today is about Rs. 45,000 per ha. But then shallow tubewells cannot be developed, for technical reasons, in hard rock regions which comprise over two-thirds of our land mass. Also, the need for replacement investment in the case of a tubewell would arise after every 15 years or so. These factors *inter alia* should caution us against using the above estimates for inferring that minor irrigation is less costly than major irrigation.

CHAPTER 9

WATER MANAGEMENT AND TECHNOLOGICAL CHANGE IN INDIAN AGRICULTURE*

Water is an extremely valuable resource. Fortunately, this precious resource is not all that exhaustible by use the way mineral resources like petroleum and metallic ores are. When we do not count sea water, water is certainly not all that plentiful. It is a limited resource which we need to use thoughtfully, avoiding wasteful and harmful practices in all sectors, including agriculture where presently over 85 per cent of total water use takes place in India.

Indian agriculture sector has two segments, an irrigated one and a rainfed one. Areawise, irrigated segment is one half of the other segment. But since production from an irrigated hectare is more than twice that of a rainfed hectare, relative share of irrigated segment in total agricultural production is more than that of the segment. Because of progress in irrigation facilities, this importance of the irrigated *vis-a-vis* rainfed segment has risen over time.

Technical change in each of these two crop segments requires different actions or measures. For technical change under unirrigated conditions, two separate problems of water management have to be tackled. In dryland farming of low rainfall regions of this country, water resources for developing irrigated farming by nature are very limited. So

---

* *Financial Express* (forthcoming).

much of the farming here, varying from two-thirds to three-fourths of the crop area, would remain under the mercy of rain gods. It is, therefore, very necessary for technical progress to occur here that extensive investments are made in integrated watershed management programme. While doing so, we should place due emphasis on irrigation component in these programmes. This is because successful cases of watershed development, like Tejpura in Bundelkhand and Sukhomajri near Chandigarh, reveal substantial development of minor irrigation works like check dams, ponds and wells.

The other problem is one of drainage congestion and flood control in high rainfall areas like the east Gangetic plains. In these areas irrigation for kharif farming is not all that necessary requirement. Farmers here are unwilling to intensity farming in the kharif season because of the double threat of flood and waterlogging of fields due to naturally poor drainage here. So water management for technical progress here requires (1) man-made improvements in drainage system, (2) some investments in protection against floods, and (3) irrigation development for supporting intensive cropping with HYV seeds during the rabi and summer seasons.

Need for economy in water use is all the greater in developing economies because demand for water in every activity rises rapidly in such an economy. Thus, any constraint of water availability can slow down further growth of income and production from agriculture. It is such a constraint that has now brought down the rate of agricultural growth in Tamil Nadu state below its rate of population rise. And it is the absence of such a constraint that the green revolution in Punjab state is still maintaining its course well ahead of the rate of growth of the state's population.

Benefits from the diverse uses of water should certainly be maximised. But while doing so we should guard against some unhealthy outcomes. In the particular case of agriculture, irrigation management should be such as to ensure equity or evenness in benefits for all farmers, between small and large farmers, as also between tail-end and top-end or head-end farmers within a canal command.

Fortunately, there is no conflict here between productivity and equity objectives of development. That is to say, achieving equity between tail-end and top-end farmers, or between small and large farmers, also enhances total farm production and farm income. This harmonious situation is the result of the operation of the Law of Diminishing Returns, according to which marginal increase in production declines as we use more and more of an input which is irrigation water in the present case.

Unfortunately, water management in our public canal irrigation is not all that good. Farmers located at the head-end of a canal system, say, a canal outlet, tend to appropriate more of irrigation supplies, to the disadvantage of their brother farmers at the end of this outlet. Besides reduction in maximum total output from canal irrigation, this unequal sharing of water leads to waterlogging and soil salinity problems, which are more visible in head-end reaches of a canal system. This brings us to the question of environmental degradation from canal irrigation development.

Waterlogging and soil salinity are undoubtedly bad both for the present as well as the future generation of farmers. These negative environmental consequences also raise problems of inter-generation equity. That is why environmentalists insist that agricultural development should take place on a durable or sustainable basis, without there occurring a fall in agricultural production in the future.

To avoid waterlogging and salinity within canal commands, good water management entails action both at the government and the individual farmer level. At individual level, an irrigator must avoid overwatering his crop. Scope for overirrigation is minimum in the lower reaches of a canal system but quite high in the upper reaches. The prevalent pricing system for canal water is partly responsible for such overuse of canal water. It is primarily the fixed nature of the canal rates that encourages farmers to apply water above the level recommended by farm scientists. It is thus not the cheapness of canal water because of which our farmers overuse canal water; it is the fixed or flat nature of canal water tariff.

Raising the level of this canal tariff would certainly improve the financial health of the irrigation departments of the state governments. But this would in no way induce farmers to use less canal water, because by doing so the irrigation department would not charge them less while sending them the water bill. So long as water is not sold by quantity or on a volumetric basis, farmers would have no financial incentive to use water in right quantities. Unfortunately, such volumetric pricing cannot be introduced in the Indian conditions. Because of the smallness of landholdings here, unlike in the U.S.A., the administrative cost of implementing such a pricing scheme is too high. The scheme has a promising possibility if farmers water users societies or associations are promoted first. Water selling by volume can be done to such associations who in turn would distribute water to individual farmer members according to their needs. But this poses another hurdle: how do we go about persuading farmers to form such water users associations?

Pricing irrigation water by volume being not all that a feasible proposition for the time being, we have to employ other means to eliminate overuse of canal waters by farmers. One way is to improve farmers' knowledge about irrigation water management. With the aid of agricultural extension workers and mass media of communications, they need to be made conscious of the long-run harmful effects of overwatering high-yielding varieties of crops.

Success in this educative drive hinges on the reliability of canal supplies. Therefore, canal management by the government engineers and administrators needs toning up. When canal supplies happen to be unreliable, farmers tend to become greedy in water application. That is to say, they want to store a lot of water in the crop root zone of their crops when they are quite uncertain about the subsequent canal deliveries of the future.

When farmers own themselves the sources of irrigation, they have greater confidence in completing their irrigation operation on time and in desired amount. Therefore, farmers in canal commands should be encouraged to acquire wells of their own. Water from these wells can be used in conjunction or combination with canal supplies. So whenever canal supply is short, a farmer can fall back on his own source of irrigation. This dependability in irrigation gives him the much needed confidence to intensify his farming, resulting in intensive use of farm inputs such as chemical fertilisers, HYV seeds, pesticides, labour, etc. This input intensification raises sharply the level of crop yields with which we nowadays identify with green revolution. It can also show up in greater cultivation of more-paying crops, as also in a rise in double cropping of land resource.

A great but incidental advantage from the development of conjunctive irrigation is that it results in balanced use of water resources. On the one hand, it prevents waterlogging. Well irrigation within canal commands gives rise to withdrawal or removal of seeped-in canal waters. Technically it is known as 'vertical' drainage, to distinguish it from conventional horizontal drainage through the construction of a network of big and small drains. Such a network of drains is a costly proposition, both in capital and maintenance costs. Investment in them be better undertaken in canals serving arid areas like those of western Rajasthan. Because, development of private well irrigation here is slow owing to the existence of saline and brackish groundwater underneath desert lands.

Since in a conjunctive irrigation system surface water, in the shape of canal or tank irrigation, is used in addition to groundwater, this leads to reduced pressure on groundwater use. As a result, chances of overexploitation of groundwater are greatly diminished, in comparison to the situation when groundwater is the sole source of irrigation. Eversince private tubewell irrigation began playing a crucial role in the rapid diffusion of bio-chemical technology in north-western wheat belt of our nation, agricultural development has become somewhat synonymous or identical with development of private well irrigation. This has encouraged explosive increase in the number of dugwells, dug-cum-bore wells, tubewells and borewells, all over the country. No wonder, then, groundwater resources of the nation have begun to be depleted here and there, more so in low rainfall tracts lacking development of surface water-based irrigation works. In the absence of state enforced regulations against overuse of groundwater, emphasis on extensive development of surface irrigation works in areas of low groundwater availability is the best guarantee against overexploitation of groundwater resource by farmers who are keen to practice intensive farming these days.

Contrary to the erroneous impression in some quarters, groundwater by nature is much less plentiful than is surface water. Fortunately, devices like sprinklers and drippers, which help a lot in water savings, are well suited for use in combination with wells and tubewells. These water economising devices save 25 to 33 per cent water in the case of sprinkler irrigation, and 40 to 60 per cent in the case of drip irrigation. These technical changes in irrigated agriculture are, of course, costly to introduce. Their introduction becomes easier in groundwater scarce areas where farming is oriented towards remunerative crops like fruits and vegetables, as indeed is the case in the state of California in the United States of America, and in Israel in the Middle East. A favourable circumstances for their use for sustaining ordinary field crops emerges when farmers' fields have uneven topography or surface. This is why sprinkler irrigation has developed in a big way in the south-western, water short tracts of Haryana state.

CHAPTER 10

UTILISATION OF CAPACITY OF SMALL-SCALE IRRIGATION*

I. Introduction

As criticism against large-scale irrigation works mounts in India, the fascination for small-scale irrigation works rises in the public mind, further adding to the swelling ranks of the critics of big dams. In such an emotive environment, legends divorced from ground reality grow. One such legend has been around capacity utilisation. According to this legend, full capacity utilisation prevails in the case of minor irrigation works in India, whereas the capacity of major irrigation works happens to be grossly underutilised.

The objective of this article is to examine critically the veracity of the impression that irrigation capacity in small-scale works is fully utilised. This verification is carried out with the help of the data gathered through the Census of Minor Irrigation Works (hereafter referred to as 'the census'). Readers must bear in mind two things: (1) the national or all-India picture revealed here is based on less than full coverage of the country, and (2) the data are based on preliminary tabulations—wherever the compilation appears suspect, it is duly pointed out. Though the census was nationwide, the available compilation is exclusive of data for some states, notably Bihar, Rajasthan and Assam. However, these excluded states and some Union Territories

---

* Abridged version published in *Facts For You*, December 1992, and January, 1993.

hardly account for 15 per cent of the national irrigation capacity of the minor irrigation segment established by the mid-eighties.

Measuring the rated capacity of an economic activity is known to be a tricky job. This has, however, not daunted scholars as well as the policy administrators from coming to grips with this problem, so as to assess the rates of capacity utilisation in various activities and sectors. In the case of industry sector of rich countries, the rate of capacity utilisation, measured month-wise, happens to be one among the principal indicators of the state of the economy.

With the onset of planning era in the country in 1951, the Plan documents began carrying the twin statistics of new irrigation capacity created and its utilisation. These statistics have been subjected to much analysis, giving rise to serious misgivings about major (and medium) irrigation on the one hand, and misplaced optimism about minor irrigation on the other. Presumably because of the inherent tremendous difficulty of computing satisfactorily the irrigation capacity of minor irrigation works, the planners adopted a working assumption that whatever area is reportedly irrigated from such works is nearer their true irrigation capability. Since ownership of such works, especially of dugwells and tubewells, is predominantly with farmers, the planners began rationalising their own working assumption on the appealing idea that an owner of a minor irrigation work would usually not allow any part of its irrigation capacity to remain unutilised.

Till the beginning of the Sixth Five Year Plan (1980-85), our plan documents went on showing merrily 100 per cent utilisation of whatever minor irrigation potential was reportedly created in a given period of planning. This irrigation capacity was usually arrived at with the help of two sets of statistics, namely, (1) number of new minor irrigation structures of various types established in a year, and (2) assumed norms of irrigation capacity for each category of work. Information on the statistic (1) is gathered from progress reports supplied by financing institutions, block development agencies, state irrigation and planning departments, etc. Information about the norm statistic (2) has been derived from sample surveys carried out in the past, plus planners' own judgements. Thus the irrigation potential norm for a shallow tubewell was periodically revised downwards because of a perception that earlier survey data pertained to farmers with larger land holdings. Likewise, irrigation potential for a dugwell was raised as more and more dugwells came to be fitted with power pumpsets instead of animal-drawn waterlifts.

These background remarks should wisen us to treat the estimates of irrigation potential from minor irrigation works with abundant caution. Moreover, we should not deem the phenomenon of 100 per cent capacity utilisation in the case of minor irrigation works for the period prior to the Sixth Plan as founded in facts. Even today, the official picture of nine-tenths utilisation of capacity of minor irrigation need not be taken at its face value.

II. Composition of Minor Irrigation

Minor or small-scale irrigation works comprise a variety of structures and contrivances. In the recent census of such works these have been distinguished by five broad types as follows:

1. Dugwells
2. Shallow tubewells
3. Deep tubewells
4. Surface-water flow irrigation schemes
5. Surface-water lift irrigation schemes

Shallow tubewells, which are mostly owned by farmers themselves, usually individually instead of jointly/collectively, now constitute the single most important minor source of irrigation from the viewpoint of created or established irrigation capacity, particularly more so from the viewpoint of area actually irrigated. According to this census, these tubewells accounted for half the gross (i.e., crop) area irrigated from all minor irrigation works during 1986-87. These area figures are inclusive of area under supplementary irrigation. Irrigation from open wells, i.e., dugwells, which have been increasingly replaced by shallow tubewells in north Indian plains, is now much less important, being no more than half that from shallow tubewells. Four-fifths of minor irrigation is now from groundwater, a source which has expanded impressively during the course of Indian planning and which has come to be identified with a thriving modern agriculture.

Surface water based lift irrigation schemes, which have been commended to the water planners by the dam critics, are as yet of least significance in total minor irrigation segment, even below deep tubewells which are, with the exception of Gujarat, mostly in the public sector.[1] Flow or gravity schemes based on surface water, which include tank irrigation and 'kuhls', now account for hardly one-eighth of total minor irrigation. Typewise statistics of minor irrigation capacity, actual irrigated area and the rate of capacity utilisation are set out in Table 1.

TABLE 1

TYPEWISE MINOR IRRIGATION CAPACITY AND ITS UTILISATION, 1986-87

S.No.	*Type*	*Created capacity (000 ha.)*	*Utilisation (000ha.)*			*Per cent rate of capacity utilisation*
			Sole	*Supple-mentary*	*Total*	
1	2	3	4	5	6	7
1.	Shallow tubewells	14,920	15,226	2,115	17,341	102-116
2.	Deep tubewells	3,011	2,224	306	2,530	74-84
3.	Dugwells	11,253	8,090	596	8,686	72-77
4.	Groundwater (1 to 3)	29,184	25,540	3,017	28,557	88-98
5.	Surface water:					
	(i) flow[1]	6,244	4,249	277	4,526	68-72
	(ii) lift	1,482	1,017	200	1,217	69-82
	(iii) total	7,726	5,266	477	5,743	68-74
	All India[2] (1 to 5)	36,910	30,806	3,494	34,300	83-93

Note: These statistics, based on the Census of Minor Irrigation Works (1986-87), are preliminary.

1. Exclusive of data of West Bengal and Kerala.
2. Excludes Assam, Bihar, Rajasthan, Manipur, Meghalaya, and the Union Territories of Delhi and Lakshadweep. On the basis of official data on minor irrigation potential created upto the end of Sixth Five Year Plan (i.e., 1984-85), these excluded states accounted for about 15 per cent of the all-India potential.

At the individual crop level, a minor irrigation source in the count.'y is predominantly used in solo, that is, singly. Its use in conjunction with any other source of irrigation, known as supplementary role, accounted for about one-tenth of total utilisation during 1986-87.[2]

The productive value of irrigation water is much more if such water is available in dry seasons of the agricultural year, more so during the rabi season. For, irrigation to crops during the wet season tends to be largely protective against rainfall failure, especially in high rainfall areas. Therefore, seasonal orientation of an irrigation work is of considerable importance. The census data reveals that almost half the area benefitted by minor irrigation works during 1986-87 was for crops of the rabi season[3]. Irrigation for Kharif crops accounted for two fifths of total irrigation. Seasonality in utilisation by irrigation category is highlighted in Table 2. It is only in the case of flow irrigation works based on surface water that Kharif irrigation is of great importance, accounting for 66 per cent of total irrigated area. That throws some light on why the productive impact of such works, especially tanks, turns out to be lower *vis-a-vis* well or lift irrigation.

TABLE 2

SEASONWISE UTILISATION OF MINOR IRRIGATION, 1986-87

S.No. Type of Irrigation	*Sole irrigated area (000 ha.)*				
	Kharif	*Rabi*	*Annual*	*Others*	*Total*
1. Shallow tubewells	5,716	8,421	593	495	15,226
	(38)	(55)	(4)	(3)	(100)
2. Deep tubewells	737	1,241	97	150	2,224
	(33)	(56)	(4)	(7)	(100)
3. Dugwells	2,973	3,904	771	442	8,090
	(37)	(48)	(10)	(6)	(100)
4. Groundwater (1 to 3)	9,426	13,566	1,461	1,087	25,540
	(37)	(53)	(6)	(4)	(100)

5. Surface water :					
(a) flow	2,796	1,256	121	76	4,249
	(66)	(29)	(3)	(2)	(100)
(b) lift	370	472	132	43	1,017
	(36)	(47)	(13)	(4)	(100)
(c) total	3,166	1,728	253	119	5,266
	(60)	(33)	(5)	(2)	(100)
All Sources	12,592	15,294	1,714	1,206	30,806
	(41)	(50)	(6)	(3)	(100)

Notes: (*i*) Figures in parentheses are percent shares.
(*ii*) All cautionary notes of Table 1 apply to this Table also.

III. Level of Capacity Utilisation

The measurement of capacity utilisation from the census data is complicated by an added factor, namely, the supplementary area. While its exclusion from the reckoning would understate the rate of capacity utilisation for minor irrigation works, its inclusion in total utilisation figures would overstate the picture of capacity utilisation. For, such area has also benefitted from major and medium sources of irrigation. No less importantly, some of this area is of intra minor irrigation segment nature, e.g., when a dugwell is used in conjunction with tank irrigation. Such conjunctive use might get reported as supplementary area under both the categories of irrigation, namely, tanks and dugwells. In view of such double counting on the one hand and minor irrigation being a partial source of irrigation when used in conjunction with major and medium irrigation works on the other, the likely level of capacity utilisation is somewhere in the range formed by area utilisation figures which first exclude supplementary area and then includes it.

3.1 *Overall Picture*

The aggregative picture of capacity utilisation in the minor irrigation segment is not all that bad, as somewhere between 83 and 93 percent of the irrigation capacity was utilised during

1986-87, a year when there was general deficiency in rainfall all over the country.[4] The rate of capacity utilisation for groundwater sources, taken together, was much better (88-98 per cent) than for surface water irrigation (68-74 per cent).

3.2 *Shallow Tubewells*

Within the sub-segment of groundwater irrigation, one discerns an interesting contrast in capacity utilisation. While there is significant underutilisation in the case of dugwells and also deep tubewells, one comes across the interesting phenomenon of overutilisation of capacity (2-16 per cent) in respect to shallow tubewells. Bearing in mind the preliminary status of the data, still two observations are worth making. First, the rate of utilisation in a given year can be affected by weather conditions deviating from normal in that year. *A priori*, one can say that drought would adversely affect the capacity utilisation in surface irrigation works, though the adverse impact is bound to be less deleterious in large-scale than small-scale works. Small stream flows are liable to large dimunition during drought. The probability of a like dimunition in a big stream flow is inherently much less. To a great extent, water availability during drought will be low in the case of shallow dugwells, more so in low rainfall regions. Resultant reduction in capacity utilisation is primarily owing to a reduction in water availability due to drought—and, to some extent, due to simultaneous reduction in hydel power for operating electric pumpsets. The reference year of the census was indeed a year of moderate drought when all five regions of the country experienced below normal rainfall during the wet season (June to September) as follows:

West	(-) 22 per cent
North	(-) 11 per cent
East	(-) 16 per cent
South	(-) 10 per cent
Central	(-) 13 per cent
All India	(-) 15 per cent

The underutilisation of capacity in small-scale irrigation works other than shallow tubewells can be simply understood in terms of vulnerability of such works to the drought of 1986-87. But this explanation cannot be fully invoked in the case of overutilisation of capacity for shallow tubewells. For that, one has to seek some other convincing framework of explanation. Admittedly, drought does not materially affect groundwater availability in the case of tubewells which penetrate quite down to lower aquifers that are not adversely affected by drought of the current period. In fact, tubewells, as also deep dugwells with pit borings, have a sort of built in flexibility to overdraw on groundwater stocks even during drought years. These can thus irrigate some extra area during a drought year provided there is no energy constraint at the same time. (On this point of flexibility, readers may refer to my book, *Irrigation in India's Agricultural Development*, pp. 184-88 and 193-95). In view of this flexibility angle one can explain, upto a point, the phenomenon of overutilisation in the case of shallow tubewells. This author, however, feels that part of the explanation might be in the emergence of groundwater markets, to which attention is drawn in the observation that follows.

Second, the utilisation of irrigation capacity improves to the extent a tubewell owning farmer is able to sell surplus tubewell water to his fellow farmers. This surplus arises because of the financial viability of investment in a tubewell even when only a part of its intrinsic irrigation potential is utilised by its owner. The mean value of irrigation capacity per shallow tubewell in use during 1986-87, as per the census statistics, works out to about 4.5 hectares of crop area. This is well below the technical capability of a minimum size tubewell which can irrigate about 4 ha. crop area in each of the two main crop seasons of an agricultural year, plus some additional 2 to 3 hectares during the summer season.[5] It is this excess or slack in capacity that enables many tubewell owners to meet other farmers' demand for irrigation water, a demand that does become keen at the time of rainfall failure.

Among the states where overutilisation of shallow tubewell capacity occurred as per the census data are Gujarat, Uttar

TABLE 3

STATES EXPERIENCING MORE THAN FULL UTILISATION OF IRRIGATION CAPACITY OF SHALLOW TUBEWELLS

S.No.	*State*	*Irrigation capacity (000 ha.)*	*Utilisation (000 ha.)*			*Rate of utilisation (%)*
			Sole	*Supplementary*	*Total*	
1.	Gujarat	53	725	5	730	1377
2.	Haryana	1,806	1,612	344	1,956	89-108
3.	H.P.	7	6	3	9	85-129
4.	Jammu & Kashmir	2	2	1	3	100-150
5.	Madhya Pradesh	96	97	4	101	101-105
6.	Maharashtra	10	10	3	13	100-130
7.	Punjab	4,660	4,490	1,061	5,551	96-119
8.	Tamil Nadu	171	163	60	223	95-130
9.	Tripura	4	4	-	5	100-125
10.	U.P.	6,670	6,867	581	7,448	102-112

Caution: Figures of capacity/utilisation are rounded off to nearest one thousand ha. Therefore, for states with small areas the rates of utilisation are to be taken with caution.

Pradesh, Madhya Pradesh, Punjab and Haryana, for which the picture of potential and utilisation is shown in Table 3. Here, one would like to comment on the incredibly high rate of overutilisation of tubewell capacity in the state of Gujarat. Possibly, it is an outcome of some totalling error. The sole area irrigated during the rabi season, as per the census compilation, is excessively high in comparison to that under Kharif or other seasons as per the following seasonwise statistics for this state:

	Sole area irrigated by shallow tubewells (ha.)
Kharif crops	10,587
Rabi crops	703,384

Annual crops	971
Other crops	9,601
Total for all crops	724,543

The census shows 5,352 shallow tubewells in Gujarat. When the reported irrigation potential of about 53 thousand hectares is divided by this number of tubewells, we obtain average irrigation potential per tubewell to be of the order of 10 hectares. Repeating a similar exercise for actual irrigated area (including supplementary area), we get an incredible figure of 136 hectares of irrigated area per tubewell. Even if one duly reckons with the unique phenomenon of investments made in tubewell irrigation in this state with a view to water selling as the dominant motive (even water companies have been constituted for purpose of this agro-business), one cannot accept the incredible data on utilisation being over 100 hectares per tubewell of shallow depth.

But this phenomenon of groundwater selling underscores another point, namely, the difficulty of assessing firmly the irrigation capacity of a tubewell. Should one be guided in this by the actual command area under an installed tubewell, or by its potential / technical capability? It appears that in the present census the assessment of created irrigation potential is based on actual culturable command area of the owner of a tubewell, which comes to hardly 3 ha. (per tubewell in use) for all the states taken together. The command area per tubewell has considerable variability across States (within brackets is recorded created irrigation potential per tubewell):

1. U.P.	3.2 (4.1) ha.
2. Punjab	3.0 (4.8) ha.
3. Gujarat	11.0 (12.0) ha.
4. M.P.	5.7 (5.4) ha.
5. Haryana	5.0 (5.1) ha.

6.	West Bengal	1.7 (2.7) ha.
7.	Andhra Pradesh	2.1 (2.6) ha.
8.	Tamil Nadu	2.1 (2.0) ha.
9.	Karnataka	1.9 (2.4) ha.
10.	Orissa	6.5 (9.9) ha.

3.3 *Dugwells*

In contrast to barely 35 thousand out of about 35 lakh tubewells (i.e., about one per cent) being out of use in 1986-87, nearly one-fifth (14 lakh out of about 72 lakh) of dugwells were reportedly out of use in that year. As a result of below normal rainfall in 1986-87, some shallow wells would have possibly gone dry. This possibility could be high in Gujarat where rainfall deficiency was 50 per cent and where more than half the dugwells (4.6 lakh out of 8.4 lakh) were reportedly not in use in this state in the census year. Another reason behind wells being out of use could be their owners acquiring access to some newer source of irrigation which is either much cheaper (e.g., canal water), or more adequate in quantity and quality (e.g., a shallow tubewell of one's own). Finally, some dugwells might have become dysfunctional due to serious overexploitation of groundwater, including intrusion of saline waters, such as the well known ingress of sea water into wells in the coastal region of Saurashtra (Gujarat).

3.4 *Deep Tubewells*

Out of nearly 90 thousand deep tubewells over 6 thousand (nearly 7 per cent) were not in use. The census picture of 74-84 per cent capacity utilisation in respect of them turns out to be much less dismal than known earlier through survey and evaluation studies on state tubewells. Therefore, it need not be taken at its face value. For example, statistics for public tubewells for 1983-85 period, as reported by R.S. Saksena, the former chief of Minor Irrigation Division of the Ministry of Water Resources, reveal as low as 6 per cent utilisation in Bihar, 30 to 40 percent in Andhra Pradesh, Orissa and Haryana states; 49 to 54 per cent in Gujarat and West Bengal states, and 75 per cent in Punjab. This calls for some probing into the census data.

First of all, it needs to be noted that the census totals are exclusive of Bihar state, whose public tubewells accounted for one-tenth of all the 63,000 public tubewells in India at the end of the Seventh Five Year Plan. It is the public tubewells of this state whose utilisation is said to be the poorest in the country. Second, the measurement of capacity utilisation in survey reports is often done on the basis of performance as per the annual running hours per tubewell. And it is known to be much less satisfactory than the one based on irrigated area statistics. Thirdly, the rather good capacity utilisation (nearly 73 per cent) for Gujarat state is really not for government tubewells. For, bulk of the 23,000 deep tubewells of this state are in the private sector.

Fourthly, census data shows comparatively higher rate of capacity utilisation (91 per cent) of 29,000 deep tubewells in U.P., for which other studies place the same rate in the neighbourhood of 40 per cent. This divergence could be due to the peculiar practice of the Irrigation Department of this state, whereby area under long duration crops, notably sugarcane, is counted more than once. So, the agricultural year here is divided into three 4-monthly segments (kharif, rabi and summer, i.e., 'zaid'), and area benefitted from a public tubewell is taken as the sum of these seasonwise areas. Thus one crop hectare under sugarcane gets reported as three hectares while compiling utilisation statistics — the same procedure is not followed at the stage of assessing irrigation capacity.

3.5 Flow Irrigation

The census data reveals lowest capacity utilisation for this class of works, namely, 68-72 per cent. As many as 48,000 flow irrigation schemes were found to be not in use during the census year. These constituted nearly one-eighth of all such schemes in existence. This fraction was nearer one-third mark in the case of Karnataka state, for which we know from another investigative study by the Indian Institute of Management, Bangalore, that "over half of the estimated 43,000 odd tanks in

Karnataka state have been found to be more or less completely silted up, resulting in area of 2.5 lakh ha. having lost to irrigation (Source: *Report of the Working Group on Minor Irrigation for the Eighth Plan 1990-95, p. 17*). This means that a transient factor like rainfall deficiency could not be blamed for such silted up tanks being out of use during 1986-87.

Most of the flow irrigation works are not individually farmer owned in the manner of dugwells and shallow tubewells. Nearly 46 percent of them are owned by government departments, 35 per cent by farmers' societies, and the rest by public or community organisations. The last one is a predominant mode of ownership in Nagaland, while farmers' societies are preponderant in Gujarat, Himachal Pradesh, West Bengal and U.P., and government ownership is predominant in southern states and Madhya Pradesh.

A majority of the minor flow irrigation schemes are based on storage works, and the rest are based on stream diversion— both pucca and temporary diversion works are equal in numbers. More precisely, nearly two-thirds of the 357 thousand flow irrigation works in use have storage backup. This fraction is higher, especially in the southern states known for tank irrigation since time immemorial: nine-tenths in Andhra Pradesh, Tamil Nadu and West Bengal; and over seven-tenths in Karnataka and Andhra Pradesh. Diversion works are predominant in Himachal Pradesh, Jammu and Kashmir, Nagaland, Sikkim and hilly parts of U.P. and many other states.

3.6 *Lift Irrigation*

Lastly, we come to lift irrigation schemes based on surface water sources such as rivers, nallahs, drains, ponds, lakes, tanks, and large reservoirs. According to the census, there were over 633 thousand such lift irrigation works. Most of these were found to be in use during 1986-87—those out of use constituted only about one per cent of the total in existence. West Bengal accounts for almost one-third of the schemes, closely followed by the state of Uttar Pradesh. States like Maharashtra and Madhya Pradesh, where modern lift irrigation schemes involving the use of power pumpsets have come up in the recent period, account for hardly one-tenth each in the national total : 66 thousand for Madhya Pradesh, 57 thousand for Maharashtra, 52 thousand in Kerala. These three states, however, account for nearly 60 per cent of all the 173 thousand lift schemes operated with the help of electric power, the cheapest source of energy for farm operations in India. Diesel-operated schemes, numbering over 203 thousand, were predominantly found in West Bengal (105 thousand), Uttar Pradesh (32 thousand) and Madhya Pradesh (34 thousand), mainly because of lower development of rural electrification in these states. Nearly 40 per cent of the lift schemes were operated with animate power derived from animals or from human beings, or both. Such traditional lifts generally entail low heights through which water is lifted. In contrast, lifts based on power pumpsets are used for heights upto 50 metres (much more in case of lifts meant for civic uses of water).

A majority of the lift schemes are operated by farmers and societies. Their ownershipwise breakup is as follows:

1.	Private/society	398,717
2.	Government	42,125
3.	Public organisations	40,811
4.	Unspecified[6]	151,393
	Total	633,046

The compilation or tabulation task appears to be far from complete and firm. This is inferred from two observations. First, the data on irrigation potential and its utilisation in respect of West Bengal and Kerala are not included in the all-India total. Second, the lift irrigation potential (116,846 ha.) for U.P., low as it is for 186,000 schemes for the state, comes out to be 10 times the culturable area commanded by these schemes, namely, 11,870 ha. In view of these factors, the perfo-mance picture for lift irrigation works, as revealed by the census data, needs to be taken with caution. States, for which data appears to be free from discrepancies, reveal following interesting facts.

A majority of the lift schemes are based on water stored in tanks, followed by flowing water in river and in drains and canals. This is particularly so in the two states of West Bengal and U.P. But once we exclude these two states from the aggregative analysis, river-based schemes appear to be more preponderant. This is evident from the following disaggregative data.

No. of lift schemes by source of water supply (000)

		River	Drain/ canal	Tank	Total
1.	West Bengal	12	22	168	203
2.	U.P.	7	8	166	181
3.	Rest of India	169	17	55	240
4.	All-India	188	47	389	624

Though the phenomenon of lifts being out of use is quite low at the all-India level (vide Table 4), it is of considerable significance in some states. For example, one-fifth of about 1500

TABLE 4

EXTENT OF MINOR IRRIGATION WORKS FOUND OUT OF USE IN INDIA DURING 1986-87

Sl. No.	*Type of work*	*Number of works out of use (000)*	*Total number in existence (000)*	*Per cent out of use*
1.	Dugwells	1426	7221	20
2.	Shallow tubewells	35	3362	1
3.	Deep tubewells	6	90	7
4.	Surface flow irrigation	48	406	12
5.	Surface lift irrigation	9	633	1
6.	All types (1 to 5)	1524	11712	13

lifts of Gujarat were not in use during 1986-87, presumably because of low availability of water in rivers, tanks, drains, etc. due to severe drought in this year. In Orissa, one-eighth of the lifts were reportedly not in use during the reference year. To what extent this was due to pumpsets being out of order during 1986-87 is not known (both in Orissa and Gujarat lift schemes are wholly pumpset operated). Anyway, the rates of capacity utilisation in these two states were much lower than the aggregate rate of 82 per cent (the rate was 27 per cent in the case of Gujarat lifts and 41 per cent for the Orissa lifts). The low utilisation in the case of Gujarat might be mainly due to the drought factor. In the case of Orissa, a NABARD study (*Public Tubewells and River Lifts in Orissa,* 1984) also revealed poor rate of capacity utilisation during the following three years prior to the reference year of the census:

	% utilisation of capacity		
	Kharif	*Rabi*	*Total*
1978-79	Nil	31	31
1979-80 (drought year*)	12	45	57
1980-81	2	36	38

* 54% rainfall deficiency.

It will be noticed that the phenomenon of underutilisation of capacity is mainly one of lack of utilisation of the wet season capacity. This is because in good rainfall years, there is no demand for kharif irrigation, and in very bad rainfall years the emergent demand cannot be met fully because of paucity of water for irrigation.

Maharashtra's data reveals an exceedingly good performance of lift capacity utilisation. The created irrigation potential for about 56,000 lift schemes, all fitted with pumpsets, is of the order of 296 thousand hectares (surprisingly, the culturable command area is somewhat higher, namely, 304 thousand ha.). In sole irrigation, these lifts benefitted totar crop area to the extent of 286 thousand ha. Also, these provided supplementary irrigation to another 133 thousand crop hectares. So, in all 419 thousand ha. were irrigated during 1986-87, giving rise to a situation of overutilisation of capacity. Such overutilisation, questionable as it is, emerges despite heavily irrigated annual crops like sugarcane claiming an important share in total benefitted area, as is revealed by the following data:

	Kharif area	*Rabi area*	*Annual crop area 000 ha.*	*Others*	*Total area*
1. Sole irrigation	83	96	92	16	286
2. Supplementary irrigation	23	103	6	2	133
Total lift irrigation	106	199	98	18	419

IV. Performance During Drought

As already mentioned, rainfall during the reference year 1986-87 was perceptibly below normal in many parts of India. This deficiency was comparatively severe in the case of Gujarat state, with actual rainfall being half of the normal level of the state. Though rainfall deficiency in the subsequent year was even more (59 per cent in Gujarat division and 81 per cent in Saurashtra and Kutch division), it must be borne in mind that drought of 1986-87 came as a sequence of droughts in the preceding two years as well, as is evident from the following rainfall data:

	Gujarat division (N= 846 mm)	*Saurashtra & Kutch division* (N=609 mm)
1984	751mm	478mm
1985	538mm	326mm
1986	407mm	326mm
1987	347mm	116mm

According to the census, there were 869 thousand minor irrigation works in Gujarat in 1986-87, commanding a culturable area of nearly 3.1 million ha. The combined irrigation potential of these works is reckoned at nearly 4 million ha. of crop land. This appears to be on the high side. This apprehension arises because of the corresponding estimate in the Plan documents being much lower. For 1984-85 the official estimate of created minor irrigation potential for Gujarat is of the order of 1.7 million ha. only. This wide discrepancy between two data sets once again emphasizes the fragile basis of the estimates of irrigation capacity of this nation.

Hardly 55 per cent of this potential could be gainfully used during 1986-87. And if we exclude shallow tubewells from the reckoning because of the suspect nature of data on incredibly high utilisation for this category of minor irrigation works, the rate of capacity utilisation further reduces to 37 per cent. This harsh fact underscores the great vulnerability of minor irrigation works (other than tubewells and deep dugwells with pit-borings) to a severe drought, and thus their great limitation in affording protection to farm production and farm incomes during drought time.[7]

Because of hard rock geology of the state, groundwater irrigation here has per force to be mainly from dugwells. There were 839 thousand dugwells in 1986-87, which commanded over 2.3 million ha. of land area. In contrast, there were only about 28 thousand tubewells, of which 23 thousand were deep ones, which commanded an area of about 0.53 million ha. Dugwells and tubewells together constitute the mainstay of minor irrigation in the state because surface water based irrigation works account for hardly 5 per cent of the total minor irrigation capacity.

Composition of minor irrigation works—in terms of number of works, area commanded, irrigation potential and its utilisation—is listed in Table 5 which also shows the number of works found not in use during 1986-87. There was a large proportion of dugwells as well as surface flow irrigation works which were not in use, presumably because of meagre availability of water in shallow dugwells and surface water sources.

V. Summary and Conclusions

Notwithstanding the intractable problem of measuring satisfactorily capacity of a small-scale irrigation work, one finds that the Indian minor irrigation segment is not free from the incidence of underutilisation of capacity. At the aggregate national level, somewhere between 7 and 17 per cent of the minor irrigation potential established by 1986-87 was unutilised in that year. The lower bound of this range estimate is based on the somewhat unrealistic assumption of counting fully all the supplementary area benefitted by such works when these are used in conjunction with either major and medium irrigation works or among themselves, that is, say, a farmer uses irrigation from both a dugwell and a tank in watering a given plot of his land. The upper bound of 17 per cent underutilisation of capacity excludes such supplementary area and is based on sole irrigated area statistics only. Even this level of underutilisation is almost twice the level conveyed by official statistics in our Plan documents.

Among the five principal categories of minor irrigation works, the incidence of underutilisation of capacity is mainly found in the case of dugwells, deep tubewells, surface flow and lift irrigation schemes. In the case of shallow tubewells, one discerns some signs of overutilisation of capacity. This curious phenomenon could be attributed to two factors. First, the irrigation capacity of such tubewells happens to be underestimated. Because of the rise of groundwater markets, in which owners of shallow tubewells are playing a major role, such benefitted area

TABLE 5

PERFORMANCE OF SMALL-SCALE IRRIGATION IN GUJARAT DURING THE DROUGHT OF 1986-87

Sl. No.	Type	Total number (000)	Not in use: No. (000)	Not in use: As % of total no.	Total area comm-anded (000 ha.)	Irri-gation poten-tial (000 ha.)	Area irrigated (000 ha.): Sole	Area irrigated (000 ha.): Supple-mentary	Area irrigated (000 ha.): Total	% capa-city utili-sation
1.	Dugwells	839	464	55	2340	3022	984	22	1006	33
2.	Shallow tubewells	5.35	0.75	14	51	55	725	4	729	1325
3.	Deep tubewells	22.9	1.3	6	478	551	397	6	403	72-73
4.	Surface flow irrigation	0.36	0.53	68	203	194	12	Neg.	12	9
5.	Surface lift irrigation	1.50	0.30	20	28	32	8	-	8	25
6.	All types (1 to 5)	869	467	54	3100	3854 (3799)	2126	32	2158 (1429)	55 (37)

Note: Figures in parentheses are exclusive of data for shallow tubewells.

is not fully reckoned with while assessing irrigation capacity in which primary importance gets attached to a tubewell owner's own farm area. Second, because of drought conditions prevailing during 1986-87 tubewell owners might have overdrawn on groundwater resource, an attribute for which these are well recognised.

The extent of capacity utilisation among four types of minor irrigation works suffering unmistakably from underutilisation of irrigation potential varies as follows:

1.	Dugwells	72-77 per cent
2.	Surface flow irrigation	68-72 per cent
3.	Surface lift irrigation	69-82 per cent
4.	Deep tubewells	74-84 per cent

The estimated rate of capacity utilisation for deep tubewells appears to be seriously biased upwards and should be taken with circumspection, more so if it is to be used as a measure of performance of government owned or public tubewells of the country. Below par utilisation in their case can be attributed to (i) poor management under public aegis, and (ii) inadequacies of electricity supply system. The factor (i) applies also to minor surface irrigation works, especially tanks, maintained largely by government or community agencies like panchayats. Another factor behind underutilisation is the sizable number of works being not in use during 1986-87, partly because of drought conditions. The severe drought in Gujarat put almost half the minor works out of use during 1986-87. This incidence of works not found in use was higher in the case of dugwells, one-fifth of them being not in use during 1986-87. While shallow dugwells could be out of use because of drought rendering them dry holes, some could have fallen into disuse because of their owners acquiring access to other superior irrigation sources e.g., in Punjab, U.P. and Haryana the high incidence of dugwells not in use during 1986-87 could be linked to the pervasive rise of private tubewell irrigation in these states. By category of works the incidence of disuse varied as follows:

		Per cent out of use
1.	Dugwells	20
2.	Surface flow works	12
3.	Deep tubewells	7
4.	Shallow tubewells	1
5.	Surface lift irrigation	1
6.	All works	13

Barring tubewells, all other categories of minor irrigation works are quite undependable source of irrigation during drought time. This vulnerability to drought is particularly marked in the case of shallow dugwells and surface water based irrigation schemes, with the possible exception of lift schemes based on big reservoirs. The very high vulnerability in the case of Gujarat state, as revealed by the census data, need to be taken with a pinch of salt.

Lastly, a minor caveat may be added. The results are based on preliminary tabulations of the census data. Also, the all India picture too may undergo revision when data for the excluded states of Assam, Bihar, and Rajasthan, and the Union Territories (accounting for 15% in total minor irrigation) are reckoned with.[8]

NOTES

1. Deep tubewells constructed in India usually extend to a depth of 100 metres and more, and are designed to give a water discharge of 100-200 cubic metres per hour (about 6 to 8 times that of a shallow tubewell).
2. In the official statistics on irrigated area, compiled and revealed annually by the Ministry of Agriculture as well as the Planning Commission, there is no place for supplementary irrigated area. In a situation of crop/land area receiving watering from more than one source, such area is classified under one head only, that is under a source which accounts for a majority share in total watering from all irrigation sources.
3. Rabi season is a dry season in most states, the single exception

being Tamil Nadu where Kharif season is much less wet, thanks to NE monsoons being stronger than SW monsoons in this state.

4. The all India rainfall deficiency of this year, though 4 per cent point higher than that experienced during the severe drought of 1987, was less severe in all regions except east India where 4 per cent above normal rainfall was experienced. (Source :*Economic Survey*, 1989-90).
5. According to a NABARD study, a shallow tubewell of 0.44 cusec capacity could irrigate 8.4 ha. area during the rabi season, 60 per cent under sugarcane and 40 per cent under wheat. For more details as to how technical irrigation capability of a tubewell can be worked out, see chapter VI, alongwith Annexure I, of this study (NABARD, 1987)
6. Most of the lift schemes under the unspecified ownership are found located in Uttar Pradesh (149, 783), and presumably these are under the individual ownership of farmers. But, then, it is incredible that such ownership should be practically non-existent in other states of the nation. Possibly, there is some compilation error here.
7. There is a nagging feeling that the picture of dismal performance of minor irrigation segment of Gujarat during 1986-87 might be exaggerated to the extent the census compilers from the state deliberately overassessed the irrigation capacity from minor works, with a view to putting them in bad light *vis-a vis* major irrigation works which are portrayed as saviours of Gujarat during drought years.
8. The Government of India has been very slow in processing the census of minor irrigation data. One wonders whether the census report itself would finally come out for public use.

CHAPTER 11

WHAT IS WRONG WITH TEHRI DAM*?

This article is being written with a specific objective that needs to be clearly understood at the outset. This objective is to help an interested reader to get at, so to speak, the rub of the matter of the Tehri dam issue. The idea is what follows is not so much as to pass a final verdict on this extremely controversial issue but to pinpoint what exactly has gone wrong with this ill-fated project. This exercise might prove instructive in comprehending some other raging controversies about big dams in this country.

Deficiencies of Planning

Parameters of Tehri project have undergone noteworthy changes over time. Since such changes occur commonly in water projects in India, this need not be normally a cause for anxiety. The changes become inevitable as the first project reports are usually based on insufficient investigative work. Anywhere from 5 to 8 years can be taken up in such pre-project investigation. Because of the compulsions to expand quickly the irrigation and power base of the nation, much of the investigative work now begins after getting a project clearance, in principle, from the central planners. It appears that the promoters of the Tehri dam have possibly misused the valid opportunity for later revision of the parameters.

---

* Published in *Facts For You*, October, 1992.

For an erstwhile Member (Agriculture) of the Planning Commission informally informed this author about three years ago that the Tehri project then being implemented was totally different from the one first proposed to and cleared by the Yojana Bhavan, e.g., the installed power generating capacity, he said, had been raised fourfold from the proposed/ cleared one of 600 mega watts (MW).

By enlarging the scope of the project manifold, the promoters certainly enhanced the benefits from this multipurpose project. On face, this enlargement of power production is sensible because there has emerged for long an acute imbalance in demand for electricity in the state of Uttar Pradesh, where supply of power is increasing at 6 to 7 per cent per annum (quite below the national rate of 9 to 10 per cent). What causes concern is the tremendous rise in project "costs".

The project "costs" are really more than the nominal value of outlays or investments in a project. The latter are presently placed in the range Rs. 3,500 - 4,000 crores at the ongoing prices of construction inputs. While this estimate would include the financial compensation paid to the dam oustees (and other displaced or uprooted persons), and the funds expended in their relocation and rehabilitation, it does not reckon with the trauma of being uprooted and facing an uncertain future in new environs. Nor does it include the agony of the non-displaced families whose (i) lands are partially submerged, (ii) relations are uprooted and relocated at far-off places, and (iii) cohesiveness of social life is seriously disrupted as they have to travel along the huge reservoir in order to meet their relations and friends across the river. These psychic and pecuniary costs do reduce sense of well being or welfare on the upstream of the dam.

Thus opposition to Tehri dam emanates both from the dam oustees and the non-oustees who are adversely affected on the upstream of the dam site. Better provision for the care of the dam oustees—thanks to the environmental activists—does little good to the other affected group. After all, the generated annual power of the order of 4000 million units (KWH) and irrigation benefit for 2.7 lakh crop hectare area (plus improvement in irrigation availability on 6.7. lakh ha.) are meant essentially for villages and towns on the downstream side of the dam. This is where part of the opposition to Tehri dam arises, a point effectively brought home to the author a year ago.

The Himachal Institute of Public Administration (HIPA) had organised a two-day national seminar on cost benefit aspects of hydel power projects located in hills. Sunderlal Bahuguna, the veteran opponent of the Tehri project, was also invited to this seminar where most participants happened to be senior power engineers who I found, during the course of my chairing three session, very articulate (much more than irrigation engineers with whom I have had far more interface in seminars, symposia, and conventions).

When Bahugunaji complained that hill people gain nothing from the dams and are only losers all the way, the engineers present at the seminar pointed out that 12 per cent of power generation was given free of charge to the state in which a power project was located. As I suggested that this share be earmarked wholly for the benefit of the people situated on the upstream of a dam, Bahugunaji got excited and promptly announced that he could forthwith give up his opposition to the Tehri dam provided 20 per cent of the power output was given free to them for their local use.

The engineers, of course, quickly objected that the higher percentage might render hydel power projects economically unviable. To this, my response was two-fold. First, the real issue is not one of the optimum percentage share of power to be given free to hill states in which hydel power schemes are being located. What Bahugunaji was pressing for is the issue of conferring some benefits out of a project investment to the local people on the upstream side of a dam. So, what needs to be done in hydel power planning from now onwards is that whatever be the percentage of power share for a hill state, it be specifically earmarked for use on the upstream side, and not for the state as a whole. To ensure this, necessary action is required in the portals of the Yojana Bhavan. This free power may be used for a variety of purposes: water, lifting from the reservoir for irrigation and drinking purposes; provision of cableways to enable people to move across the reservoir; for industrial estates, etc. As irrigation with water lifted from the reservoir enhances land productivity by a factor of two to three — such enhancement has been of the order of five times in the case of Maharashtra reservoirs from which adjacent villages have been allowed to lift water (on payment)— dam affected people (other than oustees) would feel a sense of sharing in the project benefits.

Second, the ongoing procedures used by the Planning Commission for judging economic viability of power projects are very conservative. Whereas the Commission abandoned in 1964 the narrow financial criterion for appraising irrigation projects, it continues to persist with it in the case of power projects. Dr. Kohli, head of the project appraisal division of the Planning Commission, readily conceded my contention but expressed reservation about measuring satisfactorily social benefits from power. While one cannot readily accept the contention of Mr. Naidu of National Hydro Corporation that social benefits (multiplier effects') from power are ten times the price at which power output from a hydel scheme is evaluated in an evaluation exercise, there is force in his underlying argument that power needs fuller evaluation, an objective that is best fulfilled by resorting to social cost-benefit analysis. In such an analysis, price at which power is sold to consumers is as irrelevant as is the irrigation charge paid by a farmer in a like analysis for major irrigation projects — in the latter case the net increase in farm income by using irrigation on one crop hectare of area is the relevant value of irrigation water.

In a large river basin, people living on the upstream of a dam are usually poorer in comparison to those living on the downstream side. They, therefore, deserve a better deal in any planned development effort. If they have failed to get this in the case of Indian planning, the blame for the same ought to be squarely laid at the door of the Planning Commission, much less at the door of water and power engineers. By reducing the scale of expenditure on each big dam project, the funds so saved could have been earmarked for intensifying multifarious developmental activities — roads, communications, education, a agricultural extension services, integrated watershed development programmes, etc. — on the upstream side. At the same time, some allocation of power output from the dam for lifting of water for irrigation and civic uses could go a long way in blunting opposition to the big dam idea.

Case for Large Reservoirs

Because of the monsoonal flows in Indian rivers there is large variation in river flow during a single year, the peak flows occurring in the monsoon months and the low flows during the summer months. Whereas demand for electricity is almost steady throughout the year, this is not so with our irrigation demand which begins to rise after the end of the monsoon season. In view of this contrast or divergence between demand and supply positions, construction of large reservoirs becomes self evident if we have to cater to our post-monsoon irrigation requirements for a stable and growing agriculture. To a lesser extent this holds good also for water needs for civic and industrial uses. Therefore, there are no alternatives to building big dams.

Run-of-the-river hydel schemes, as also micro hydel power schemes, should be built for meeting power needs. Likewise, small and medium dams must be built for meeting our irrigation needs. But we must recognise the techno-economic limits of these options, as also of other suggested alternatives such as traditional water harvesting technologies, dryland and natural/organic farming and groundwater irrigation. Leaving aside the case of run-of-the-river power schemes based on large fall (natural or man-made) in a river, other options are of a small-scale character better suited for meeting local needs of power/irrigation. Emphasis on their development, to the exclusion of large reservoirs, raises the relevant question of how the planners are going to meet the large needs of the people in the valley plains.

Though the case for large reservoirs is strong, yet it does not give, so to speak, unbridled license to dam builders and our water planners to build the largest possible dam / reservoir at a given dam site, as has indeed been done in the U.S.A. where giant dams and mega reservoirs have been generally built. Such dams truly dam up a river not allowing even above-normal year flows (that cause flood havoc) to pass over the spillway system of the dam. Thus, the reservoir capacity of the Hoover dam is three times the average annual flow of the Colorado at Boulder dam site. Such giant or mega reservoirs are all right so long as the submergence costs are not high, a condition that is far more easily fulfilled in a country like the U.S.A. than in India where populations near dam sites are high — in the case of Hoover dam there was no question of any dam oustees, nor of submergence of forests and cultivated lands.

Economic Viability

Economic viability of big dams is no more being taken for granted. When the author met last year Don Gambles, a member of the Independent Review Team constituted by the World Bank for the Sardar Sarovar Project (Navgam dam), he asked me how come that few expost evaluation studies have been carried out in respect of Indian major irrigation works. I told him that till the beginning of the eighties few people expressed doubts about the realised benefits from major irrigation being incommensurate with the incurred costs. As environmental consciousness heightened during the eighties, some expost evaluation studies of major irrigation works were indeed initiated, notably by the Central Water commission.

Unfortunately, these studies have remained in very restricted circulation. This author is thus in no position to offer a firm critique based on these studies. His impression, however, is that these studies do not lend credence to the rosy picture of cost-benefit ratio portrayed in the approved project reports. At the same time, nor do these seem to cast serious aspersion on the economic viability of major irrigation works. For instance, in the one published report for the Mula irrigation project (Maharashtra), N. Rath and Ashok Mitra (of the Gokhale Institute of Politics and Economics, Pune) place the expost (discounted) BC ratio to be marginally above unity.

Before we look at the BC ratio for the Tehri project, attention may be drawn to two aspects that have sown seeds of doubt in the public mind about the economic viability of big dams in India. One relates to the incessant escalation in the project costs and the other to costs of environmental loss in the shape of submergence of forest lands and the land degradation occurring within canal commands. To the extent the cost escalation is the result of (a) general price inflation, and (b) enlargement in the size or scale of a project, one need not unduly worry about the viability question. Because, both the forces (a) and (b) work likewise on the benefits side also, that is, general price inflation raises the nominal value of additional crop output — the consequence of (b) on benefits is self evident. It is primarily the attempt to reckon with the environmental costs of a project that can seriously erode the viability of a project.

I have basically no objection to reckoning with the environmental costs. This is the need of the hour. But the estimational work in this regard needs to be carried out firmly and to its logical end. Let me first expand a bit on this logical aspect. If major irrigation development helps in improving our environment in some respects, these improvements should be either included in the project benefits or deducted from the costs. For example, introduction of surface water irrigation in groundwater scarce, low rainfall regions improves groundwater availability,thereby sustaining the establishment of extra wells in such regions. I have shown elsewhere that the additional crop production on account of such improved groundwater availability can be as much as the one resulting directly from the use of surface irrigation. In the particular case of the Mula project, the BC ratio can nearly double when such indirect benefits are reckoned with.

As for firmness in estimation, critics of Narmada dams have overstepped very badly in evaluating environmental cost due to loss of forest cover. Even if one grants that project promoters are grossly underassessing such costs, these critics swung to the other extreme in their zeal to make a valid correction in the cost-benefit ratio. Thus the BC ratios for four major dams of the Narmada valley tumble down to far below one when each hectare of submerged forest land was assigned an astronomical price tag of Rs. 1.26 crores (as compared to Rs. 300/ha. used by the project promoters) by Ramesh Billorey and Claud Alvares. Here, a reasonable cost would be in the neighbourhood of Rs. 55,000/ha. (Source: Kanchan Chopra, my colleague).

Let us now look into the BC results for the Tehri project. For this purpose we would go by data given in Vijay Paranjpye's study, entitled *Evaluating the Tehri Dam* (INTACH, 1988). While its rate of return on power segment is placed by him at 6.89 per cent (well below the anticipated rate of 11.59 per cent as per the project promoters), its (undiscounted) BC ratio for the irrigation segment is reckoned at only 1.28 (below 3.49 as per the project report). For the project as a whole, the discounted BC ratio works out to only 0.56.

Kanchan Chopra, using more appropriate methods of BC analysis than those employed by Paranjpye, arrived at BC ratio of 0.89, which still indicates unviability of the project on strict economic grounds. This author too has carefully probed into the evaluative work of both Paranjpye and Chopra, and found the project quite a viable proposition. Here I cannot fully go into the reasons why my findings are at variance with theirs (Interested readers may see my article in *Economic and Political Weekly*, August 31, 1991, reproduced in chapter 16). However, the following points need to be stated briefly.

My reassessment or re-evaluation of Tehri dam centres round two things: (1) the valuation of hydel power by Paranjpye and Chopra, and (2) Paranjpye's computations of irrigation benefits. We begin with no.1. Leaving aside his dim appreciation of the power needs of U.P., Paranjpye does not alter the price of 48 paise per KWH at which electricity was sold in U.P. and on which basis it was valued in Tehri project report as per the procedure laid down in this regard by the Planning Commission. Chopra values this power on the alternative cost principle, namely, the cost of generating coal-based thermal power, which is about 82 paise/kwh. It is basically as a result of this 70 per cent enhancement in the price of hydel power that her BC ratio for the project rises to 0.87.

Chopra's valuation of hydro power at the resource cost of thermal power makes sense in the context of cost effectiveness, that is, while making a choice among techniques of production with the tacit assumption that product remains the same (or exact substitute) in each technique. That is not so in the present case as hydel power stations (backed with storage reservoirs) are well suited to meeting peak power loads in power system. For this reason, such flexible power needs to be given a higher price tag than that on thermal power where average cost of power generation becomes lower only because of high rate of capacity utilisation (i.e., 'plant factor') owing to reliance on thermal stations for meeting the base load of a power system.

Paranjpye revises downwards the value of annual irrigation benefits from the Tehri project, from Rs. 158 crores to about Rs. 65 crores only. A reduction of the order of Rs. 44 crores occurs because of his unjustified assumption that this much income would have accrued to farmers in any case under rainfed conditions from 0.27 million ha. of additional crop area brought under irrigation through Tehri project. Since 92 per cent of this area is anticipated to be in the rabi season, project promoters are quite justified that in the low rainfall conditions of western U.P. land would remain fallow during rabi season once a kharif crop has been matured under rainfed farming. (Of course, Paranjpye is not the first economist to commit such an error of underassessing such benefits from irrigation).

His other downward revisions lack supporting evidence. Knowing as I do about the irrigated agriculture of western

U.P., I am more inclined to go along with the project promoters' than his calculus. So his downward revision of irrigation benefits is open to serious doubt (his capitalising the interest costs on investments during the gestation phase of the Tehri project is acceptable, though the need for this cumbersome capitalisation is obviated in the standard discounted BC framework).

In view of the foregoing discussion the doubt cast on the economic viability of Tehri dam project is not well founded in facts. So the case for this project on economic grounds is not all that weak as portrayed in the INTACH study. Its economic viability is reasonably good.

Non-economic Angles

Non-economic considerations now loom large in the calculus of those who are strongly opposed to the big dams. For the sake of convenience in analysis, these may be broadly divided into two categories: (1) environmental, and (2) seismic dangers. Whereas the environmental considerations tend to underline (a) the pecuniary as well as non-pecuniary costs of environmental degradation following the construction of big reservoir, and (b) the sufferings of the tribal and other poorer classes for the benefit of the mainstream population, the seismic angle underscores the potentially high danger of disaster from a dam burst resulting from an earthquake.

I have already dealt with some aspects of these environmental costs, and would presently concentrate on the seismic hazard which, in my view, is a crucial issue that needs satisfactory resolution one way or the other. Before taking it up for a detailed discussion, I would like to record here that with improved and enhanced canal irrigation due to the Tehri project there would be noteworthy improvement in groundwater regime within the semi-arid west U.P. region. Because of the protective nature of the existing canals here groundwater resource here is being heavily exploited by farmers who have gone in a big way for private tubewell irrigation since the mid-sixties. So far, two factors have militated against groundwater depletion here on an extensive scale. One is the paucity of electricity for pumpsets, and the other is the substantial groundwater recharge from the canal network. Added canal supplies from the Tehri reservoir would improve groundwater recharge—waterlogging/salinity are no problems in the existing canals, thanks to the vertical drainage incidentally provided by the multitude of tubewells in this region.

One is struck, if not surprised, by the difference in expert assessment on the matter of earthquake hazard posed by the Tehri dam. Eminent earth scientists/engineers like Prof. Jai Krishna consider this rock-filled dam structure quite safe, capable of withstanding a seismic shock of high intensity that is not an improbable event in this part of the western Himalayas. This optimism, however, is not shared by some other renowned experts like Prof. Bruno of the U.S.A. This author is really at his wits ends on this vital issue, and cannot see an easy way out of this kind of impasse.

Possibly, if at the early stage of this raging controversy an impartial review of the matter had been carried out by the Centre, the issue might have been clinched one way or the other. There is no denying that the Centre has not followed impartial, above-board policy and procedures in the clearance of water projects. Anyway, even if the review were indeed fairly conducted, there is no guarantee that a unanimous, jury-like verdict would have emerged.

This apprehension stems from the observation that nowadays expert assessments and opinions in every discipline do tend to diverge not infrequently. Why this happens is not so germane to discuss right now; the recognition of the phenomenon is all that matters presently. This is a situation of great dilemma for decision makers, raising the question: who is better qualified to take a final view on an issue lacking concurrence among experts themselves? There are no easy answers here. In what follows I am sharing my loud thinking on this question.

Whenever experts differ widely, I would proceed as follows. If the situation is one of foregoing benefits *vis-a-vis* some possible environmental degradation that is remediable later on at some investment cost, I would appraise this cost against the benefits likely to be foregone, attaching due importance to the probabilities of the two things. But if the situation is one of development versus great disaster, say, from a likely dam burst due to earthquake, I shall go along-with those experts who fear devastation through a dam. A situation of predicament still exists when the environmental degradation apprehended by some experts is of the irreversible or non-remedial type. How does one go about sorting out this kind of situation?

CHAPTER 12

CONJUNCTIVE IRRIGATION : SARDAR SAROVAR*

Conjunctive use of water resources is today the watchword among Indian irrigation planners. It usually connotes that irrigational needs of an area be met jointly from an area's surface water as well as groundwater resources. But lately, in the context of the issue of small-scale versus large-scale irrigation works for exploiting surface water resources of a big river basin, the conjunctive idea has been extended onto the joint development of micro/mini, medium and major dams. The key idea here is that the long run sustainability of irrigated agriculture based on a big dam would be lower in the absence of effective watershed management work in the river catchment upstream of the dam. Along with afforestation and soil conservation, small dams play a crucial role in arresting the silt that threatens the life of the reservoir behind the big dam.

Here in this paper, the focus is on conjunctive use of surface water irrigation and groundwater irrigation in the command area downstream of a big dam. It is worthwhile to know whether surface water planners or the groundwater planners are in the vanguard of the conjunctive irrigation proposition. In India, it is primarily the former who are

---

* Appeared in *Financial Express*, 10 September, 1990.

pleading for conjunctive irrigation. They appear to be doing so for two reasons, one strategic and one tactical.

The strategic consideration stems from the bogey of waterlogging developing in canal commands due to the inevitable seepage of canal waters down to groundwater table. By pleading for groundwater development within a canal command the goal is to acheive vertical drainage of the seeped-in canal waters, so as to prevent rise in water table to within crop root zone of the command area. Incidentally, this obviates the need for sizable public investment in conventional horizontal drainage system within the canal command.

The ploy

As for the tactical play, the plea for conjunctive irrigation helps the surface water planners in fending off the groundwater cause lobbyists who have been arguing vociferously for much more emphasis on groundwater than on big canal irrigation works. The ploy has worked at least with groundwater scientists of the groundwater institutions who also now blithely talk of conjunctive use of groundwater and surface water.

In such a scheme, the groundwater reservoir of an area is not simply a balancing reservoir. Instead, it is tapped, as in the western United States, as a main source of meeting water needs, thereby allowing the groundwater reservoir to be depleted well beyond the 'safe yield' limit (i.e., normal annual recharge to groundwater reserves). As a result, the high periodic shortages in suface water availability are not allowed to impinge adversely on irrigated agriculture of an area. In point of fact, the years in which abundant supply of surface water becomes available to an area, say, a water district, it is diverted to both current usage as well as to the empty storage spaces underneath the land through artificial groundwater recharge methods.

The Sardar Sarovar Project (SSP) is probably the first major irrigation work for which a planned attempt has been made by the project promoters themselves to incorporate the idea of conjunctive irrigation within the SSP planning. Therefore, it would be instructive to examine the project for its conjunctive irrigation content. Such an examination might help us in appreciating the promoters' claim that not a single hectare within the SSP command in Gujarat state would be allowed to be waterlogged from the seeped-in canal waters.

The SSP is truly a gigantic irrigation scheme with a command area of over three million hectares, of which nearly two-thirds is culturable, i.e., fit for crop farming. In this large command, most of which is within Gujarat, the SSP is expected, as per present plans, to provide additional irrigation to the extent of 1.8 million hectares of crop area. Towards this objective, nearly nine million acre-feet (MAF) of Narmada waters would be diverted to the Gujarat plains.

Further Loss

This diversion will be done by damming the Narmada at Navgam and creating the Sardar Sarovar reservoir, which would feed the 40,000 cusecs, 445 km. long main canal. The 'live' storage capacity of the SS reservoir is only 4.7 MAF - it would receive some water from the Narmada Sagar proposed to be built by Madhya Pradesh by damming the Narmada 240 km. upstream of the Navgam dam. This augmentation in water availability from SS reservoir arises because the Narmada Sagar would be largely storing water for power generation, and much less for consumptive use in the agriculture sector.

Canals in India, more so in northern India where these are primarily unlined and are designed for promoting extensive/protective farming, are very leaky, with barely 25 to 50 per cent of the water released into them managing to reach farmers' fields. At the field level, a further loss — from the viewpoint of crops evapo-transpiration needs better known as the consumptive requirements of plants — occurs mainly in the shape of percolation of water down to groundwater table that is well beyond the reach of root system of a crop (but not of a well established tree). This field percolation loss, which varies with porosity and water holding capacity of the soil and is usually in the range of 15 to 20 per cent for low water using crops and twice as much for paddy, can rise when farmers tend to over-irrigate their crops in the mistaken notion that they are storing extra amount of canal water in the crop root zone of their crops (generally reckoned at top five feet of the soil profile). The SSP planners hope to reduce substantially the leakiness in conveyance as well as the field percolation, and envisage an efficiency in water use of the order of 60 per cent. That is to say, 60 per cent of the water released from the headworks at Navgam dam would be fruitfully used for meeting consumptive needs of the crops. Whereas conveyance losses are to be contained through extensive lining (right upto eight hectare outlet point) of the canal network, the excessive field percolation may be contained if the SSP command farmers live up to the expectations of the SSP planners of not applying more than two inches (five cm.) of depth of water in each watering to a field.

The SSP planners anticipate that nearly a third of the tapped Narmada water (i.e., 2.7 MAF) would go towards raising groundwater table. So, they have provided for groundwater development for irrigation purpose to the same extent. Groundwater development within the SSP command is anticipated both within private and public aegis. The annual abstraction/extraction of groundwater resource for irrigation purpose is placed at 2.71 MAF (3.351 million m^3 or 0.335 million hectare - metres), of which nearly six-tenths would be through dugwells and tubewells owned and operated by farmers themselves. While each dugwell equipped with a 7.5 HP pumpset and costing Rs. 30,000 in capital outlay is anticipated to extract 0.8 hectare metres (ham.) of groundwater annually, the corresponding withdrawal by a privately owned 20 HP tubewell installed at a cost of Rs. 150,000 is placed at 10 ham. — 20 ham. in the case of 25 HP public sector tubewell costing Rs. 200,000. The capital and annual recurring costs of groundwater development of the order of 2.71 MAF are placed at as follows:

	Number of structures	Capital cost (Rs. crore)	Recurring cost* (Rs. crore)
1. Dugwells with pumpsets	115,920	348	83
2. Private tubewells	2,216	33	2
3. Public tubewells	5,624	112	7
Total (1 to 3)		493	92

* Energy cost plus repairs and maintenance.

It may be pointed out that some of the above mentioned costs are already incurred. For, nearly one third of 2.7 MAF were being withdrawn by wells existing in the SSP during 1981-82. Adjusting for this factor, the added costs of groundwater extraction are reckoned at Rs. 150 crore in capital outlays and Rs. 16 crore in recurring charges. (There is something amiss here because the additional cost of extracting two-thirds of groundwater is far smaller than the 1981-82 cost of extracting a third of groundwater. On a pro-rata basis, more plausible estimates of additional costs of additional groundwater development would be around Rs. 350 crore in capital outlay and Rs. 61 crore in recurring terms).

SSP Planning

As a sizeable part of the SSP command is underlain with saline groundwater, private groundwater development in such saline tracts/pockets is not likely to occur. So, the project planners have wisely provided for 2710 large capacity (75 m^3/hour or 30 ham. per year) Government tubewells, each costing Rs. 175,000 in capital costs and Rs. 20,000 in annual operation, thereby lifting 813 million m^3 (nearly 0.6

MAF-, of groundwater. This vertical drainage would entail Rs. 47 crore in capital costs and Rs. 5.4 crore in annual operations.

The foregoing review shows that if the anticipations of the SSP planners are realised in practice the groundwater balance of the SSP command would not be affected adversely by the introduction of huge quantities of Narmada waters into it — it is an altogether different matter that the anticipated costs on account of conjunctive groundwater irrigation are underassesed by them. But if the anticipations go awry — either because canal seepage through lined channels turns out to be more or the field percolation loss exceeds expectations, or both — one has to provide for extra costs for withdrawing the extra seepage-cum-percolation addition to groundwater table.

Leaving aside the apprehension that these extra costs may be of the same order as provided for in the SSP calculus presently (namely, Rs. 400 crore on capital account and Rs. 66 crore on recurring basis), the moot point to ask is whether the requisite private investment in dugwells and tubewells would be forthcoming in the SSP command. The unqualified answer to this query is 'yes'. This assessment is based on several considerations of which the following ones need mentioning here.

Overdrawal

The SSP proposes to deliver a rather modest quantity of canal water for each unit of land in its command. For a culturable command area of over two million hactares about one million ham. (8 MAF) of canal water is provided for irrigation in the whole year. This comes to an irrigation delta of barely 50 cm. per unit of land area. If a good deal of it fails to reach the farmer, he would have strong compulsion to make up for the deficiency in water requirements. This can be achieved by investing in groundwater, as has been done by farmers in Punjab, Haryana and western U.P. where canal deliveries as well as the agro-climatic conditions are not much different from those of the SSP command. The development of a good market in groundwater in Gujarat should be an added facilitating factor for requisite investments in private well irrigation.

I am not unduly worried about waterlogging-salinity problems raising their ugly heads within the SSP command following the introduction of massive Narmada waters in its fields. In point of fact, my worry is on another count, namely, development of intensive irrigated farming that may strain the groundwater resource of the SSP command. The farmer here is resourceful and well tuned to market opportunities. If he takes to heavy water using crops like paddy, sugarcane, fruits, etc., on the same scale as has been done by the Punjab-Haryana farmer for paddy, he would overdraw on groundwater resource. Such overdrawal can lead to intrusion of saline bodies of water, say, from the sea (as has happened in Saurashtra coastal region) into sweet groundwater aquifers. One sure way of containing the rise of sugarcane cultivation is to be restrictive in allocating licences for new sugar mills whose establishment invariably boosts canecultivation in their neighbourhood.

PART II

REVIEWS OF REPORTS/STUDIES

CHAPTER 13

FAULTY ICSSR SURVEY OF INDIAN IRRIGATION*

Research activity in all disciplines, including economics, is expanding at an explosive rate. This necessitates periodic surveys of literature; and in sponsoring these a signal role has to be played by professional associations of research workers and other apex bodies. The Indian Council of Social Science Research (ICSSR), which is a major funding agency for research in social sciences in India, has rightly taken upon itself this function. It sponsored a second survey of the literature in the eighties. Late Professor Krishna Bharadwaj's study: *Irrigation in India: Alternative Perspectives* is a part of this fresh effort.

The second round survey pertaining to economics has twenty nine papers under preparation. It is not supposed to be a conventional survey of the state of research. According to late Professor Sukhomoy Chakravarty: "The second Survey of Research in Economics is in a way substantially different from the first. Most of the contributions in the first survey had a significant *bibliographical orientation* and covered relevant literature generated within a specific period of time — that is upto 1970. The *form has been changed in the second survey which seeks to elucidate and enlarge the analytical issues pertaining to a major development theme*. While the analysis is not limited to any specific period, greater attention has

---

* *Journal of Indian School of Political Economy*, July-September, 1992.

been given to recent writings, especially in India". (p.v.; emphasis added).

Bharadwaj's report on irrigation in India was completed and submitted to the ICSSR in late 1985. (One fails to understand why the ICSSR took five years to bring out this 73 page document). It consists of three sections, besides an introduction by the author and a foreward by Prof. Chakravarty, former Chairman of ICSSR and also of the economists Advisory Committee for the second survey. Section one is titled 'Growth of Irrigation in India'. The state of research on irrigation is the subject matter of section two. Section 3 is mainly an expository writeup on different types of irrigation, with heavy emphasis on their technical aspects. Finally, we have a one page sumup, entitled 'Concluding Remarks: Tasks Ahead'. A short bibliography of about 125 references is provided at the end, as also an index.

The new conception of the survey certainly freed Bharadwaj from being meticulous in presenting an exhaustive list of research contributions that would be otherwise so imperative in a conventional survey of the literature. But this does not give her freedom to be arbitrary about choosing the works she consults and presents in a select bibliography for the survey. This selection must satisfy some basic criteria, such as 'significant contributions to research, in the area of irrigation in India', which she herself states at the outset of the study. Any discerning researcher would be shocked by the manner in which she applied the yardstick. Her report and the Select Bibliography, which ignore so many major issues, developments and works relating to Indian irrigation, however include a news item in the *Indian Express* and the following entries:

1. Agenda of 28th meeting of the Board of Directors, Punjab State Tubewell Corporation (PSTC), 1976.
2. *File* on Maintenance and Operation of Tubewells, PSTC, 1976-1979.
3. *File* on Tubewells installed under Emergency Programme, PSTC, 1978.
4. *File* on Financial Affairs, PSTC, 1982.

In view of the brief enjoined upon the author by the commissioning agency, it is somewhat pointless to enumerate here some noteworthy omissions of significant contributions from the select bibliography. Yet, whatever has been proffered by her as a survey of the literature is far from a thorough job. She remains on good wicket only so long as she is using authoritative sources like the reports of the first or second Irrigation Commission, National Commission on Agriculture, Royal Commission on Agriculture and the Central Board of Irrigation and Power. But the moment she ventures out on her own, she stumbles pitifully. Let us take her interpretation of the plan statistics on investments in irrigation sector which have been misinterpreted by legions of writers.

Subscribing to the widely-held but erroneous view that Indian water planning in the post-Independence period has been one of a continuation of the earlier one bearing a heavy tilt in favour of major (i.e., large-scale) as against minor (i.e., small-scale) irrigation works, Bharadwaj falters in handling the data on irrigation given in plan documents. First, she quotes very approvingly from Niranjan Pant's paper as follows: "During the Fourth and the following plans, investment in new major and medium schemes has again picked up: the Sixth Plan envisaged an outlay of Rs. 109,700 million for major and medium irrigation, which is *47.64 per cent more than the total amount (Rs. 74,000 million) spent on the same during thirty years preceding 1981*, Pant, 1982, p. A-34; see Table 2 for plan-wise expenditure on irrigation" (p. 11, emphasis added).

This is a clear case of the author trying to dramatise the mounting emphasis on the development of major (and medium irrigation) by our planners. But without doing the adjustment for the gradual depreciation of the Rupee due to price inflation over the planning period, the inference gets faulted. The dire need for bringing investment outlays at constant prices for making comparison between Plans is, alas, not realised by many writers who are usually non-economists (Pant is a public administration scholar). In the present case, however, the author even does not bother to look into her own cited Table 2 on p. 55 which is culled from P. Roger's study. This table shows *annual* average outlay on major and medium irrigation for each Plan period *at 1970-71 prices*. Though such data on investment in *real terms* does show a five-fold rise between the first and the sixth Five Year Plan, yet it does not lend credence to the erroneous impression being foisted by Pant, and endorsed by Bharadwaj in her survey. At 1970-71 prices, the targeted outlay for the sixth Plan works out to about Rs. 37 billion, whereas the cumulative total for the investment on major and medium irrigation comes to about Rs. 62 billion which is about 86 per cent higher than Rs. 37 billion.

Second, the author subscribes to the untenable view that minor irrigation has been neglected in Indian irrigation planning since 1951. Scores of writers, sold on the idea 'small is beautiful', have tried to sustain this view by parading the fact that the proportion of Plan outlays on minor irrigation account is low. Bharadwaj too follows this well-beaten but erroneous path. She writes as follows:

"Minor irrigation has suffered relatively overall neglect in terms of priorities of the public irrigation policy. Although a purposive shift to minor irrigation did take place during the Third Plan, with a significant rise in outlay on minor irrigation, ... the achievements... remained unsatisfactory.... It has been estimated that during the (Sixth) Plan period upto 1980-81, although 49 per cent of the irrigation potential was created through the major/medium schemes, they absorbed 76 per cent of the total outlay (Pant, 1983, p. 1315)." (p. 14-15).

Neither Pant nor Bharadwaj realises the elementary fact that much of the minor irrigation development is under farmers' own aegis. As plan outlays on minor irrigation do not include outlays on private account, it is inappropriate to judge planners' emphasis on minor irrigation development merely from the plan data on investment for minor irrigation *vis-a-vis* major and medium irrigation (which is entirely in the public sector). Whether or not emphasis on minor irrigation development is missing in our planning has to be judged by ascertaining answers to two questions. First, what is the relative share of minor irrigation in total irrigation potential created during the course of planning in India since 1951? Second, what is the desirable value for this relative share in any optimal water planning for the country? The author time and again encounters actual share in any plan period to be nearly 50 per cent (see, for example, pages 11, 13). As she is unware that this share is very near the optimal[1] share, as suggested by the estimates of *ultimate* irrigation potential of the country from minor and major irrigation, she needlessly keeps on stressing throughout her paper, directly or obliquely, that minor irrigation has not received due attention in Indian irrigation development in the post-Independence period.

Bharadwaj's one lament throughout the survey is that technical aspects of irrigation have received too much emphasis in the irrigation research literature, whereas social or class aspect of irrigation development have been neglected. In her concluding observations she candidly writes: "A common refrain in our discussions above has been our viewpoint that these 'technological' considerations of costs and benefits need to be placed within the context of socio-economic relations and conditions of production and exchange of user community. More research needs to be done on the interaction between the irrigation technology and the social relations in a region" (p. 51). While this reviewer could not agree with her more on this research agenda, he would like to caution that without proper knowledge of the technical aspects of irrigation[2] the resultant social analysis might become faulty. Indian economists have been considerably handicapped in coming to grips with technical aspects of irrigation, with the result that the literature on the economics of Indian irrigation lacks both in depth and width.

Bharadwaj's contention that researchers in irrigation economics have not paid any noteworthy attention to the class aspect of irrigation development and its impact on different classes in the countryside, should have led her to ponder over as to why this has happened, instead of merely reiterating it in the whole paper. In point of fact, her paper is laced with three major observations: (1) lack of full utilisation of irrigation potential created during a plan period, (2) inefficient operation and maintenance of public irrigation works, especially canal systems, and (3) resource-poor farmers benefiting much less from irrigation development. She uses one or more of these three minus points of irrigation experience in India to belittle too often any noteworthy achievement she comes across in the literature. For example, to the beneficial impact of irrigation and investments in public irrigation on crop production reported in some research papers she responds as follows: "These results, while not wrong in emphasizing the importance of public irrigation, are too broad to generate meaningful policy prescriptions. The aggregative treatment of irrigation in terms of investment (and confining it to public investment) bypasses important issues regarding the level of operation and effectiveness of the potential so created" (p. 18).

In making inferential observations, the survey lacks spatial coverage. This raises the issue of general validity of these observations. Let me illustrate this important point with the help of a concrete example. The survey relating to deep tubewells is based primarily on the Punjab experience with which Jasveen Jairath is familiar; and Jairath's help is acknowledged by Bharadwaj: "In the preparation of this research paper, the author received enthusiastic and fruitful cooperation from Dr. Jaswin (sic) Jairath." Since (a) Punjab accounts for hardly 5 per cent of such tubewells in the country, and (b) the experiences of installing them and operating them under public aegis has been far from uniform all over the country, the survey lacks in coverage as well as representation of the national picture. If only 20 per cent of the irrigation potential was found to be used in Punjab during 1971-74 by Bharadwaj or Jairath, the same rate was much higher (nearly 50 per cent) in U.P., the state with lion's share of deep tubewells of the nation. Though a number of research reports on the problem of underutilisation of capacity of such tubewells in U.P. had been carried out prior[3] to the commencement of this survey report, none is cited while assuring the reader that "similar evidence is available from Uttar Pradesh"[4] (p. 40).

The survey of the literature on shallow tubewell is also coloured unduly by the Punjab-related literature/experience. Ours is a country of continental diversity. Unless the author had gone about selecting her bibliography on the subject in a systematic manner, she was bound to give us a very partial — and at places distorted - picture of the literature on Indian irrigation. She is so preoccupied with essaying her own limited and biassed viewpoint on the subject of irrigation that she does not transcend beyond the few writings known to her prior to commencing the task of surveying the literature. These known writings prove handy in buttressing her own particular viewpoint on a given matter in the irrigation literature.

The author draws rather too much on her own (and Jairath's) work, so much so that sometimes it appears as if she is succumbing to the natural weakness of writers to over project their own writings, including the not so significant ones, given an opportunity to comment on the literature in a given area. Here one faces a dilemma of sorts. If one calls upon a scholar to do the survey in his or her own research area, he or she may fall prey to the above weakness, as also be biased in the critique (in praise as well as in criticism) of other scholars' work. But he or she would have the signal advantage of both familiarity with and better access to the literature, especially the unpublished one, thereby minimising the problem of errors of omission in the survey. In this tradeoff, I would rather entrust the task to such a scholar than to one placed at the fringe of the subject, however eminent he or she may otherwise be. This is all the more imperative for a subject like Irrigation where the literature is spread in journals/books of very diverse disciplines. Any scholar lacking familiarity and access is bound to commit grave errors of omission and commission.

Bharadwaj has not followed a correct policy of listing the authors of the cited works in the Bibliography. While it is all right to identify the co-authored works by the first author's name (adding, *et.al.*, of course) in the main text, the same practice is indefensible in the Bibliography where all the authors must figure *as the they are listed in the original works.* For example, from the fertiliser study by K.S. Parikh, *et.al.*, one cannot know who the other authors are. The printing space in Bibliography need not be economised even if the number of authors is too large, as in the case of the study 'Impact of Irrigation: Studies of Canal, Well and Tank Irrigation in Karnataka'[5] is listed under by Nadkarni, M.V., *et.al.*, This is unfair to the other 10 authors. Worse still is the reduction of the first name of some of the authors to initials only. Thus Dharm Narain and Shyamal Roy's signal contribution on the relationship between irrigation and intensity of cropping is listed under D. Narain and S. Roy.[6] Worst of all, it is when studies are cited in the text but do not find any listing in the bibliography. For example, there is a very favourable account given on pages 19-20 of some of my studies of 1983 but none figures in the Bibliography.[7]

For fulfilling the expectations of the kind that the second survey was meant it is necessary that the surveying scholar be himself/herself one with some noteworthy contributions in the area being surveyed. Admittedly, this condition would have been less imperative had the survey been of a conventional kind with 'bibliographical orientation', But not so in the following situations:

1. The area to be surveyed has specificities that demand more than a nodding familiarity with the subject matter of the survey.
2. A good deal of the literature is unpublished and available in mimeo form, Ph.D. and M.Phil theses of the universities, etc. Even access to the published literature may not be all that easy if scholars use diverse discipline outlets and journals for publishing their work.

This applies to Indian irrigation literature. The reviewer, having put in over 25 years in research in irrigation economics, is quite baffled by the ICSSR for selecting Bharadwaj as much as her agreeing to undertake the survey of irrigation literature. It is crucial drawback and is hardly mitigated by the association of Jasveen Jairath, an irrigation economist with engineering background (she has earlier served in the Irrigation Department of Punjab). Barring a singular inclusion of her Ph.D. thesis on Punjab irrigation of 1984, none other figures in the survey.

NOTES

1. The ultimate irrigation potential of the country is reckoned at 113 million ha. of which minor irrigation (tanks, tubewells, dugwells, etc.) is placed at 55 million ha. and major/medium irrigation at 58 million ha. Applying the principle of conjunctive development, the relative emphasis has to be determined by these relative shares in ultimate potential.
2. Though the author bemoans the irrigation scholars' pre-occupation with technical aspects, she does precisely this in section 3 of the book, where she writes extensively about the technical aspects of multipurpose projects, deep tubewells and shallow tubewells.
3. My book, entitled *Development of Tubewells in India* (published in 1981 by Agricole Academy, New Delhi and (reprinted in 1982), mentions at least a dozen research studies on deep tubewells of U.P. alone. Presumably, its 'technological' contents turned off the author who does not refer to it at all.
4. The singular study pertaining to deep tubewells that is cited at the end of the sub-section on deep tubewells is one by Kripa Shankar, the context being different, viz, "a decline in the use of public tubewells as a result of farmers' installation of their own shallow tubewells" (p.41).
5. A portion of the title ('studies of') is missing in the Bibliography.
6. The author, as also Jairath, is innocent about the research value of this study, as she never comments on it. It is mentioned only once on p.22, without any perceptive observation about it.
7. The one shown for 1983 against my name is not the one discussed on pp. 19-20. The two missing studies being commented upon by the author are: (1) Productivity Impact of Irrigation in India, and (2) Sourcewise Productivity Impact of Irrigation, both in mimeo form. These constitute the core of my book *Irrigation in India's Agricultural Development (1988)* but were made available to the author through a colleague of mine who conveyed Bharadwaj's request for my writings on irrigation.

CHAPTER 14

CSE REPORT ON FLOODS IN THE HIMALAYAN RIVERS*

India is a country of such continental diversity that one can form contrary impressions or opinions about any one of its major characteristics. When a periodic drought occurs, a feeling that Nature has been too niggardly in the matter of water endowment comes over to many of us. As news of flood havoc in years of excessive rainfall pours in, we begin feeling a sense of tyranny of our water bounty. In between these fluctuating mental moods, we get occasionally baffled by the seemingly paradoxical phenomenon of simultaneous occurrence of drought and flood in the same calendar year, sometimes in the same state!

It is these extreme oscillations in natural phenomenon that give rise to the pertinent question: why cannot the government undertake major water conservation measures, whereby surplus flood waters get effectively stored up, to be used later either in rainless months of the year, or carried over to subsequent years to cope with drought in the main monsoon season period? Another related question is: why can't we harness the huge surplus waters of our highly flood-prone eastern Indo-Gangetic plains, presently flowing to the Bay of Bengal, so as to relieve *inter alia* the great natural water scarcity in the drought prone tracts of the western and southern parts of the country? Though these

---

* Appeared in *Economic and Political Weekly*, May 1, 1993.

two questions have not been squarely answered in the third Citizens' Report on the State of India's Environment, entitled *Floods, Flood Plains and Environmental Myths,*[1] released recently by the Centre for Science and Environment (CSE), New Delhi, yet one can conclude that the CSE's answers to these questions are primarily in the negative. For, its central message for the nation is that it must learn to cope with the periodic flood hazard. In point of fact, the authors are so overwhelmed by their stunning research findings that they dedicate the Report to people who have learnt, over the ages, the art of living with floods.

Before elaborating the contents of this signal contribution to the Indian research literature on floods, some observations about the CSE itself are necessary. First, the prefatory remarks of the Series Editors, Anil Agarwal and Sunita Narain, announce the CSE's decision to now transform itself from essentially a compiler-cum-diffuser of ongoing transformations of Indian environment to a policy research body.

It is possibly this change that has emboldened the authors to live upto the image of a researcher, namely, to tell the truth as he discovers it through painstaking research endeavours, without fear of upsetting holders of contrary views however numerous they be. No wonder, this Report has caused much dismay and disbelief to those who have for long believed in the 'sponge effect' of forests in eradicating the flood menace. 'Dam the Himalayas with forest cover, not with engineering dams' has indeed been one of the main slogans of those who are opposed to the idea of big dams in the Himalayas, as also elsewhere in the country as well as in the world as a whole. To put it bluntly, the CSE has shown that environmentalists and the Indian media supporting them have been propagating sheer environmental myth when they plead for afforestation of the Himalayas as a *pucca* or sustainable solution to the flood problem of the vast plains in northern and eastern Indian sub-continent. Little wonder, then, that the Report has been coldly received by the environmentalist groups. Before long, a critique of the CSE volume too would emerge, in the process enriching the literature in this area. This is an inevitable paradigm of advancement in the research world. Therefore, the CSE ought to take the criticism, bitter or otherwise, in its stride.[2]

The second observation pertains to the CSE announcement about the contents of its future reports on the nation's environment. "We now find that completed chapters go out of date even before we reach half the book. The result is an unending chase to document changing events in an ambitious attempt to produce a comprehensive report... Having gone through a difficult experience over the last five years to produce the third report, chasing events which continue to move with considerable rapidity, we have now decided to publish the third report not as a comprehensive report but as a series of reports on specific issues". The present one on floods is, therefore, the first of this new series.

For an organisation to "move away from journalism into policy research" is a radical transformation, requiring in the first place a sea change in mindset. Among other things, it demands both patience and perseverance in probing something akin to 'art for art's sake'. It requires a curb on the craving to publicise paradoxical discoveries, striking discrepancies in data base, glaring contradictions, etc. so as to attract public attention. Furthermore, requirements of quality research poses the problem of creating an in-house expertise of specialists in diverse disciplines. Without requisite support of scarce financial funds on a durable basis — not to mention of still scarcer resource persons — the quality of research and the substantive content of the subsequent reports may be difficult to ensure. Too much dependence on short-run project support from outside agencies, and on outside experts, has its own perils.

It would appear that the CSE has largely opted for the latter course in bringing out the present research report. This is suggested by the numerous contributions listed at the place that carries author's names. Twenty six names from the Gangetic-Brahamputra basins are listed for the concrete inputs supplied by them ("This report would not have been possible without the support of ..."). Anil Agarwal and Ajit

Chak did both the coordination and editing work, and the writing of the report has been done by Anil Agarwal, Neeraj Labh and V.A. Nambi" with the help of additional contributions from Mukul Sharma, Ajit Chak and Sangeeta Synghal." To make a sensible amalgam out of diverse contributions is a hazardous task, more so in the research world. To guard against the risks of misperceptions, misplaced emphasis, or outright mis-reporting (these risks are unduly high while dealing with an immensely complex resource like water), the CSE might have held a seminar to which select flood water experts (more so from the government bodies which figure adversely in the report) could be invited. The need for this kind of filtration of a compounded research document prior to its publication is all the greater because CSE's reports tend to be read widely and quoted avidly but uncritically, more so by those who happen to be outside the academic portals. This poses the danger that some of its own weak/soft conclusions might become a source of new half-truths, if not outright myths. Let me concretise this point with a pertinent example.

On flood damages, the authors have assiduously compiled the yearwise statistics for the period 1953-87, giving the mean value of damage per year plus the maximum value for the worst year. Since they do not adjust for the persistent price inflation that occurred in this period — this is something that is so routinely done in applied economic research — the entire analysis gets distorted. Assuming that Indian Rupee depreciated to ten paise between the fifties and the eighties, the extent of rise in the value of flood damage would be nearly fourfold, not fortyfold. Because of this neglect of inflation factor, the computation of the mean value of damages per year and the identification of the worst year of flood damages become misleading exercises. Without price adjustment, it is open to question whether the incidence of flood damage is rising over time.[3]

This illustrative criticism is not to detract from the central proposition of this report that is reproduced below in the authors' own cautious wording. "....floods in the plains below the vast Himalayan ranges may .not be greatly exacerbated by deforestation. Floods are, in fact, and will remain, an inherent feature of these plains whether the Himalayan mountains are well clad with a green cover or whether they are deforestead and barren. The Himalayan mountains constitute an extremely fragile ecological system. They are the youngest mountains of the world and, therefore, highly erodible. They are lashed by rainstorms of an intensity that probably no other mountain system faces. They are extremely seismic, periodically witnessing some of the world's worst earthquakes. Water and silt, therefore, move out of these mountains in explosive waves. Floods and shifting of river courses is, therefore, inevitable.

Deforestation can aggravate the problem but *afforestation cannot get rid of it*. Now this may not be true with other flood plains with different watershed characteristics, hydrological conditions, rainfall parameters and other ecological characteristics. In fact, the information presented in this report lead us to the inevitable conclusion *that the societal susceptibility to the flood problem in the Indo-Gangetic plains has increased more because of the enormous social and ecological changes that have taken place in the flood plains than the changes that have taken place in the higher reaches* of the Himalayan watersheds." (p. vi, emphasis added)

So what has been amiss (a) with our earlier faith or belief in the role of forests in averting floods, and (b) in our ongoing planning of building multipurpose dams and network of embankments along rivers for containing the periodic floods? The authors provide cogent and convincing arguments/evidence on the futility of constructing river embankments and covering Himalayan slopes with forest cover as protection against the ravages of Himalayan rivers. The same, however, cannot be said categorically about their negative perceptions about the utility of big storage reservoirs in flood proofing task. Before dwelling on this debatable point, let us grasp the argument as to why the sponge effect of the forests fails to work out fully in the case of the Himalayan rivers.[4] Since there is nothing new or novel about the other argument about the ultimate futility of embankments in the case of rivers with large silt load and volatile fluctuations in day-to-day flows, this aspect needs no more than a passing reference in what follows.

Though rainfall, in the ultimate analysis, is the source of water flows of a river, yet analytically it is useful to distinguish different components of such flows. One component is the 'base' flow which is a sort of minimal flow that is often seen in a river despite the absence of any current rainfall precipitation in the catchment area. This flow originates from some natural storage bodies in the river catchment. Two such noteworthy storage bodies are snow mountains and water held underneath in the soils, including soft rocks and the crevices/cracks of hard rocks. Snow melt and water discharge from groundwater table into a river are the two principal sources of the base flow, which does vary depending *inter alia* upon solar activity and the height of groundwater table above the river bed. Snow melt tends to peak during summer season precisely when groundwater component of the base flow tends to be minimum.

Occasional breaches[5] in natural lakes formed by landslides blocking the course of a river in its upper reaches with high gradients lead to additions to the base flow. If such a breach is in the nature of a dam burst, it can lead to flash floods in the upper reaches. But most commonly flood in the lower plains of a river basin results from surface water runoff in the wake of a downpour. As this rainfall runoff gets superimposed on the base flow (about 15 to 20 per cent of the mean annual flow), the river swells in size, the extent of swelling depending on the volume and intensity of the runoff water which in turn depend on three distinct factors; (1) quantity, intensity and simultaneity of rainfall, (2) the slope or gradient of the land mass and the relative share of mountainous catchment, and (3) soil depth and soil cover, especially on the hillsides.

Needless to say, these three factors (as also some less important factors not mentioned here) have an interacting impact on the runoff. Thus a rainfall of high intensity (given the same slope of land and soil depth) would still generate lesser runoff when the land is well covered with trees and grasses which blunt the force with which rain drops strike the ground, thereby facilitating its infiltration into the soil. However, the depth of the soil and the porous space within it determine how much (infiltrated) water would get stored up in the soil. Once this storage limit is reached, the subsequent rainfall must *wholly* runoff to the river channel down below, irrespective of the extent of the forest cover. From this point onwards, forests, bushes, grasses and other vegetation no more impede the water runoff phenomenon. Such flora, however, do continue to impede the other runoff phenomenon, namely, soil erosion from land surface, better known as *sheet* erosion which has to be distinguished from other kind of soil erosion, such as hillsides toppling over in the shape of big land slips or landslides that block, partially or wholly, stream channels.

It is this thickness (and porosity) of the weathered soil on the mountainous slopes that essentially determines how much of the rainfall will be stored up ('dammed up' in Sundar Lal Bahuguna's terminology) in the upper, hilly catchments of a river basin. Thus the sponge effect of vegetative cover tends to diminish as one moves up a hillside because depth of soil diminishes from bottom valley to the hill top. Likewise, the sponge effect tends to be inversely related to amount of rainfall. In other words, afforestation or integrated watershed management programme is likely to prove *ceteris paribus* much more effective in conserving water *in situ* in low rather than high rainfall, hilly terrains. It is this perception or experience about low rainfall tracts that has probably sustained the widely-held view of forests functioning everywhere or universally as sponges for absorbing rainfall which would otherwise end up as floods in the valleys and the plains down below.

In passing, it may be pointed out that runoff of surface water can occur even before the porous space is fully saturated with infiltrated rain water. The likelihood of such a phenomenon is all the more when intensity of rainfall is high, that is to say, when rainfall drops come in intense succession in a short span of time. When this intensity is low, rainfall infiltration occurs in a smooth fashion. That is to say, infiltrated water, pulled by the force of earth's gravity, has enough time to travel inside the porous voids of the weather mantle of the earth.

Not only the rainfall but also geologic conditions of the Himalayas are unfavourable for effectively arresting, through afforestation, the soil as well as water erosion. True, the storage space for rain water here at places is often unusually large owing to much less compaction of soils having occurred in the Himalayas. But this looseness of soil militates against the stability of the hillsides once these get impregnated with infiltrated water inside their bodies or bowels. In the absence of solid, rocky walls to hold back such stored waters, two things happen. First, subsurface runoff occurs in a big way, carrying with it both the infiltrated water and the loose soil. That is to say, we have a case of leaky storage, the leaks becoming gushing muddy subterranean channels owing to the force of earth's gravity, ending up finally into surface streams at the valley floor.[8] Second, the phenomenon of landslides and toppling of hillsides into surface streams is hastened by the inner movements of silt/debris-laden water. So the more we promote rainfall infiltration via vegetative covering of the hillsides, the greater the danger of landslides toppling, more so in a seismically active region like the Himalayas.

The authors of the Report underscore the surface hydrology, geology and hydrogeology of the Himalayas in order to bring home the following crucial point. "Landslides contribute more to soil loss in the Himalayas than surface erosion. Deforestation is often blamed for landslides, but forests can only inhibit shallow landslides. They have little effect on deep landslides." (p.40). When heavy rainfall over a two or three day period occurs, there is neither enough time for infiltration of rain water into the soils nor is there enough soil depth in hills to store such huge quantities of water even in geologically compacted mountains. For storing 82 cm. of rainstorm of 18 September, 1980 (as occurred, according to the Report, in central Himalaya over a two day duration with its centre at Nagina in Bijnor district of Uttar Pradesh) one needs 4 to 5 metres thick *dry soil* which is almost an impossibility at the fag end of a monsoon season.[9] No wonder, such intense rainstorms produce devastating swelling in river flows. For instance, the three-day rainstorm of late September of 1924 in the western Himalayas (Simla-Kumaon hills) gave rise to the following consequences:

"The Yamuna catchment upto Tajewala received heavy rains during the first two days. A peak discharge of 14,000 cumecs (about half lakh cusecs) passed down Tajewala headworks on September 28, and 22 km. upstream the Yamuna at Paonta rose by 13.1 m. (about 45 feet) on the same day. Four days later, on October 2, the water level rose by 0.94 m. above the danger level at Delhi railway bridge. Hundreds of people and thousands of head of cattle were washed away in Dehradun, Saharanpur, Ambala and Karnal districts." (p.33, box item titled 'Rains of Terror').

We might rightly ask at this stage: why not create man-made storage reservoirs to hold back the flood waters? This is indeed a sensible idea, which has been not well explored in the Report. There are techno-economic limits to this option.[10] First, rivers cannot be dammed usefully once these have emerged from the hills onto the flat or deltaic plains. Low height dams here do not create any worthwhile storage of flood waters in high rainfall basins. On the other hand, construction of high dams here would submerge very large tracts of valuable land with many human settlements. Roughly speaking, each hectare of land area benefitted with irrigation from such stored waters would mean another productive hectare of land going under the reservoir, not to mention the large-scale uprooting of masses on these high density lands. It is only in the hilly portion of a river basin that the ratio of submerged land to benefitted land can be kept at tolerably low levels. Typically, a big dam in India submerges land equal to 5 to 10 per cent of the benefitted land, whereas a small dam, like the one used in South India for tank irrigation, submerges area equal to 15 to 20 per cent of the land it benefits.

Second, dam sites for erecting big dams are naturally rather scarce. Because of this scarcity dam engineers are tempted to build mega dams on few dam sites identified through survey and investigation work in a river basin. However, this temptation is greatly tempered by technical parameters (rock geology, hydrology, meteorology, soil characteristics, etc.) on the one hand and socio-economic factors on the other. If a dam site can sustain a huge reservoir both technically and socio-economically, why not build one to have the maximal multipurpose benefits of flood control, hydel power generation, irrigation, water for industrial and municipal uses, etc? Hoover dam on the mighty Colorado river (USA) is a good example of such a mega reservoir that can store *three times* the normal or average annual flow of that river. This widely acclaimed feat of American engineering of the 20th century[11] effectively stores up most of the above-normal flood waters, as do most other big American dams which are designed with storages far higher than the mean annual flows of their rivers.[12] Such dams truly "kill" a river in the words of Baba Amte, the veteran opponent of the big dam idea on the sacred Narmada river, that is to say, these mega dams fully harness river water resources for economic prosperity, allowing little loss of river water to the seas.

In contrast, few Indian reservoirs are so designed. These are mostly designed on '75 per cent dependability' basis, whereby their storage is inherently incapable of impounding any above-normal inflows into them. Owing to this, their managers are forced to let out such excess inflows through the dam spillway system, only to be berated in public fora for aggravating the flood problem instead of controlling it. The authors of the study under review too harbour such misgivings, writing, as they do in bold letters on the billboard page preceding each chapter, the categorical sentence that "dams have become an important cause of floods." (page before chapter 1).[13] In what follows the Damodar Valley (DVC) case is taken up for an instructive analysis of why dams can occasionally aggravate the flood menace in the Indian conditions.

The DVC project, consisting of a few big dams and a strong component of soil and water conservation programme in the upper erodible reaches of the Damodar river basin, is patterned after the famed, multipurpose Tennesse Valley

Project (TVP) of the United States of America, with flood control as one express objective, to achieve which a part of the storage behind dams is *exclusively earmarked* for flood water storage. With such an allocation of storage capacity, the conflict between economic uses (irrigation, power generation and navigation) and flood control gets eliminated. But unfortunately the DVC management has not been allowed to use this earmarked storage. Why? Because the state administrations of this inter-state project have been unsuccessful in fully completing the task of shifting many of the dam oustees from the reservoir areas. These unshifted oustee villages, located at higher elevation in the catchment area, would be submerged in the reservoirs if the reservoirs are filled up to the full dam heights. As a result, excess inflows in years of exceptional rainfall (in amount as well time of the year) have per force to be let out, though these can be impounded provided the DVC management is enabled to utilise the hitherto *unutilised* flood storage capacity of its system. This brings us to the pertinent question as to why the state administrations, under the aegis of the state politicians, fail to carry out the eviction task as per the original project plans. Thus we come face to face with the socio-economic factors that have a great bearing on the decision about the size of a big dam to be built on a given dam site.

When population density is low, land (including forest land) resource is plentiful in relation to population resource. In such favourable resource endowment, costs on account of land submergence and the resultant dislocation of human populations by big reservoirs tend to be low. For instance, in the United States some reservoir sites were totally berefet of human settlements, as in the case of the Hoover dam, the highest dam of the world (till the construction of Naurek dam in the Soviet Union in recent years). In other sites, the unfortunate, dislocated people could be easily relocated on a land-for-land basis and that too very near their original place of habitation. It is thus not surprising that mega dams, with storages capable of impounding even exceptionally high inflows, are the order of the day in the U.S.A.

But these circumstances do not prevail in densely populated nations like India where the number of dam-disrupted persons is usually sizeable and convenient alternative locations for their rehabilitation practically non-existent. As a result, these persons are very adversely affected by the development of dam-based irrigation/power projects. Hence, one encounters widespread opposition to the proposed big dams on the mighty rivers like the Ganga and the Narmada. In a way, this opposition brings poignantly home the meaning of the great rider on cost-benefit analysis, namely, whose costs and whose benefits?

Economic theory offers no satisfactory solution to this intractable problem; economists here offer mere sops in the form of financial compensation to the dam oustees. As ability to handle finance of the low-educated people living in great isolation from the mainstream is fragile, they are, by and large, unable to restart life once they are uprooted from their original environs.[14] This is one inhuman face of the development process that has dismayed many a sensitive soul.

In an engineer's calculus of the height of a dam, the benefits of a multipurpose dam *ceteris paribus* increase much faster than the proportionate rise in the dam height almost in an accelerated manner (i.e., the relationship is non-linear, probably quadratic).[15] But so is the relationship between land submergence/number of affected persons and the dam height. Thus, the more the multifarious benefits we attempt to confer on villages and towns on the *downstream side* of a dam, the higher become the costs of submergence and dislocation on the *upstream side* of the dam. It is a well known geographical fact that the density of population, when already high, tends to rise as one moves away from the *flood zone* of a river basin. This crucial factor militates strongly against Indian dam builders' desire to emulate their American counterparts in building mega reservoirs, each with a storage capacity well above the annual flow in a river. The DVC failure to utilise the flood storage spaces in its dams is to be understood in this aforesaid social milieu of the country.

Let us return to the issue of dams being a cause also of floods. As a multipurpose dam comes up on a river in a given region an impression goes round that floods would become a thing of the past on downstream side of that dam. The impression is fostered both by the engineering fraternity and the regional politicians, irrespective of whether flood control is a specific objective in building the dam. This encourages land-hungry populations to begin settling down in the *flood zone* area of a river basin.

If so happens that even when there is no express provision for storing flood waters in the reservoir, the extent to which *a part* of the flood waters originating on the upstream side of the dam are held back in the reservoir for irrigation and hydel generation, it reduces the flows to the downstream plains, thereby reducing the area of flood zone. But people moving into the flood zone for settling down permanently have no idea where exactly the new boundary of the diminished flood zone lies. The resource-poor among them, and more so those who are already eking out a precarious living out of the *khadar* lands of a river, tend to overspill, knowingly or unknowingly, into the newly defined (but undelineated by any government agency) flood zone area. These people suffer not only in the event of even a normal flood in the river, but most devastatingly (in life, cattle, standing crops, assets, etc.) from an exceptional flood. The situation is best summed up by the proverbial saying: deed has in it the seed of destruction. The partial security against floods afforded by a dam becomes a means of destruction for the unwary.

This spillover or encroachment into the flood zone of rivers, especially in the Gangetic plains, has been occurring ever since the density of population has been rising inexorably. It is this population pressure related encroachment of the flood zones that is the root cause of rising flood-related losses (even when nominal values are adjusted for price inflation) in India.[16] Disaster management experts in general and Indian geographers in particular have been urging the Centre in vain, time and again, to enact flood zoning laws. Can governments meaningfully enforce such laws in the face of burgeoning population for which opportunities for gainful absorption lack in, both agricultural and non-agricultural occupations outside the flood zones?

Because of our socio-economic compulsions we cannot build mega dams that can truly hold back both the exceptionally high water inflows and vast quantities of silt and debris following the occurrence of intense rainstorms at the fag end of the monsoon season. With extra storage for water as well as for silt and debris, the multipurpose mega dams provide not only surer and greater economic benefits but also provide these on a far more sustainable basis. We are per force to do without such mega dams. As a matter of fact, we actually need to scale down a bit of the heights of our planned dams, so as to keep the serious problem of dam oustees within manageable limits. Such scaled down dams would still remain big dams but with substantially reduced economic benefits and flood prevention role. Even so, these could help in combating the flood menace to some extent. In point of fact, the administrative backup needed for the recommended CSE option of living with the floods in the Himalayan river plains would be much less exacting than that without (a) some big dams, (b) selected afforestation programmes, (c) massive integrated watershed programmes, and (d) selective embankment and river training investments. But without the component (a), living with floods would be horrid. Therefore, we need to look afresh at the CSE-ruled out option of big dams in the Himalayas, without over-reacting to the seismic hazard posed by such dams.

NOTES

1. It is available, both in paper back (Rs. 150) and hard bound (Rs. 350), from the CSE.
2. A telephonic conversation with Anil Agarwal on 22nd April, 1992 (after he had been sent the first draft of this paper three weeks earlier) revealed that he was quite exercised over the criticism of the report, more so from Vandana Shiva and N.D. Jayal. I have seen only the review by Jayal in *India Today* and did not appreciate his highminded advice that such reports would weaken the environmental movement. Jayal's own body, INTACH, has not always advanced the cause of truth.

Its own two anti-big dam studies, under the authorship of Vijay Paranjpye, are full of half-truths, not to mention their weak analytical content on economic points. For more details, see my reviews of these (*EPW*, August 31, 1991 and *Journal of the Indian School of Political Economy*, Vol. 4, No. 1, January-March, 1992 both are reproduced in chapters 15 and 16.

3. This illustration be better taken as a response to editors' solicitation that "comments, as before, would always be welcome".
4. The exposition from now onwards is based on the reviewer's own understanding, now and then reinforced with data from the CSE report.
5. These breaches usually occur at the point of confluence of two tributories of a stream. At this point the process of sedimentation gathers strength because of slowdown in the pace of the smaller of the two tributory.
6. By 'in situ' conservation the connotation is that water is stored near about the place where rain drops fall on the ground. Water conservation, however, has a broader usage that includes water harvesting (in farm ponds or in large metallic containers), and construction of percolation tanks, irrigation tanks, diversion works, major reservoirs, etc.
7. The speed of this infiltrated water is very low, more so in sticky or clayey soils.
8. Those who have visited the famed Sukhomajri watershed near Chandigarh might have observed land subsidence near the edges of the watershed. Such subsidence is due to heavy soil erosion underneath the land, where subsurface water channels remove a great deal of soil too.
9. The monsoon normally ends by the middle of September. It was such a post-monsoon storm in the Bhakra catchment that created havoc in 1988 in part of the Punjab plains falling in the Sutlej basin. For more details, see p. 12 of the Report.
10. The expository writeup from this point onwards is once again this reviewer's handiwork.
11. For an excellent, highly readable account, see Joseph E. Stevens' *Hoover Dam: An American Adventure* (University of Okhlahama Press, Norman and London, 1988). For a review, see chapter 20, section II.
12. For half a dozen big dams each in the U.S.A. and India, Z. Hasan gave ratios of storage to mean annual inflow, while presenting his paper on Surface Water (jointly with R.S. Prasad and O.K. Rao) at the Third National Water Convention at Nagpur, 5 and 6 February, 1992.

13. Later in the chapter they conclude on a less unacceptable note when they state that "the Indian experience, therefore, shows that dams are only a mixed blessing as far as flood control is concerned" (p.13). No less interestingly they cite instance of dam burst for all categories of dams: the big dam at Mutha (Maharashtra), the medium dam at Morvi (Gujarat) and a small dam at Gopinatham (Karnataka).
14. Sometimes, tribal forest dwellers among the uprooted people in India have been resettled in other forested tracts so as to minimise for them the hardship of restarting life in dissimilar environs. Since the forest cover of the nation too is already below the needed level, the option of relocating tribal populations in suitable habitats has become very problematic.
15. Some of the Narmada Bachao Andolan activities are lately veering round to the view that heights of Narmada dams can be reduced, a point also commended by this reviewer to water planners for the last two years. But they are incorrect when they assert that lowering of the Navgam dam by 15 per cent, from 455 to 388 feet, would not materially affect Gujarat's irrigation benefits from this dam.
16. Reported statistics on the value of economic losses from natural disasters need to be taken with a pinch of salt because states have been increasingly inflating such losses, so as to get more central assistance which has become now an important source for meeting their budget deficits.

CHAPTER 15

INTACH EVALUATION OF THE TEHRI DAM PROJECT*

Two Remarks

At the very outset two things need to be stated. First, the case chosen here is a multipurpose project, yielding benefits both in the shape of hydel power and irrigation. Yet, it is widely viewed as a hydel project because it is primarily conceived as power augmenting scheme (an analogy in the reverse is the multipurpose Bhakra Nangal Project planned primarily for irrigation augmentation). Second, it is not my objective to pass here any final verdict on this highly controversial big dam project. That verdict cannot rest solely on benefit-cost ratio of the project, however sophisticated may be the BC analysis. On the one hand, the seismic hazard posed by this project needs fuller investigation by technical experts. If either by thickening the base width of the dam (as per the Russian advice), or by lowering the height of the dam, the seismic hazard could be brought within acceptable limits, the benefit-cost ratio has to be reworked with enhanced costs/reduced benefits.

Scope of the Paper. The Tehri Dam project was conceived in 1949, and detailed investigations were carried out in 1963. As the parameters of the project have undergone change, we

---

* First presented at the Seminar on Social Cost Benefit of Hydro Electric Projects in Hills, held during 7 to 9 May 1991 under HIPA auspices at Shimla-12. Published in *EPW*, Aug. 31, 1991.

must be clear about the version being reviewed here. It is the one evaluated by INTACH and authored by Vijay Paranjpye, an economist better known in environmental activist circles as well as to the print media. This review's focus is on the subtitle of the INTACH study *Evaluating the Tehri Dam: An Extended Cost Benefit Appraisal*, as finally published in 1989. The review takes note of only one serious review of this study by Kanchan Chopra, my colleague, which she prepared for the big dam book edited by me. (Dhawan, 1990)

Resume of Project Costs and Returns

As per the project planners' report, the Tehri project is Rs. 1475 crore investment proposal. From its Stage I installed generating capacity of 1000 MW (1000 MW more to be added in Stage II), about 3000 million KWh of hydel power would be available per year, much of it to cater to the peak load demand of U.P. State. The annual working expenses are placed at about Rs. 25 crores. Besides hydel power, the project would improve onfarm income on about 0.6 million ha. of area already irrigated by the Ganga canal system, as also bring 0.27 million ha. additional area under irrigation in the same canal system. The important point to note here is that the newly irrigated area is mostly rabi area when arable land is likely to remain fallow in the absence of irrigation in the semi-arid plains of western Uttar Pradesh

The project report envisages a net revenue of about Rs. 124 crores per annum from the sale of power. While this constitutes 11.59 per cent on the investment share of power segment of the project, the important point to note is that it accrues to the state department under whose aegis the project comes up. A BC ratio of 3.49 for irrigation segment is mentioned. The value of increased farmers' income from the Tehri waters is placed at Rs. 158 crores or thereabouts, accruing wholly to farmers and not to the project authority. No wonder, then these two components of benefits from the project, lacking additivity as these do, are not combined into a single one measure in the project report.

In short, the project meets the Central planners' rate of return criterion for power projects (above 10 per cent) as well as the benefit-cost ratio criterion for major irrigation projects (BC ratio above 1.50).

Paranjpye's Appraisal

Paranjpye, utilising pertinent and not so pertinent arguments as well as data base, questions the aforesaid estimates of costs, returns, benefit-cost ratio, etc. He basically raises the capital costs of the project on the one hand and drastically lowers the benefits from irrigation on the other. As a result, the viability of the project vanishes on both counts: the rate of return on capital in the case of the power segments gets diminished to about 6.89 per cent,[1] and the BC ratio for irrigation segment comes down to 1.28. When he combines the two disparate components of returns from Tehri project into one, the overall BC ratio for the whole project works out only 0.56 (He claims on p. 133 that a BC ratio of about 4.8 is mentioned for the project in an affidavit filed by the state of U.P. in the Supreme Court).

More specifically, his major revised estimates are as follows. First, he finds that the investment cost of the project is about Rs. 1,740 crores, about 18 per cent above the project estimate. Truly damaging to the Tehri project planners' case is his attempt to assess the interest cost on investments during the 11-year gestation period (reckoned at 12 per cent per annum on a compounding basis). As he capitalises these interest charges, the capital cost of the project shoots up to nearly Rs. 3,023 crores (four-fifths more than Rs. 1,740 crores as the investment outlay).

On the benefit side, he leaves intact the gross revenue figure from sale of power but enhances the working expenses. Thus, the net revenue from power diminishes, but marginally (by 2 per cent). However, he brings down the benefits from irrigation to Rs. 65 crores, a reduction of the order of Rs. 93 crores.

Chopra's BC Analysis

Kanchan Chopra had a close look at Paranjpye's evaluation of the Tehri project. While leaving undisturbed his estimate of income benefits from irrigation, she concentrated *inter alia* on his estimate of benefits from hydel power. Throwing overboard his arguments, which are very weak indeed, she proceeds to revalue hydel power at 82 instead of 48 paise per KWh. This higher price is the resource cost of generating thermal power, an alternative to hydel power development in the state. But departing from Paranjpye's rather traditional or a bit outdated procedure of computing undiscounted benefit-cost ratio, she does the standard BC analysis in which a discounted BC ratio as well as an estimate of internal rate of return (IRR) is obtained. In her words, "... we did our own calculations using UNIDO methodology and social prices obtained by giving distribution weights to different commodities and to different category of consumers".[2] (Chopra, 1990, p. 189). So, her (discounted) BC ratio comes to 0.87[3] but with an IRR of 10.38 per cent. Thus Paranjpye's conclusion of unviability of the project remains undisturbed.

This Author's Critique

Professionally, I have been time and again raising the unconventional viewpoint that benefit-cost analysis is essentially speculative in character, notwithstanding the valiant efforts in economic theories to minimise the speculative element. The room for speculation rises manifold when an evaluator or BC analyst is motivated one way or the other. While project promoters are known to oversell a project by underplaying project costs and overplaying its benefit side, economists tend to be conservative in this area, that is, they tend to overdo on the cost side and underplay the benefits. Evidently, if you have an economist who is motivated to kill a project proposal, he can be quite successful if his criticism is favourably received and projected by the mass media. If Tehri dam project promoters can be charged with selling an unviable project to the Centre, Paranjpye cannot escape a like charge in the reverse, that is, killing probably a viable project, as shown below. The subsequent critique centres round (a) a close look at the onfarm benefits of irrigation, (b) methodology of BC analysis, and (c) the problem of valuation of benefits from hydel power. I shall begin with the point (c) first.

Paranjpye has goofed in utilising economic theory of pricing. Still worse, he has shown little understanding of growing demand for electricity in the economy of Uttar Pradesh. While under monopoly conditions a firm can overprice its product, over and above its resource cost, a public utility is prevented from doing so. This is true the world over. Underpricing of power (and irrigation) in India is well recognised, and the State Electricity Board of Uttar Pradesh is no exception in this matter. In fact, his own calculation for the Tehri power is that its generation alone would cost 73 paise per KWh (p. 65, item 6 in the tabular data), whereas it would be sold only at 48 paise per KWh. How can then he make the following preposterous statement: "Since the Government is in the position of a monopoly producer, it has been passing on the higher costs of generation to the consumer, unilaterally raising prices". (p.63, 3rd para).

As regards his understanding of the power position in U.P., the less said the better. Blithely forgetting the distinction between 'demand for a good' and 'actual consumption of that good' (the latter is less than the former in a regime of scarcity), he unwarrantedly makes the following observations:

> We also feel that the energy forecasts provided by the authorities to justify the need for building a peak station are overestimates. For instance, in 1983-84, 9,642.3 million units of energy were consumed in U.P., when the actual production was 11,683.2 million units. But in 1985-86, the authorities expect that the demand will be 21,369 million units. These estimates further assume that demand for energy will grow at a rate of 9 per cent per annum whereas the *demand* has grown only at 4.8 per cent per annum between 1973-74 and 1983-84" (emphasis added, p. 64).

When power is in short supply (and when it is underpriced also), the hiatus between actual consumption and demand is bound to be wide. Therefore, the rate of growth of actual consumption of power is no measure of likely rate of growth in demand for power. Knowing as I do know how power shortages have been hampering tubewell irrigation both within private and public aegis in U.P., I am really astounded by Paranjpye's perceptions on power needs. There has been veritable explosion in tubewell irrigation in the state: the number of shallow private tubewells rose from 3 thousand in 1950-51 to 353 thousand in 1973-74, 1,586 thousand in 1984-85, and nearly 2400 thousand in 1989-90. It is because of power shortage that farmers had to opt for diesel pumpsets, whose number in 1989-90 was nearly 1900 thousand as compared to only about 600 electric pumpsets.

Even so, the consumption of power in the State's agriculture sector in 1986-87 stood at 99.75 GWH (average price realised = 27 paise/KWh), constituting 37 per cent of total state consumption of power.[4] The power shortages, however, prevented electric tubewell owners to do the needed irrigation.[5] For example, a survey of 230 electric tubewells in 1982-83 showed that their owners could not irrigate their main crops of wheat, sugarcane and paddy upto the levels recommended by farm scientists (see Table 1 for details).

TABLE 1

CROPWISE AND REGIONWISE NUMBER OF WATERINGS BY PRIVATE ELECTRIC TUBEWELL OWNERS IN U.P., 1982-83

S. No.	*Crop*	*Recommended no. of waterings*	*Actual No. of waterings*		
			West U.P.	*East U.P.*	*Central U.P.*
1.	Wheat	5	3.66	3.27	3.47
2.	Paddy	5	3.00	2.64	2.54
3.	Sugarcane	7	4.62	3.53	3.96
4.	Maize	3	1.77	1.33	1.25
5.	Other crops	-	1.25	1.10	1.20
	Weighted average	-	2.93	2.76	2.64

Source: Dhawan (1989, p. 54).

As regards Chopra's valuation of hydro power at the resource cost of thermal power, it makes sense in the context of cost effectiveness, that is, while making a choice among techniques of production, with the tacit assumption that product remains the same (or exact substitute) in each technique. That is not so in the present case, as hydel power stations (backed with storage reservoirs) are well suited to meeting peak power loads in power system. For this reason, such *flexible* power needs to be given a higher price tag than that on thermal power where average (unit) cost of power generation becomes lower only because of high rate of capacity utilisation (i.e., 'plant factor') due to use of thermal stations for meeting the 'base load' of a power system.

Time has come when power projects are evaluated with fuller economic cost benefit criteria. Such a change in criteria, from rate of return criterion to cost benefit criterion, has already taken place in the case of irrigation projects since Independence. This transition was commended by the veteran economist Dr. D.R. Gadgil, a pioneer in evaluating major irrigation works in India. In fact, this approach is relevant for all public investment proposals where benefits to the economy at large far exceed the departmental net returns on such investment. I think that electric power is now in that class.[6] As infrastructural service par excellence, projects providing power need to be appraised by pricing power at its marginal value product in the economy. This value today in U.P. is far more than 82 paise/KWh.

My second major comment pertains to Paranjpye's remeasurement of irrigation benefits, an area of central pursuit in my research work of nearly last two decades. Since I have been writing for long that such benefits have been underassessed in the Indian benefit-cost exercises. I am, therefore, impelled to look closely (and harshly) at his substantial downward revision of the Tehri project planners' estimate in this regard. He has terribly goofed here. Instead of revising the benefits downwards, he ought to have enhanced them upwards. I do not wish to bore you with the tedious calculus in this regard. Here, I present the thrust of my two-fold argument.

The first is about the direct output impact of any source of irrigation. In working out this impact (and the resultant income and employment effects), a simple differencing of irrigated and unirrigated yield data would understate the output augmenting role of irrigation (Dhawan, 1988, chapter 3). To avoid this underassessment, I have suggested one summary procedure and one season-by-season measurement. In the latter procedure, one computes the output augmentation separately for each crop season (kharif crops, rabi crops and summer crops) and then add them up. In the summary procedure, one uses the seasonal orientation of an irrigation source to measure the excess of aggregate irrigated yield over aggregate rainfed (unirrigated) field. If 'K' stands for the proportion of crop area under kharif irrigation, the yield impact (from the viewpoint of output augmentation) is given by $Y_1 — K.Y_0$ where Y_1 and Y_0 stand for aggregate irrigated and unirrigated yield, respectively. 'K' for the 0.27 million ha. additional irrigated area for Tehri dam project is nearer zero (0.08 to be precise) because only 0.021 million ha. out of total 0.27 million ha. of additional irrigation is from kharif sugarcane. Thus the Tehri project planners are justified in assuming that the entire additional net output/income from 0.27 million ha. area (placed at Rs. 64 crores vide Statements 1 and 2 of Table IV on p. 83) is additional benefit from the project. Therefore, Paranjpye's contention that it should be reduced by the estimated value of about Rs. 44 crores (vide calculus shown on p. 78) presently realised from 0.27 million ha. is invalid.[7] Wit this modification alone, the irrigation benefits, as estimated by Paranjpye, would move back to about Rs. 109 crores.

The second aspect of my argument pertains to indirect output impact of canal waters, through substantial increase in groundwater recharge that sustains more of groundwater-based agriculture in low rainfall regions having naturally poor groundwater availability. As this indirect output impact can be as much as the direct output impact (Dhawan, 1989, chapter 6, 7 and 9), the true on-farm income benefits can be twice as much as the direct ones. Since the Western U.P. area to be served by the Tehri project is a low rainfall area with poor groundwater recharge from rainfall infiltration, it would be defensible to raise *ceteris paribus* the onfarm income benefits of the projects to a level of about Rs. 200 crores (43 crores above the level estimated in the project report, and Rs. 136 crores above the level measured by Paranjpye).

Finally, I would like to comment on the improved methodology employed by Paranjpye. One cannot fault him with his attempt to reckon with interest charges of the project gestation period. Despite his use of annuity approach to annualise capital costs, he remains within the traditional domain of undiscounted BC analysis. A major lament of the Indian economists (since the publication of the Indian Irrigation Commission's Report in 1972) against the government BC analysis has been its undiscounted nature, whereby the stream of future incomes after project completion and the stream of incurred costs of the project gestation period are not brought to comparable present values or worth. In an undiscounted analysis, the annual value of the incomes from a project is simply divided by annual costs (one-shot capital outlay is annualised by applying an interest rate plus a depreciation rate, and this 'fixed cost' is then added to working/recurring expenses per annum), so as to obtain a BC ratio which is then adjudged against a cutoff value, e.g., 1.5 is now the cutoff value for major and medium irrigation projects in India. Had discounting been done and the present value of income benefits divided by the present value of project costs, the BC ratio so obtained would be adjudged or appraised against unity. Thus, it is clear that an undiscounted BC ratio, when appraised against a value set above one (e.g., 1.5 for major irrigation projects), is not all that improper. The procedure implicitly recognises (a) the quick and easy manner in which undiscounted *vis-a-vis* discounted BC ratio is worked out; and (b) the time lag between the two streams of costs and benefits.[8] Now that computer facilities are available rather readily and pervasively, prudence should prevail over pragmatism, that is to say, discounted BC ratio be computed - this obviates the need for any arbitrary cutoff norms against which BC ratio is to be appraised.

Main Conclusions

Time has come to view power as an input with wider ramifications in the economy at large, and thus appraise power projects on the basis of marginal value product of power. In other words, such projects need be appraised within the framework of economic benefit-cost analysis similar to that used in the case of major irrigation projects. It is inappropriate to value hydel power from storage works either at the average price realised by a State Electricity Board or at the alternative cost of thermal generation.

Irrigation benefits from Tehri project have been unwarrantedly scaled down by Paranjpye in his cumbersome exercise in re-evaluation. These are, in fact, not fully measured even in the Tehri dam report. A common error in cost benefit analysis in India has been to ignore tremendous increase in groundwater-based farm output due to seeped-in canal waters in low rainfall tracts. Thus, the doubt cast on the economic viability of Tehri project by Paranjpye is not well founded in facts.

NOTES

1. This percentage is thrice mentioned on pages 42, 65 and 137. Yet, something is amiss with it, because the underlying exercise data on p. 65 would suggest a rate of 9.59% (Rs. 12121.81 lakh as per cent of Rs. 126,431.34 lakhs).
2. The weights used are as follows. Power is given a weight of 1.2 as it is in short supply in the economy. Further, consumers of power are given a weight of 0.8 and of irrigation water a weight of 1.2.
3. If we were to work this ratio by the methodology of Paranjpye (without distributional weights), the BC ratio would be 0.83 when power is priced at 82 paise/KWh.
4. Power consumers in other sectors of the economy know too well how power needs of agriculture sector come to acquire priority at sowing and maturing stages of crops, thereby leading to a spillover effect of power shortages in agriculture.
5. In a flat, horse power linked tariff, tubewell owners are expected to cross the level of recommended waterings for water loving crops like sugarcane and paddy.

6. Here I am reminded of Professor K.N.Raj (formerly of Delhi School of Economics and associated with the formulation of the First Five Year Plan) questioning the investment in Bhakra Nangal as he could not foresee the value of its huge power output for the economy of Punjab — the state has been experiencing power shortages since the green revolution.
7. Paranjpye does not realize that his method of estimating this number is grossly in error. He has assumed it to be 44.7% of Rs. 9,829.28 lakhs, the estimated value of net income from 6.04 lakh ha. of already irrigated land. And 2.7 lakh ha. is exactly 44.7 percent of 6.04 lakh ha. By this method, he is assuming that each unirrigated ha. gives an income of Rs. 1,627, which is too high (for an irrigated ha. his figure averages only Rs. 2,387).
8. A measure similar to simple rate of return (RR) on investment in an industry is the IRR which duly takes care of this time lag. A simple RR is net revenue as a per cent of capital outlay or investment. Net revenue is the excess of annual gross revenue over annual working costs plus depreciation charge. It can be shown that larger the time lag, the higher is RR over IRR (Dhawan, 1982).

REFERENCES

Chopra, Kanchan (1990). 'Large Dams and Cost-Benefit Analysis: Some Analytical Aspects and Policy Implications', in Dhawan (1990), pp. 185-200.

Dhawan, B.D. (1990). (ed), *Big Dams : Claims, Counter-claims,* Commonwealth Publishers, New Delhi.

———————— (1989). *Studies in Irrigation and Water Management,* Commonwealth, New Delhi.

———————— (1988). *Irrigation in India's Agricultural Development,* Sage, New Delhi.

———————— (1982). *Development of Tubewell Irrigation in India,* Agricole Academy, New Delhi.

Paranjpye, Vijay (1988). *Evaluating the Tehri Dam,* Studies in Ecology and Sustainable Development, No. 1, INTACH Series, Indian National Trust for Art and Cultural Heritage, 71, Lodi Estate, New Delhi-3.

Statistics of Minor Irrigation Development (1989). Publication No. 212, Central Board of Irrigation and Power, Chanakyapuri, New Delhi-21.

CHAPTER 16

INTACH EVALUATION OF NARMADA DAMS*

The book** under review is the third in the INTACH series on ecology and sustainable development. Whereas the first one focussed on the Tehri dam, this one focusses on the Sardar Sarovar Project (SSP) and the Indira or Narmada Sagar Project (NSP) under which the waters of the Narmada rivers are to be tapped with the help of two big dams at Navgam and Punasa, respectively. Like the Tehri project, the SSP too has become very controversial. The present study gives the reader a good account of why there is so much opposition to the big dam idea from diverse angles: economic, political, social, seismic, ecological, environmental, cultural and religious.

The book consists of ten chapters, besides an interesting editorial by N.D. Jayal, a supportive foreword by Professor Satish Dhawan, and a prologue by the author. The author provides an acknowledgement list of his own that underlines the marvellous multi-disciplinary support accorded to him in the preparation of this holistic study. He being an economist,

---

* Published in *Journal of Indian School of Political Economy*, January-March, 1992.

** Vijay Paranjpye, *High Dams on the Narmada: A Holistic Analysis of the River Valley Projects*, Indian National Trust for Art and Cultural Heritage, 71 Lodhi Estate, New Delhi- 110 003, 1990, pp. 320+xxvii, Price. Rs. 75/-.

economic analysis receives top billing. And the reviewer being an economist, the review too gets oriented that way.

Chapter 1 briefly delves into the cultural ethos and the legend around the sacred rivers in general and the Narmada in particular. This is followed by a short account of irrigation development efforts in the past within the Narmada valley, highlighting both the pre-Narmada Water Disputes Tribunal (NWDT) controversy on height of the Navgam or the SSP dam between Gujarat and Madhya Pradesh, and the controversy and popular opposition since the Tribunal's award in 1978. In Chapter 3, the author discusses the NWDT award. Besides revealing the roles played by politicians at the helm of affairs, irrigation and power planning engineers, and the judiciary in sorting out inter-state differences in sharing waters of this inter-state river, this chapter throws up two, somewhat inter-linked, questions about (1) the very quantum of the river flow, and (2) the optimum height of the SSP dam.

Paranjpye rightly objects to the quantum of Narmada water being simply a matter of agreement between the chief ministers of the three concerned states who declared in 1974, presumably for the Tribunal's use, the Narmada flow to be 28 million acre feet (MAF). Fortunately, this figure is close to the experts' estimates (28.92 MAF by the Khosla Committee and 27.22 MAF by the Technical Experts appointed by the Tribunal). He is unjustifiably inclined to the lower estimate of 22.22 MAF, which was arrived at by the Tribunal, at an early stage, on the basis of flow data for mere 22 years of the most recent period. Since the experts' estimates are based on a far longer series (70 to 80 year period), these cannot but be accorded greater credence over those based on a short series which might be less balanced in terms of good and bad rainfall years. This elementary hydrological truth needs pointing out here because time and again one comes across many a Narmada activist expressing unwarranted grouse over this matter.

Unfortunately, the other issue about the dam height has not attracted the due attention it deserves in the post-NWDT

Award phase of the debate. Paranjpye has done well to point out how this vital parameter was raised or lowered at various stages before the Tribunal pegged it down to the present level of 455 feet for the SSP dam. In 1956, a height of 160 feet, for the first stage of the dam, emerged in the CWC investigative work (even at this height irrigation potential of 4.4 lakh ha. exists). In 1959, it was lifted to *300* feet for the second stage. The Planning Commission, while sanctioning in 1960 the first stage of the project, approved a height of *320* feet for the second stage. When the Government of Gujarat thereafter pressed for a much higher level of at least *460* feet, the then Union Minister of Irrigation and Power intervened and the stillborn Bhopal Agreement between the Chief Ministers of Gujarat and Madhya Pradesh was reached in 1963, wherein a height of *425* feet was envisaged. As the MP Chief Minister promptly afterwards questioned the veracity of the agreement and insisted on a height of *162* feet only, Dr. Khosla Committee was constituted to look into the whole matter. This Committee recommended in 1965 a height of *500* feet. As both the states of Madhya Pradesh and Maharashtra rejected outright the recommendations of this technical Committee, the Centre appointed in 1969 the NWDT.

From Paranjpye's writeup one gets some inkling into host of factors behind dam height. He, however, is disinclined to reveal his own position on this vexing issue. That lower height reduces sharply both the extent of land submergence (and the RR problem of oustees thereof) and the risk of dam-induced seismicity needs wider and closer attention than has hitherto been the case. Can the height be reduced at this stage? Yes, provided the concerned states jointly approach the Centre to undo the binding nature of the Tribunal's Award in this regard. In a very narrow sense, the issue of small-scale versus large-scale surface waterbased irrigation works is one of height of dams or bunds, as irrigation (and hydel power generation) capacity rises sharply with the height of a dam/bund.

Chapter 4 is entitled 'The Economics of Dams in India'. It is laced with assorted writeups or observations on water resources and irrigation in India. The attempt is to apprise the reader with serious shortcomings in irrigation planning and implementation. Towards this end, the author makes an extensive use of the PAC reports, which have received publicity in newspapers quite out of proportion to their intrinsic content and merit.

Unfortunately, the chapter brims with half-truths, unfounded assertions, unwarranted statements, inferences contrary to cited evidence, etc. So, a reader would have to be very wary. The two following examples would suffice. The claim that "even at constant prices the small-scale irrigation (both surface as well as sub-soil) is far more cost efficient" (p.86) is the result of a faulty use of data in Tables 12 and 13. Firstly, the plan investment figures for minor irrigation are exclusive of huge investment on private or farmers' account. Secondly, these do not reckon with very high supporting investment costs of rural electrification (typical estimates: Rs. 30,000 per pumpset) and power generation (typical estimate = Rs. 90,000 per pumpset) required for the millions of electric pumpsets that now constitute the mainstay of *newer* minor irrigation works based on groundwater as well as surface water.

It is a singular aspect of debaters that they take a simple demolition or rebuttal of their rival's standpoint as enough for establishing the validity of their cause. The critics of big dams have drawn attention to numerous ills of major irrigation works, but shied away from an equally critical scrutiny of minor irrigation works, where too the ground reality is none too rosy. I have already pointed out that the much-publicised cost advantage of minor over major irrigation is not well-founded in facts.[1] Likewise, the much paraded advantage in capacity utilisation is of doubtful validity. It is unfortunate that some *working assumptions* of the Planning Commission in this matter have been mistaken for empirical reality by scores of analysts, including Paranjpye.[2] In this case, he is dimly aware of the limitations of the data base (vide his footnote to Table 9), and yet he chooses to take an alarming view of the fact that the all-India rate of capacity utilisation for major irrigation was only 84.3 per cent as against 94.1 per cent for minor irrigation works. Proponents of minor irrigation cause, especially of small-scale surface-water based schemes, would receive a jolt whenever *pucca* estimates of capacity utilisation turn up one of these days. This is being asserted on the basis of limited survey-based results this reviewer has seen. Some inkling into the same is provided later in the review when we discuss lift irrigation in Panchmahals as an alternative to big dams.

Chapter 5 focusses on irrigation development in Gujarat state, the main beneficiary state from the SSP. It highlights the seemy side of major irrigation development in the past, namely, unutilised capacity, the engineers-contractors' nexus to defraud the exchequer, time and cost over-runs in project completion, departmental inefficiencies, waterlogging, dam failure (Machhu dam), corruption and bribery, rising project costs, financial losses due to low irrigation rates, etc. Not unexpectedly, the author refrains from giving an account of the minor irrigation development in the State. He is, however, aware that (a) there has been overdevelopment in groundwater irrigation, leading to ingress of sea water into coastal Saurashtra, and (b) farmers' willingness to pay more for canal water as signified by the high cost they incur in well irrigation (owned as well as purchased).

Economic analysis of the SSP is taken up in Chapter 6, which is not well written. Since the project is centrally approved, it means (a) the *undiscounted* BC ratio is at least 1.5 for the irrigation segment, and (b) the rate of return on investment in the hydel power segment is above 12 per cent. The anticipated values of these two parameters or criteria as per the project promoters' assessment are not ascertainable from the INTACH report, presumably because Paranjpye could not get access to the project reports submitted to the Planning Commission (see the editorial, p. vii).

As for the irrigation portion of the SSP, the undiscounted BC ratio is said to be 2.08 for the Gujarat state. This is underpinned by Rs. 1,165 crores of annual onfarm income benefits and Rs. 559 crores of annualised costs, both computed at 1986-87 prices (*Source:* Narmada Development Authority).

Paranjpye proceeds to evaluate the SSP within the *discounted* BC framework, using 12 per cent as the rate of discount. After closely looking at the assumptions of the project promoters — and altering them where necessary — he comes up with a BC ratio of 0.66, and an IRR of 9.2 per cent for the project as a whole. Since this BC ratio is below one and the IRR is also below the rate of discount of 12 per cent, he finds the SSP an economically unviable proposition.

While this reviewer agrees with his altered assumption that project costs would exceed by a factor of almost one-third, he is disinclined to do so in respect of Paranjpye's other two major alterations, namely, (1) the gestation period of the project would be 27 instead of 22 years, and (2) the onfarm benefits from irrigation would be one-fifth less. Admittedly, he has advanced some plausible arguments for making the altered assumptions. But one cannot dismiss lightly the resolve of the Government of Gujarat to hasten the completion of the SSP, though their target of 10 years time is certainly ambitious. Likewise, his perception that 20 per cent of the 1.7 million ha. of irrigation potential would be lost due to waterlogging-salinity problems is off the mark in view of explicit planning for vertical drainage within the SSP command. This reviewer rather fears overdrawal of groundwater in the SSP command before long.[3]

At any rate, even a 9.2 per cent IRR cannot be dismissed lightly, more so for projects with long life and for the purpose of enhancing and stabilising agricultural production. After all, Nitin Desai Committee (1984) thinks 9 per cent IRR a worthwhile rate for agricultural projects. Paranjpye does not realise that this cutoff value is determined by social rate of discount, and not by interest rate to be paid to lending institutions — the World Bank would charge 12 per cent on its dollar 450 million loan for the SSP.

The focus in chapter 7 is on the problem of resettlement and rehabilitation (RR) of the people adversely affected by dams. In this reviewer's opinion, it is this negative side of the dams that should constitute the crux of the opposition to the big dam idea. This opposition reminds us of the proverbial limitation of BC analysis as a tool for judging economic viability of an investment project, namely, 'whose costs, and whose benfits', to which Paranjpye alludes in the preceding chapter. Our track record in RR activity has been dismal. Whether we will break new ground in the case of this project only time will tell. Although, thanks to the sustained intervention on this score from the World Bank, handsome financial provisions are being made, the Gujarat lobby is being naive in asserting that the envisaged RR job would actually improve the lot of the dam oustees.

I have no basic differences with the author about the RR issue, but wish that he had dealt with an important aspect, namely, how lowering of the dam height reduces the scale of the RR problem. Admittedly, even 10 per cent reduction in dam height reduces reservoir capacity more than proportionately, thereby reducing the irrigation potential of a dam more than proportionately. According to K.C. Thomas, a former Chairman of the Central Water Commission, the lowering of height by 10 per cent in the case of two Narmada dams would give rise to the following order of reductions in storage capacity and land submergence[4]:

	in storage	*in submerged area*
1. SSP	57.2	61.6
2. NSP	42.7	43.6

Though these estimates need to be viewed with some caution, it is unfortunate that benefits and costs are not assessed in Indian water planning against feasible variations in the height of a dam. As to submergence at different heights, we have some interesting data from *Human Resettlement in Lower Narmada Basin* (1985) prepared by S.C. Varma for the Narmada Valley Development Authority of the Government of Madhya Pradesh. In the case of Narmada Sagar, the submergence-height relationship exists as follows:

Dam height (metres)	*Submerged area (hectares)*	*Incremental area submerged per metre increase in dam height (ha.)*
190	1,000	-
210	2,000	50
230	24,000	1,100
244	46,000	1,571
261	80,340	2,020

Instead of such a relationship for the SSP Mr. Varma mentions that in the first stage submergence when the dam height would be 106.70 metres (350 feet) the number of affected villages would be 23 (with 84 affected families), rising to 182 when the Sardar Sarovar attains its stipulated height of 138.7 metres (455 feet). Thus the number of oustee families rises disproportionately and steeply with the rise in dam height.

Another no small factor of advantage in reducing dam height is the reduction in seismic risk. One viewpoint, to which expression has been given by Prof. U.R. Rao, Chairman, ISRO, is that the risk of earthquake disaster from a dam rises manifold after the height of a dam has crossed a certain threshold level.[5] This security angle calls for a fresh look at the whole concept of optimum height of a dam. If this optimum height allows lot of water to flow down to the sea without conferring any irrigation or power benefit to the society, such water may still keep intact the ecology of the river on the downstream of the dam, about which apprehensions have been expressed by some ecologists.

Chapter 8 concentrates on the NSP, for which the officially computed BC ratio is 1.85.[6] In Paranjpye's assessment, the realistic BC ratio would be 0.27 at 12 per cent rate of discount. However, the corresponding IRR is placed by him at 9 per cent. If one reckons with the external economy of this project on the SSP, the national returns from the project as distinguished from the State-level returns to Madhya Pradesh would be higher than 9 per cent. In view of the close linkage between the two projects, a joint IRR for both the investment projects taken together ought to have been computed also.

Paranjpye rightly questions the Department of Environment (DOEn) norm of pricing the loss of forest cover due to dam building at the incredibly high value of over Rupees one crore per ha. In this connection, his following observations are noteworthy:

> "So far, no justification has been provided or no rationale has been given as to how this magic figure of Rs. 126.7 lakhs has been derived. Alvares and Billorey have used this figure and 'derived' a B/C ratio for NSP of 0.017. Apart from incorrect, simplistic methodology used, by using this figure for environmental loss they fall into a trap. In the case of the controversial Tehri project in Uttar Pradesh, the authorities had calculated a B/C ratio of 4.785:1 for the dam by *considering environmental benefits and losses*. Without environment benefits/losses it was turning out to be 3.49, i.e., by incorporating the provisions of DOEn guidelines, the project was actually showing an improved BC ratio. The 'logic' used by the authorities was simple. if every ha. of forest felled for the project generates environmental losses, then every ha. of planted forest (under compensatory afforestation) would ultimately generate environmental benefits..." (p. 225).

Before the summary view presented in the final chapter 10, the penultimate chapter is devoted to a discussion of alternatives. It brings together some ideas and suggestions which have been floated by the dam critics to meet the charge of the major irrigation promoters in India that there is no alternative but to build big dams for harnessing the water resources of the nation. Evidently, it is a tough task. Whatever be the limitations of this chapter, both Paranjpye and the INTACH deserve credit for their endeavours in this regard. The following five specific problem areas are discussed at length:

1. Meeting irrigation needs of the tribal people in the hilly, eastern Gujarat state;
2. Meeting irrigation and development needs of the Kachchh (Kutch) region;
3. Alternatives to hydel power needs;
4. Meeting civic and industrial water needs;
5. Development of land and water resources of the Saurashtra region.

At the face of it, the suggested alternatives seem sensible and appealing. However, these do require more thorough appraisal and also confirmation by various knowledgeable persons. As an illustrative case, I provide a critical appreciation of lift irrigation alternative for tribal areas. But before I do that, I would make two pertinent observations. First, the alternatives and the SSP lack comparability. Take, for instance, the irrigation objective of the SSP, namely, providing irrigation to 1.7 million ha. of crop area. Alternatives for tribal areas envisage 0.2 million ha. irrigation at an investment outlay of Rs. 240 crores. Likewise, the proposed alternative programmes of development for the Kachchh and Saurashtra regions envisage additional irrigation of 0.075 million ha. and 0.25 million ha., respectively. This adds up to only about half a million ha. of irrigation potential.

Second, the investment outlays for the SSP are so large that these would crowd out many other programmes of agricultural development.[7] The needed funds for the alternative schemes can come from the hide of the SSP, through reduction in its investment size by lowering its dam height. Such redevelopment of investment resources will eminently meet the social objectives of development so intensely put forward in this chapter.

Paranjpye devotes considerable space to commend lift irrigation. In this context, he draws attention to the development of such schemes in tribal Panchmahal district. He is particularly impressed by lift irrigation development under the auspices of the Sadguru Water Development Foundation (SWDF), a non-governmental organisation promoted and nurtured by the industrial house of the Mafatlal Group. For reasons better known to him, he emphasises SWDF as an NGO or voluntary field organisation, without referring to its link with the industrial house whose backup of engineering skills and finance have proved critical in the efficient working of the lift schemes sponsored by it. He commends the SWDF long-range proposal submitted to the state government, that 500 more lift irrigation schemes (over and above 225 schemes already executed by the SWDF) could be established at a cost of Rs. 35 crores, benefitting 1.25 lakh crop ha. area of 62,000 farmers.

Girija Sharan and Sandeep Kayastha of the Indian Institute of Management, Ahmedabad, mention in Appendix A-2 of their study *Lift Irrigation in Panchmahal* (Report No. 144 of the Centre for Management in Agriculture, January 1990) some more details about 215 lifts to be established in the first phase of this proposal. These 215 lifts, sites for which have been identified by the SWDF, are anticipated to cover a crop area of about 42,000 ha. at a capital cost of about Rs. 19 crores. Of this irrigation potential, nearly 20,000 ha. each is in the kharif and rabi seasons, and the rest (1801 ha.) under summer irrigation. As per the detailed investigations by Sharan and Kayastha, the lift irrigation potential for the kharif and summer seasons is of doubtful value. During summer season there is no water to be lifted; during normal rainfall years the demand for kharif irrigation is zero. For the Shakarpura lift, a great success story, they find that the firm irrigation capacity is for 129 ha. of crop area only, and not 360 ha. as per the SWDF assessment (140 ha. each in kharif and rabi seasons, and 80 ha. during the summer season). Thus the realistic capacity is 36 per cent of the rated capacity. And only 103 ha., on the average, were actually irrigated between 1980 and 1986. In other words, the actual irrigated area is only 29 per cent of the rated potential. This percentage of utilisation is far below the 75 per cent utilisation assumed by Paranjpye.

The INTACH is to be complimented for bringing out this publication. Because of its holistic character it is rather longish and unwieldy in its presentation. However, what an unwary reader would need to guard against is many numbers which are wrong either in magnitude or in the units of measurement. This is partly the handiwork of the printer's devil, but also a result of hastiness in writing and production. Not infrequently, expressing 'lakhs' and 'crores into 'millions' (and *vice versa*) has been erroneously done (not an uncommon infirmity in Indian writing). For example, irrigation potential of the SSP is wrongly mentioned as 17.9 million ha, on p. 254, and data in Tables on pages 173-76 are listed in crores of Rupees while these ought to be lakhs of Rupees. At several places, the disappearance of the decimal point (e.g., on p. 301 in capacity utilisation parameter), or its replacement by a comma (e.g., on p. 170 the astronomical figure of Rs. 17,169 crores as the cost of compensatory afforestation), plays havoc with an estimate. The attempt to insert some nicely printed slips of errata is half-hearted; and on some occasions it appears needless (e.g., on pp. 301 and 306).

NOTES

1. For more details on this aspect, see B.D. Dhawan, Major and Minor Irrigation Works : Cost Aspects of the Controversy, *Economic and Political Weekly* (Review of Agriculture), 30 September, 1989.
2. For more details, see B.D. Dhawan, Trends in Unutilised Irrigation Capacity in India, *IASSI Quarterly*, Vol. 9, No. 3, January-March, 1991.
3. See, B.D. Dhawan, Trends and New Tendencies of Indian Irrigated Agriculture. Commonwealth, Publishers, New Delhi, 1993, chapter 8.
4. Source : B.D. Dhawan (ed.), *Big Dams : Claims, Counterclaims,* Chapter 10, Commonwealth Publishers, New Delhi, 1990.
5. Source : Personal Communication, January 30, 1991. Professor Rao writes "the frequency of earth quake shows practically no increase upto a particular height and then exponentially increases beyond the critical height. The critical height itself varies from region to region, being dependent upon the topography, soil characteristics and the existence of fault zones. The general shape of the curve, however, is practically the same at all places".

6. It is not clear from the text whether it is discounted or undiscounted ratio — most likely, it is the latter one.
7. This crowding out effect, more at the stage of actual allocations of investible funds than at the sectoral Plan formulation, has earned irrigation engineers both bitter hostility and unhealthy envy from soil conservation scientists, dryland farm experts, tribal and backward area programmers, etc.

CHAPTER 17

TALE OF TWO STUDIES: EVALUATIONS OF SARDAR SAROVAR PROJECT*

Introduction

Big dam idea has become controversial all over the globe. Proposals for all new dams in India, for irrigation or hydel power purpose, have been increasingly questioned for their merits, and their demerits pointed out vigorously. Questioning the merits of major irrigation schemes is certainly not a post-Independence phenomenon. As early as the mid-nineteenth century, Sir Arthur Cotton, of the Godavari Barrage fame, questioned intensely the wisdom of his counterpart in Northern India, Sir Thomas Cautley, for undertaking the construction of the famous Ganges Canal system. After Independence, the Damodar Valley Project, a multipurpose scheme, was opposed in the fifties. What is new about the present-day opposition is the element of activism in opposition from organised groups, through the print media, public meetings, rallies and threats to physically stopping the survey/construction activity related to a controversial dam. From this angle, the Tehri dam and the Sardar Sarovar Project (SSP) are presently the two most controversial investment schemes.

---

* Prepared for a public lecture under Narmada Control Authority at Indore on April 10, 1992. Appeared (without notes) in *Facts For You*, May, 1992.

The SSP envisages a 455 feet high dam on the Narmada at Navgam in Gujarat, so as to meet irrigation, power, drinking water and industrial/urban needs of this droughtprone, water-short state. Its approval or clearance came after a long, chequered disputation with Madhya Pradesh through which flows the Narmada before entering Gujarat. This period (1958-78) of controversy, prior to the Narmada Water Disputes Tribunal Award in 1978, is not of much concern here. Our central concern is with the two exante evaluation studies. As their findings are contrary to each other, these have played a role in the acrimonious debate on the SSP.

Background of the Studies

One study is by the reputed Tata Economic Consultancy Services (TECS), a Bombay based profit making firm offering consultancy services primarily to industry and trade. This agency was approached by the Narmada Planning Group (NPG), a multi-disciplinary group specially constituted by the Government of Gujarat for formulating and appraising the SSP. Its mandate was to carry out an economic evaluation of the SSP. It gave a clean chit to the SSP, as also singing a lot of paeans to the SSP scheme in its *Economic Appraisal of Sardar Sarovar Project* prepared in May 1983.

The TECS has done a job that would certainly please the sponsoring NPG and its members. Both were guided in the evaluation by a desire to obtain the World Bank funding for the SSP, for which the Government of Gujarat had approached the World Bank. The following acknowledgements in the report are quite noteworthy :

> "While it is difficult to mention names (of NPG members) of all those we owe our gratitude, we owe a special debt to Dr. Y.K. Alagh, Dr. S.R. Hashim and Mr. B.J. Desai for their encouragement and guidance.
>
> We have also greatly benefitted from interaction with the members of the World Bank team. Many practical

> suggestions were made on several issues during the course of the study. We owe our gratitude to the members of the team, in particular to its leader Dr. L. Jung.
>
> The study was carried out by two independent teams led by Mr. R.K. Koti and Dr. M.G. Pavaskar, respectively..." (p.vi, phrase within brackets added by this author).

And it does not enthuse or reassure this author when he comes across some erstwhile member of this NPG making eulogistic references to the TECS report with regard to its favourable findings, or about its sophistication in benefit-cost exercises : for, it is afterall a collaborative evaluation of the TECS and NPG. Before giving some more pertinent background information about the TECS study, some salient facts about the other study need be stated first. This study is from the Indian National Trust for Art and Cultural Heritage, better known by its fascinating acronym INTACH. Its report, *High Dams on the Narmada : A Holistic Analysis of the River Valley Projects*, is credited to Vijay Paranjpye, an economist who had earlier carried out the INTACH report on Tehri Dam, entitled : *Evaluating the Tehri Dam : An Extended Cost Benefit Appraisal.*

The INTACH is located in New Delhi, and is a wholly autonomous body, registered under the Society Act, for the conservation of natural and cultural heritage. "The Society aims, with the active participation of its members, to create an awareness among the public for preservation of this heritage, by acting as a *pressure group* when any part of it is threatened by damage or destruction arising either out of private acts or public policy" (emphasis added). As the Narmada dams are going to inundate many places of worship and of pre-historic culture along the river course, INTACH's concern about, if not hostility to, the proposed dam is understandable. Although the two major dams, one at Navgam and the other at Punasa in M.P., are inter-linked in conception and design — the latter is a sort of a backup dam for the former — INTACH's opposition to the latter dam is no less forceful. And given Paranjpye's anti-big dam position during the eighties, one should not be surprised to get from him in mid-1990 an unfavourable report on the SSP, both on economic and non-economic grounds. So, we have two evaluation reports on the same project, each one being rather one-sided in spirit and conclusions.

The Friedrich Naumann Foundation of the Federal Republic of Germany is acknowledged by N.D. Jayal, the Director of National Heritage of INTACH and the Editor of the INTACH Series 'Studies in Ecology and Sustainable Development', "for the generous financial support which made this study possible". Further, it "is a non-profit making private institution, primarily engaged in the strengthening of democratic and pluralist developments, both in the industrialised and the developing world. In India the Friedrich Naumann Foundation is supporting projects in the field of environmental protection. One of its major partners is the INTACH" (p. xi). This external connection, if charitably viewed, signifies the internationalism in the environmental movements of today. But it has not been taken kindly by the irrigation and hydel power engineering fraternity in India. The INTACH has to live down this connection, more so with those discerning persons who perceive anti-development strands in advanced countries when it comes to the development efforts in the Third World.

The INTACH study deals with the dam issue in a comprehensive frame covering economic, seismic, environmental, ecological and cultural aspects. A heroic effort is also made to work on alternatives to the SSP. For such a multi-disciplinary assessment, inputs from persons with diverse backgrounds became inevitable. Therefore, acknowledgements brim with names of persons and institutions, and with a very supportive Foreword from Professor Satish Dhawan. The two studies lack comparability in content, except in respect of economic analysis about the SSP. In what follows the focus is on this comparable portion of the two reports. Before doing that, an important aspect of the two reports needs pointing out.

The TECS report, though printed, is not a published document. Access to it has been provided on a select basis. As a result of such restrictive circulation, it became difficult for this author to appraise the claims made about its sophisticated and comprehensive BC analysis during 1989 when the controversy about the SSP was at its peak in acrimoniousness and public involvement. His request for a copy from the TECS was at first refused on the plea that the report is meant for the client (NPG) only. A copy did later arrive in mid-March, 1990, but only about 6 months after the draft report of INTACH was put in circulation for comments. (A copy of this draft came to me from INTACH in November 1988 or threabouts - the published version was released in June 1990, but came into my possession only in March 1991 when the INTACH promptly acceded to my request for a copy). Approach to the then-Member Planning Commission in charge of irrigation and who as Chairman NPG had intiated the TECS study proved in effect no more fruitful. Initially, during the course of a meeting in the Yojana Bhawan in late 1988, he simply brushed aside the request on the plea he could not part with the last copy he was left with on his shelf. On later thoughts, he allowed the author to peruse it for one hour, this being the duration for which he had come to this author's institute for delivering a talk to a group of trainees. The author, therefore, strongly shares the sense of anguish arising from denial of data and information, to which Mr. Jayal gives an apt expression in his Editorial as follows :

> "It has been our unfortunate experience that governmental agencies, despite their assurances to the contrary, do not cooperate in divulging data, thus adding immensely to our difficulties. The Planning Commission, for instance, while maintaining a public facade of openness, provided access during 1988 and 1989 to practically nothing other than the Economic Appraisal of the Sardar Sarovar Project carried out by the Tata Economic Consultancy Services Ltd. in May 1983". (p.vii)

Such denials cause bitterness. It engenders a feeling that things under wraps are suspect. As a result, the data or report seeker's judgement on a controversy can be affected, thereby further accentuating a controversy. Persons and agencies, which indulge in covert or overt games of withholding information needlessly, must, therefore, share the blame for accentuating and even distorting controversies, as also prolonging their duration.

TECS Evaluation

For a variety of considerations, the author is discussing first the TECS evaluation of the SSP. For one, the other report by INTACH takes issues with some of its assumptions. For another, it excites the author more, partly for its having been not in the public domain - the INTACH's is a priced document — and partly for its state-of-the-arts in respect of benefit-cost analysis. It is divided in nine chapters that are well written. Chapter VIII deals with the final project appraisal.

At market prices prevailing during 1981-82 the discounted benefit-cost ratio for the *entire* SSP project works out to be 1.39, the rate of discount being 12 per cent. The benefits are inclusive of benefits from non-agricultural (i.e., municipal and industrial) uses of water. And this BC ratio improves to 1.84 if "economic" prices are used in the evaluation. One may rightly ask : What are these "economic" prices; how do they differ from ordinary or market prices; and how have they been arrived at by the TECS experts? For that, curious readers may read the two-page Section B of the Chapter II. Here it may suffice to point out as to which costs/benefits of the SSP have been modified — and in which *direction* — by the TECs for achieving the so-called economic appraisal of this project. As a result of recourse to the United Nations Industrial Development Organisation (UNIDO) method, the project costs become almost one-sixth less from their nominal level (from Rs. 2,011 crores down to Rs. 1,669 crores on *present value basis*). This is because the "economic" prices for all project inputs (except skilled labour) are reckoned well below their market or nominal levels, as can be verified from the following (accounting) ratios of "economic" to nominal values for major items :

1.	Cement	0.64
2.	Iron and Steel	0.63
3.	Unskilled labour	0.65
4.	Electrical equipment	0.60
5.	Transport equipment	0.69
6.	Non-electrical equipment	0.75
7.	Tyres and tubes	0.46
8.	Petroleum products	0.81
9.	Skilled labour	1.00

On the benefit side, the recourse to "economic" prices of farm products leads to enhancement of the present or discounted value of benefits by nearly one-tenth (from Rs. 2,793 crores onto Rs. 3,063 crores). This arises because the "economic" prices for wheat and paddy turn out to be higher than their observed domestic levels of 1981-82. While wheat gets overpriced by 8 per cent, paddy gets overpriced by 30 per cent. Actually, the accounting ratio for paddy crop works out marginally above one (1.03) in the TECS calculus but its evaluators force it up to 1.30 by taking the plea of quality of domestic crop being superior to the one traded in the world. Similar forcing up is effected for other foodgrains, cotton and other non-foodgrains, as revealed by the following raises in the accounting ratios:

1.	Cotton	0.95 raised to 1.00
2.	Non-foodgrains	0.91 raised to 0.99
3.	Other foodgrains	1.05 raised to 1.17

There is no attempt by the TECs' evaluators to reassure the reader that such noteworthy quality premia in pricing farm products are indeed justified. All that we get is an asterisk mark on the accounting ratios table on p. 22. Other accounting ratios employed in TECS evaluation are as follows:

1.	Fertilisers	0.73
2.	Pesticides	0.60
3.	Groundnut	0.89
4.	General conversion factor	0.80

When accounting ratios of associated inputs of irrigation (i.e., farm inputs whose use goes up substantially under irrigated conditions) are taken below unity, this too leads to enhancement of benefits from irrigation. From this angle the assumed values of the accounting ratios for chemical fertilisers, pesticides, unskilled labour, etc. make the benefits picture rosier.

To use international prices in lieu of domestic prices in order to judge the economic viability of an irrigation project does not appear realistic when free trade in goods is lacking. At any rate, one has to handle carefully the twin problem of cyclical element in commodity prices as both the world prices as well as the domestic prices have cycles of ups and downs. Use of a single year's prices (e.g., in the case of domestic prices of 1981-82 in the TECS report) can give rise to avoidable errors. And if world prices are below their equilibrium level (i.e., true cost of production), say, because of dumping practices followed by some exporters, one has to duly reckon with this while working out the "border" prices.

Sophistry in analysis must be applauded provided it is in the direction of realism. Had the TECS evaluation been for different dam heights of the SSP project, theirs would have been a signal, pioneering contribution in evaluation. Admittedly, this is to expect too much from TECS. Afterall, some one from outside had to furnish them with estimated project costs and project benefits for different dam heights.

But instead of praising *ad nauseam* the SSP proposal the TECS experts should have done some exercises in warning about the project coming a cropper if certain germane assumptions do not get fulfilled. Such exercises cannot be said to be covered by mechanistic sensitivity analyses. It demands expert knowledge about the intrinsic nature of project being appraised, and not simply expertise in the rigmarole of BC analysis. Anyway, the TECS report contains no sensitivity analysis even. So, one does not know how sensitive are its BC results to various parameters. One critical parameter is the gestation or construction period of a multipurpose project. A bane of Indian multipurpose projects has been the serious time overruns in their completion which in trun has led to more than proportionate project cost overruns. So, one would like to know how many years in time overrun and how much of project cost overrun in the case of the SSP would make this project unviable.

Let me, on the other hand, give an example of trivial sophistication. In most irrigation project evaluations, the without-project existing situation (i.e., 'control') is one which is assumed as constant for future. This is not so in TECS evaluation, which envisages some rise in farm output from the observed (1981-82) level of Rs. 426 crores to Rs. 491 crores by 1990-91 (and constant thereafter). As it is netted out for cost of cultivation, it becomes a much smaller number. Since this net output is low in comparison to the net output with-project situation, the sophistry of jacking up a bit has little adverse impact on the computed value of the onfarm benefits of the SSP. What then is the point in devoting one whole chapter to such sophistication, with a view simply to departing from the usual practice of holding the 'control' constant throughout the time horizon of the SSP?

If at all a need for departing from conventions existed, it was in the case of value of agricultural output in the with-project situation. This is normally held constant for the whole time horizon of a project. The case for deviating from this beaten path would arise if one can underscore that irrigated yields of crops tend to rise over time, and not stayput at the assumed levels. In the particular case of Gujarat, the aggregate pure irrigated yield (without change in crop pattern) has risen at the rate of 1.9 per cent annum during 1970-71 to 1987-88 (1.6 per cent for foodgrains and 2.1 per cent for non-foodgrains).

As mentioned earlier, one reason why the BC ratio for the SSP is good is due to the external economy arising out of huge investment in the upstream side in the Narmada Sagar Project. Since the latter is mainly for power generation, waters released from it would be picked up by the SSP reservoir. (The linkage between the two projects requires a BC analysis *jointly* for the two projects). Delay in completing Narmada Sagar can erode the viability of the SSP.

INTACH Evaluation

INTACH's evaluation is rather longish (over 300 pages), spread over ten chapters. Economic evaluation of the SSP is set out in Chapter VI. The chapter is not a well-written presentation. At places it is so sloppy and slipshod that one misses the smoothness of the TECS report. Paranjpye is overeager to demonstrate the economic unviability of the SSP (as well as the NSP). He, unlike the TECS, does question practically most of the assumptions of the project promoters.

He places the discounted BC ratio for the SSP at about 0.66 (0.27 for the NSP). This ratio is free from any price manipulation. While this is well below the corresponding comparable value of 1.39 arrived at in the TECS report, it is not easy to specify how it compares with the project promoters' own estimate. For, they need not report any discounted BC ratio while forwarding their proposals to the project clearing authority at the Centre, which still uses the *undiscounted* BC ratio norm of 1.5 (reduced to 1.25 or so for projects for drought prone areas). The IRR (internal rate of return) for the SSP is placed at 9.2 per cent by Paranjpye, which is about 3 percentage points less than the rate at which discounting has been done by him as well as the TECS. Economic critique in the INTACH report is undoubtedly much less impressive, both in form and content. This is so despite Paranjpye's use of the discounting method of benefit-cost analysis — in his Tehri dam report he tried to innovate his BC analysis within the undiscounted framework (see the author's review in *EPW*, 31 August, 1991). Yet, at the stage of writing, interpreting and presenting, he is sloppy, giving an impression as if he does not understand the discounted framework.

One may ask: what are such critical alterations effected by Paranjpye as would lead to the lowering of the BC ratio well below unity? In a way, he has followed the same route (but in reverse direction) as the TECS has followed to raise the BC ratio from 1.39 to 1.84. While the projected benefits are reduced by one-fifth, the project costs are raised by almost one-third. Furthermore, he lengthens the gestation or construction period of the project by 5 years. No wonder, the BC ratio plummets from 1.39 to 0.66.

How plausible are the altered assumptions? Plausibility hinges *inter alia* on how good is one's understanding of the irrigation activity in general and big dam activity in particular. On p. 155 he observes that "...the average productivity even on irrigated land is very low in india", but gives no quantitative idea of how low is this level. Of course, official data in this regard cannot be cited easily because crop production in India is not distinguished by irrigated and dryland (unirrigated) status. But it is not all that difficult for a researcher to make such estimates himself from the detailed yield data based on crop cutting experiments carried out annually to estimate cropwise total yield for Indian states. Admittedly, this is a bit time-consuming (as well as expertise demanding) task. Paranjpye could have quoted other workers' research in this regard. He is aware of my own work — he does list in the Bibliography my book, *Irrigation in India's Agricultural Development* (1988), which gives such estimates for irrigated and unirrigated crop areas for India as a whole as well as for all 17 important states for 1983-84. To call the national irrigated yield of 1.98 tons/ha. for foodgrains (3.98 tons/ha. for non-foodgrains and 2.21 tons/ha. for all crops) as very low is patently unwarranted, more so when the corresponding yield on drylands is only about 0.86 tons/ha. (vide Table 4.1 on p. 84 of my book).

He unwarrantedly faults the TECS for making the assumption that "irrigated yield of paddy, cotton and tobacco, has been assumed to be twice that of the unirrigated yield" (p.149). But he has no empirical basis to substantiate the untenability of this assumption. My own work on the irrigated and the unirrigated segments of the Gujarat agriculture, as quoted in my book referred to earlier, should have been useful for enlightening him in this regard. The yield differential between the two segments during 1983-84 stood as follows:

	Food-grains	*Non-food-grains*	*All crops*
1. Irrigated yield (kg./ha.)	2,291	2,517	2,364
2. Unirrigated yield (kg./ha.)	930	919	926
3. Yield differential			
(i) absolute (kg./ha.)	1,361	1,598	1,438
(ii) relative ('1' as % of '2')	246	274	255

Differences in crop pattern between the two segments of agriculture can heighten the pure yield differential, Therefore, I give below mean values of irrigated and unirrigated yield of selected crops of Gujarat for the entire period 1970-87.

	Irrigated (kg./ha.)	*Unirrigated (kg./ha.)*	*Relative difference (unirrigated = 100)*
1. Rice	1,737	905	192
2. Cotton (in terms of lint)	311	133	234
3. Tobacco	1,800	870	207
4. Wheat	2,170	550	395

Instead of attenuating the yield effect of the SSP at the stage of recomputing BC ratio, Paranjpye tinkers with the area effect. "In the case of benefits we have assumed that 20 per cent of the net command area will not be actually irrigated by the SSP due to various reasons enumerated earlier". (p. 167). He fears the development of waterlogging-slainity problems which would put land out of use. "The irony is that the most vehement supporters of the SSP, namely, the rich farmers' lobby of the central Gujarat plains in Baroda, Kheda and Ahmedabad, will be the greatest losers when waterlogging becomes a reality. On the other hand, the farmers in the Bhal areas and the coastal plains, who are already familiar with the problems of flooding and salinity, may simply not use the canal water beyond a limit. This will then lead to underutilisation....." (p. 130-31).

Waterlogging and consequent soil salinity/alkalinity has been the bane of canal irrigation in the Indian subcontinent. No wonder, the critics of SSP have time and again aired their misgiving that the project might eventually cause much damage to the land resource. They have thus contested, with telling evidence from the Tawa project in M.P., the contention of the project promoters that not a single hectare of land would be allowed to go out of cultivation due to waterlogging. This author has looked into this controversial issue. The most appropriate thing to do would be to work out the entire scenario of build-up in groundwater table from seeped-in waters of canal origin— such seepage is quite substantial even in a fully lined canal network like the one planned for the entire SSP command. Alongside, one has to estimate the contrary force on this build-up, namely, groundwater withdrawals by the well owners within the SSP command. Only then one would be able to work out the scenario for groundwater balance, which would indicate the extent of rise in water table, if any, and when it might reach the crop root zone — this, the scientific definition of waterlogging, is reached even before visible or surface waterlogging of fields appears.

This author has come to the considered conclusion that the critics' misgivings are rather misplaced in the SSP context where conditions are altogether different from those encountered in the Tawa command in central Madhya Pradesh. For one, the groundwater balance is well worked out by the project promoters and due provisions made for the withdrawal of excess groundwater through private tubewells/wells and government-owned tubewells. Paranjpye's apprehension that requisite investments in private wells may not be forthcoming may not be shared by those whose perceptions are along the following lines.

When hardly 18 inches of Narmada water is planned to be delivered in a year to an SSP command farmer, he has strong incentive to tap groundwater resource with a view to practicing intensive farming throughout the year. And should some of the SSP farmers go in for heavily irrigated crops like sugarcane, paddy, fruits like bananas and papaya, etc., they would begin the process of serious overdrawal on groundwater resource. In fact, conditions here are similar to those in Punjab, Haryana and West U.P. protective canals within whose command intensive cropping with paddy and sugarcane has put pressure on groundwater resource. Climatewise, soilwise, and in terms of resourcefulness and enterpreneurial spirit, the situation in the SSP command is no different. Here, the rise of water sellers phenomenon would take care of groundwater needs of resource-poor farmers, or farmers with too much parcellisation of their land holdings.

The problem of under-investment in private well irrigation would arise mainly in areas underlain with saline or brackish waters. Farmers here would be rightly disinclined to tap groundwater, fearing such water would build up salt toxity in the soil. But it is precisely for such areas that vertical drainage through government tubewells is visualised by the SSP planners. Should there, however, be default in implementing this component of the SSP, the danger of waterlogging developing in such areas is truly serious. In the past, such defaults have occurred in respect of project components which are envisaged to avert problems within canal commands.

An instructive example in this regard is that of the premature silting up of the Nizamsagar reservoir in Andhra Pradesh, another oft-cited case used to argue against the lack of sustainability in dam-based developmental activity. In this case, an important component of the original project was the construction, on the upstream side, of another biggish check dam for holding back the silt and debris. As this investment was not eventually undertaken, the life of the Niazamsagar, as also its irrigation potential, has been drastically reduced. The probability of such defaults is high when fund paucity is acute. The paucity of funds is a chronic malaise in project implementation in India and thus a major cause of both cost and time overruns in completing major and medium irrigation schemes in our country. This brings us, then, to the second major altered assumption of paranjpye, namely, a time overrun of 5 years (along with the assumption that project benefits begin flowing in the 14th and not the 10th, year of construction).

Paranjpye perceives serious shortage of funds for the execution of the SSP. Hence, his justification for a 5 year slippage in project completion. Thus he anticipates the completion of SSP in 27 years as against 22 years visualised in the TECS report. On the other hand, the Government of Gujarat has shown serious intention of completing the project in another 10 years only, and the C.C. Patel Associates has carried out some exercises in this regard. In view of such urgency on the part of the government, it is not unreasonable to proceed on the assumption that there would be no time overrun and that the project would be completed in 22 years as per the original plan.

As regards the third altered assumption about project cost, Paranjpye is on a better or surer wicket. Actual project costs during the post-Independence period of project implementation have tended to exceed the planned costs by a big margin. This tendency can be traced to three factors: (a) general price inflation, (b) unforeseen project costs, and (c) deliberate underprojection of project costs with a view to improving chances for project clearance. Both the factors (a) and (b) together predominantly account for the wide gaps between the actual and the estimated costs. Lately, the factor (c) too is acquiring importance as the incidental project costs of (i) relocation and rehabilitation of dam oustees, and (ii) environmental safeguards are soaring, much of it in response to environmental groups/agencies and activist groups pleading forcefully for more effective RR package for the uprooted people, for compensatory afforestation, for catchment treatment, etc. Another reason is that project proposals are increasingly submitted with much less pre-investment investigations, mainly because of political decision to force the pace of irrigation development of the nation (especially since 1971).

Paranjpye's contention that the SSP might cost one-third more in real cost terms [that is, without reckoning with price inflation or factor (a)] is very valid. Actually, this increase in costs in a compilation by him of cost increases already announced since 1983 (after the TECS report was prepared). It is, however, not easy to list here which part of the project cost has been enhanced by how much, thanks to the inelegant manner in which he presents his cost writeup.

In view of the foregoing discussion on the changes effected by Paranjpye in his BC analysis, his IRR of 10.8 per cent for the SSP project appears more realistic, as it is computed by assuming that costs only would be 31 per cent more than those visualised by the project promoters originally. (The corresponding BC ratio is not mentioned by him, but it would be somewhat below unity). Anyway, an IRR of the order of 10.8 per cent, though certainly not exciting, does not mean bad economic viability for a project with long gestation and far longer life. For such projects, the IRR norm for project clearance has to be somewhat less than the rate of discount used by a lending institution, say, the World Bank in the present case. Instead, it has to be nearer to our *social* rate of discount (i.e., time preferences of a society), which is reckoned to be between 6 and 9 per cent. In fact, Paranjpye's arguments for disagreeing with Nitin Desai Committee's recommendation in 1984 of adopting 9 per cent IRR norm for agricultural projects are rather misplaced, as he thinks this rate is determined by the going interest rate on loanable funds.

During the course of the big dam debate, alternatives to big dams have figured prominently, naturally form the side of the critics of such dams. The INTACH and Paranjpye have undertaken in the penultimate chapter IX an exercise on alternatives, which deserve attention as well as critical appraisal from experts. Indeed, this is direly needed in respect of the non-economic contents of this report. Paranjpye draws attention to the development of lift irrigation schemes in Panchmahal district in east-central Gujarat. He cautions against their execution or implementation by contractors even though the schemes are under public aegis. He observes:

> "It is well-known that 80 to 90 per cent of existing lift irrigation schemes executed by the private contractors have totally failed due to poor quality workmanship. It must be ensured that no lift irrigation scheme fails on technical grounds" (p. 261).

He is, however, highly impressed by the lift irrigation development in the Panchmahals under the auspices of the Sadguru Water Development Foundation (SWDF), a non-governmental organisation promoted and nurtured by the industrial house of the Mafatlal Group.[1] Not showing a trace of his critical faculty, he accepts the claims as well as proposals of the SWDF for lift irrigation development in the district. Thus, he commends the SWDF long-range proposal, submitted to the state government, that 500 more lift irrigation schemes (over and above 225[2] schemes already executed by the SWDF) could be established at a cost of Rs. 35 crores, benefitting 1.25 lakh crop ha. area of 62,000 farmers. Girja Sharan and Sandeep Kayastha of the Indian Institute of Management, Ahmedabad, mention in Appendix A.2 of their study *Lift Irrigation in panchmahal* (Report No. 144 of the centre for Management in Agriculture, January 1990) some more details about 215 lifts to be established in the first phase.

Let us also take note of the benefit-cost results of Shakarpura lift, a great success story, analysed in depth by Sharan and Kayastha. The *undiscounted* BC ratio at *100 per cent utilisation of 129 ha. of irrigation potential* is 1.32 (expected value as per the project report is 1.85). This shrinks to 1.06 when 20% unutilised irrigation potential is reckoned with. This ratio may come down a bit more if it is computed on a discounted basis. And the reduction may be still more if (a) subsidy element in the electricity bill is removed, and (b) the cost of tank, built 40 years earlier, is also reckoned with. It is actually the 100 per cent subsidy in capital cost for tribal areas that makes lift irrigation a worthwhile proposition. Note also that even the ratio of 1.32 is worked out on the assumptions that (a) all the 129 ha. are devoted to wheat crop, and (b) average yield of wheat under lift irrigation is 3.7 tons/ha.[3]

Concluding Observations

Since we have not here looked at the INTACH report in all its holistic aspects, the foregoing critique should not be taken as a review of the whole report. In fact, our critique is partial in respect of even its economic content, as we have primarily focussed on its one chapter about the BC analysis of the SSP. The report deserves a fuller review for the totality of its contents, economic as well as non-economic.

The powerful role of irrigation and hydel power in the economy of Gujarat state cannot be overstressed. So, the economic viability of the SSP need not be doubted, though it may not be as rosy as portrayed in the TECS report. Most probably, the official undiscounted BC ratio of 2.08 *for the irrigation component* of the SSP is quite realistic. This viability is not likely to be disturbed even if the scale of the SSP is reduced substantially by reducing the height of its dam, say, by 10 per cent. It is such scaling down of multipurpose projects that is the need of the hour, and not the construction of a multitude of mini dams as an alternative to a big dam. Reduced heights do mean reduced benefits from our riverine water resources. On the other hand, these mean reduced project costs, reduced land submergence, reduced forest submergence, reduced RR problem, reduced dam-induced seismicity, and reduced risk of dam disaster, reduced crowding out effects of a big dam investment, etc.

NOTES

1. For reasons better known to him, he emphasises SWDF as an NGO or voluntary field organisation, without referring to its link with the industrial house whose backup of engineering skills and finances have proved a critical factor in the efficient working of the lift schemes sponsored by it.

2. There seems to be some mix-up here about numbers, for Girja Sharan and Sandeep Kayastha in their study of lift irrigation in Panchmahal district (I do not find it figuring in the non-alphabetical Bibliography) mention much smaller numbers. In 1987, there were 82 lift irrigation schemes in all — SWDF accounted for 35 only (constructed since 1975).
3. It may interest Paranjpye to know what difference to wheat yield is made by irrigation in Gujarat, as Sharan and Kayastha cite the following evidence for 1980-81 to 1984-85 for the district :

Year	*Irrigated wheat (tons/ha.)*	*Unirrigated wheat (tons/ha.)*
1980-81	1.84	1.11
1981-82	2.23	0.60
1982-83	2.04	0.58
1983-84	2.40	0.59
1984-85	3.28	1.00
Average (1980-84)	2.36	0.78

CHAPTER 18

DEVELOPMENT OF WATER RESOURCES IN NORTH-WESTERN INDIA*

In the wake of the spurt in agriculture due to HYV technology, water is now being widely perceived as the limiting factor in the farm growth process, giving rise to inter-state wrangling over sharing of common river waters. The case of Tamil Nadu is quite an instructive example in this regard. There has been a marked slowdown in this state's agricultural growth as it approached the point of full exploitation of its surface and ground water resources. Every year one hears about its pleadings with Karnataka, an upper riparian state, for the release of Cauvery waters so as to save its paddy crop in the Tanjore rice bowl. Both being water-short states, their wrangling over water is part of a universal problem of water disputation among states wherever the water endowment is poor in relation to the arable land. Our cultural plurality is only an aggravating circumstance, and not a root cause, in inter-state water disputes. After all, even a culturally homogeneous country like the United States has a long history of inter-state water disputes.

In short, we must be mentally prepared for the inevitability of water disputes. The disputation is most likely to be more intense and more prolonged whenever water scarcity is acute. Barring the water-abundant regions in eastern India

---

* *Economic and Political Weekly*, October 22, 1988.

and the long coastal strip below the Western Ghat mountains, the rest of the country, *including the Punjab-Haryana area,* is naturally water-short. The book** under review looks at some major issues of water resources development and management in north-west India which covers, besides Punjab and Haryana, the two hilly states of Himachal Pradesh and Jammu and Kashmir, the highly arid Rajasthan and the Union Territory of Delhi.

The reviewer found the contents of the book absorbing reading, for which both Dhillon and the Centre for Research in Rural and Industrial Development (CRRID), Chandigarh, need to be complimented. The CRRID has brought out this volume as a part of its *Discussion Series,* a rather unique undertaking by a research institute in India. Dhillon, a former chief irrigation engineer (Punjab), prepared, at CRRID's invitation, a working paper on the manifold issues of irrigation development in NW India. The paper, consisting of nine sections, was sent for a critique to R.S. Gill, a former senior official of the Beas Project and presently a member of the Punjab State Planning Board. In the next round, both the paper and this critique were forwarded to A.M. Singal, an erstwhile chief irrigation engineer of Haryana state for his perusal and reactions. He took the opportunity to write a definitive account of his own. The CRRID has published in the volume under review the working paper, along with the critique by Gill and the write-up by Singal. How one wishes that like comments and reactions by the officials of the governments of Rajasthan, Himachal Pradesh and Jammu and Kashmir had also been obtained by CRRID and duly published in the present volume, so as to enable impartial observers to get a more complete picture of the shared as well as non-shared perceptions of the problems of the region. Hopefully, this may be made good in the subsequent edition that ought to carry salient comments from other persons so

** *Water Resources Development and Management in North-West India: Some Issues* by Paul Singh Dhillon; Centre for Research in Rural and Industrial Development, Chandigarh, 1987; pp. 128.

enthusiastically sought by the CRIDD director in his prefatory remarks.

Acute Paucity of Water Resources

In just 92 pages Dhillon has ranged over practically every aspect — organisational, legal, technical, political, international, economic, etc — of surface irrigation, his own area of expertise and professional experience. In his brief introduction to the region and its various rivers, he asserts that almost the whole of the land in the two hilly states "is unfit for artificial irrigation because of unsuitable topography". Thanks to the Indus Water Treaty with Pakistan, Jammu and Kashmir is practically debarred from developing new sources of irrigation from its three rivers of Indus, Jhehlum and Chenab. In the Jammu area adjoining Himachal, the state would share in the Ravi waters when the Thein dam comes up. This area and Himachal Pradesh have considerable scope for added irrigation through lifting of river waters. If Haryana finds it worthwhile to lift its canal waters by almost 450 feet to meet irrigation needs of its upland tracts of the south-western parts (Singal, p. 99), why rule out such development in Himachal which is rather well endowed with cheaper hydel power potential.

Of course, in view of the comparative small size of arable land in these states, their total demand for irrigation water is going to be rather small, without making much difference to the overall picture of water requirements of the three states of the plains portion of the region, namely, Rajasthan, Punjab and Haryana. Assuming an irrigation delta of 5 feet per acre per year for double cropping the land resource (as adopted by Dhillon), these two states may need 15, and not 5, million acre feet (MAF) as compared to 50 MAF for Punjab, 45 MAF for Haryana, and 350 MAF by Rajasthan (Dhillon, p. 73).

The noteworthy point that emerges from Dhillon's section, entitled 'The Future Perspective', is one of acute paucity of water resources in this region. For double cropping under wholly irrigated conditions, the regional irrigation requirements turn out to be of the order of 450 MAF, almost nine times the water endowment of the region. This picture of paucity is not radically altered even if Rajasthan is excluded from the reckoning. For the aggregate requirements of Punjab and Haryana, the two regional states which contend the most for the waters of the three eastern rivers of the Indus system (Ravi, Beas and Sutlej), are about 60 MAF above the estimated availability of 35 MAF as per Dhillon's assessment (third footnote on p. 73). This huge water deficit can be bridged in two ways, namely, (1) transferring water from another surplus river basin, and (2) adopting measures that (a) curb the demand for water, (b) lead to economy in water use, and (c) minimise water storage and transit losses. Here, one discerns considerable divergence in the standpoints of Dhillon and Singal. This reviewer is not impressed by Gill's sketchy critique which precedes even Dhillon's presentation. On balance, Singal's assessment looks more appealing. Yet it is worthwhile to go over some salient measures for resolving the gap.

When the Eradi Tribunal award came in the wake of the Rajiv-Longowal accord on Punjab, Indian press reports indicated that the Tribunal had somewhat overestimated the Indus river flows to be shared among the states of the region. The volume under review contains no reference to this award, presumably because Dhillon's paper was written prior to the award — his own preface is dated May 30, 1986. One can easily discern that he has not been meticulous in presenting the estimates of water resources of the region. He does not indicate the basis, or the source, of his overall estimate of 55 MAF with the following break-up given in a footnote on p. 73.

	MAF
(1) Perennial streams of Punjab and Haryana	40
(2) Ghaggar and seasonal torrents	2.85
(3) Groundwater	4.50
(4) Rajasthan's own water resources	7.25
Total	54.60

In another footnote on the same page, he gives the following break-up for the combinated water resources of Punjab and Haryana:

		MAF
(1)	Sutlej	11.50
(2)	Ravi-Beas surplus	7.72
(3)	Ghaggar and seasonal torrents	3.10
(4)	Pre-partition uses of Punjab from the Indus system	1.98
(5)	Haryana's share in Yamuna waters	6.00
(6)	Groundwater	4.50
	Total	34.80

Groundwater Resources

In contrast, Singal gives a more systematic account of water availability in the region under varying assumptions. Unlike Dhillon, he takes up this issue right in the beginning of his write-up — and without relegating the matter to long footnotes. After describing water discharges in various canal systems of the area (along with capacity that is already established for transferring water from Ravi to Beas, and from Beas to Sutlej), he gives the mean flows, the dependable flows and the dry-year flows of the rivers as follows:

	Annual Flows (MAF)		
River	*Mean Value*	*Dependable Value*	*Dry-Year Value*
Ravi	6.48	5.26	3.96
Beas	12.39	9.63	6.96
Sutlej	13.36	10.99	9.06
Yamuna (Haryana's share)	8.50	5.75	4.38
Total	40.73	31.63	24.36

While the reviewer wholly accepts the thesis of paucity of water resources in the region, he would like to make two observations which suggest that both Singal and Dhillon understate the water potential of the region. First, the river flow estimates of both are much lower than those released by Central Water Commission in its new document, *Water Resources of India* (April 1987), as shown by the following data:

	Mean Annual Flow	*Utilisable Flow*
Indus (up to border)	73,305 Km^3 i.e., 59 MAF	46,000 Km^3 i.e., 37 MAF
Yamuna (excluding Chambal)	57,241 Km^3 i.e., 46 MAF	N.A.

Even if we accept Singal's figure for Haryana's share in Yamuna, the mean flows of the region (excluding Rajasthan) amount to nearly 68 MAF, and the dependable flows amount to nearly 48 MAF.

The second observation pertains to the estimate of groundwater resource given by Dhillon (Singal, for some inexplicable reason, just does not mention any estimate in this regard in his write-up). Those familiar with the crucial role played by groundwater irrigation in the agricultural transformation of Punjab and Haryana often harbour an impression that the groundwater bounty of the area is very immense. This is belied by Dhillon's estimate of 4.5 MAF for Punjab-Haryana tract whose total water resources are reckoned at 35 MAF. Of course, the available official estimates of groundwater potential are much higher, though not near the impression of groundwater being much more bountiful than river water. For instance, while the Central Groundwater Board (CGWB) reckons the groundwater potential at 13.10 km^3 (about 10.50 MAF) for Punjab and 8.80 km^3 (7.0 MAF) for Haryana, the state groundwater directorates place these at 18.15 km^3 (14.52 MAF) and 8.14 km^3 (6.4 MAF), respectively.

Groundwater is a local resource, in the sense that its utilisation is normally confined to the vicinity of its natural occurrence. States seldom wrangle over the groundwater resources of a river basin. In view of this, writers in the volume under review may have not paid much heed to the groundwater irrigation potential of NW India. A more weighty reason, however, for underplaying groundwater resource and its quantum could be traced to a widely-held view, if not bias, among surface irrigation engineers in general and hydrologists in particular, that groundwater and river water are not two distinct entities. More specifically, they deem that the estimates of volume of river flows are inclusive of annual groundwater recharge, which, unlike groundwater stock, is usually the basis for assessing groundwater resource and its irrigation potential. Both Gill (p. xvi) and Dhillon (p. 31) do subscribe to this hydrological view, the latter expressing it in the following poignant manner:

> All underground waters not only have their source in surface waters, there being no innate or primeval waters as such, but are in many cases, a physical continuation of the latter through a changed medium and to some extent even reappear as such in the form of seepage and springs, to again merge with them in a common medium of flow.

In view of this, Singal's omission of groundwater resources appears defensible. But, then Dhillon's inclusion of 4.5 MAF as groundwater resource (of Punjab and Haryana states only) appears questionable. On this issue of additivity of two categories of water resources, my own thinking is as follows. Both groundwater and surface water (river, lake or pond) do originate from a common parent, namely, precipitation (rainfall and snow), and are simultaneously highly inter-connected with each other, in the sense that what is groundwater at one point of time can acquire the form of flowing stream water later, and *vice versa*. As river water gets tapped for irrigation, a good deal of the irrigation water becomes groundwater owing to seepage from canal network and field percolation. Both Dhillon and Singal quote the following order of losses in canal irrigation:

	Per Cent
Main and branch canals	17
Distributories	8
Water courses (field channels)	20
Field seepage	17
Total loss	62

Thus nearly two-thirds of the river water released from headworks for canal irrigation end up in the groundwater table. It is because of this huge man-made ('artificial') groundwater recharge that one finds that nearly 60 to 70 per cent of annual groundwater replenishment (i.e., groundwater potential estimates of CGWB or the state groundwater directorates) is on account of extensive development of river-based canal irrigation in the two states of Punjab and Haryana. Evidently, one would be incurring an error of double counting if the seeped-in waters, which have become part of the groundwater potential, are not excluded from addition while computing total water resources of NW India. In other words, total water resources should be deemed equal to the sum of annual river flows plus net rainfall infiltration component of groundwater potential, which is reckoned as follows for Punjab and Haryana by the Second Irrigation Commission:

	Punjab	*Haryana*	*Punjab+ Haryana*
Gross rainfall infiltration to groundwater table (MAF)	5.1	3.0	8.1

Net available for irrigation after allowing 25 per cent deduction on account of evapo-transpiration and sub-surface run-off to the rivers (MAF)	3.83	2.25	6.1

Though the net groundwater estimate of 6.1 MAF is about a third higher than Dhillon's figure of 4.5 MAF, the difference need not be viewed with any serious concern, because there is a lack of firmness in the estimates of groundwater potential of this country. But the same cannot be asserted about the estimates of river water flows. Therefore, one would like to know why Dhillon and Singal's estimates have a perceptible difference in numbers, which in turn are significantly below the CWC estimates.

Large Transit Losses

In India, the water requirements for irrigating one crop ha., in comparison to US or Israeli irrigated agriculture, are rather high. This is not so much because of the problem of over-irrigation and wasteful use of water by our farmers, but because of huge losses in transit between the point of harnessing water and its inlet point in a farm field. Nearly three-fourths of the afore-mentioned total loss of 62 per cent is in the canal conveyance system, the rest being due to deep percolation of applied canal water below the crop root zone down to the groundwater table. Technically, it is possible to totally eliminate such losses, thereby eliminating artificial groundwater recharge component on the one hand and enlarging the area to be irrigated by a factor of nearly two.

Going by the national norm of 0.90 metre delta for one crop ha. for canal irrigation (as compared to 0.66 metre assumed for well irrigation), any investment that saves this 0.60 m lost in transit and field percolation would enable the community to irrigate three instead of one crop ha. On this extreme assumption, the available river flows of NW India (lying somewhere between 45 and 73 MAF), if fully tapped, would provide irrigation to 19 to 30 million ha. gross crop area of the region. Adding another 3 million ha. from 8 MAF of groundwater recharge due to rainfall, 22-33 million crop ha. of irrigation potential exists in NW India whose arable area, according to Dhillon's state-wise figures on p. 73, is of the order of 35 million ha. In other words, the water resources of the whole region even under the most optimistic conditions would barely suffice for providing irrigation to each unit of land for one crop season only.

Needless to add, it may not be worthwhile economically to strive towards the realisation of the optimistic conditions, namely, (1) to wholly prevent the seepage losses in transit, (2) to wholly eliminate field percolation losses, and (3) to grow crops which need only 30 cm. of irrigation for maturing. A wholly piped water distribution system, which alone can eliminate transit losses, appears an uneconomic proposition for a big canal system. Instead, to reduce substantially the seepage losses via canal lining with impervious material appears a better proposition. Singal favours this option without any reservation when he writes as follows:

> In this context, a question is often asked as to whether or not lining of canals and water courses should be carried out in such areas. The answer is an emphatic 'yes'. The lining of canals makes water available on the surface. There is really no point in letting the water seep in the first instance and then to pump it to bring it to the surface (p. 101).

This reviewer does not concur with Singal, except in a special case, namely, the use of canal lining for preventing seepage in areas underlain with saline waters unfit for crop activity. In such a situation, the seeped-in waters are not recoverable through groundwater development as these get mixed with saline bodies of water. In the absence of a drainage system as an adjunct to the canal system, there is a gradual build-up of groundwater table that ultimately gives rise to problems of waterlogging and soil salinisation. Such a build-up of groundwater table has already occurred in the cotton belt of NW India which is underlain with saline waters, and would occur in the Rajasthan canal command also unless canal seepage is controlled.

Dhillon, unlike Singal, has some reservations about conserving canal waters through the medium of canal lining. He rightly cautions against taking up the second phase of the World Bank-assisted canal lining programme, as he apprehends threat to groundwater-irrigated agriculture sustained by seeped-in canal waters. He observes as follows in his 4th section of the paper, entitled 'Integrated Development of Surface and Underground Waters':

> Of late, a concerted drive is under way all over the region for the lining of field channels and old unlined channels constructed under the diversion projects...The whole question of lining needs to be weighed against its effect on water balance to ensure that in our effort to conserve losses, we do not over-shoot the mark and violently destabilise the water balance, turning surplus into actually deficit areas, thereby depriving the affected lands of their existing source of irrigation (p. 36).

The expert opinion on the issue, whether to line or not to line a part or whole of the canal network, is indeed quite divided, and Dhillon is right in suggesting more deliberation on the matter. This reviewer, however, is unequivocally inclined against canal lining under the following circumstances which do prevail in the Western Indo-Gangetic alluvium (excluding tracts underlain with saline and brackish waters):

(i) existence of a protective canal system, along with canal irrigators' inclination to invest in their own private wells;

(ii) natural availability of groundwater being unfavourable, e.g., depth to water table may be high, or water-yield of shallow wells is low in normal rainfall years and very precarious during drought years; or probability of striking a dry hole is high, etc.

(iii) proneness of groundwater resource to over-exploitation, partly because of absence of statutory groundwater regulation provisions and partly due to faulty tariff for power pumps that encourage farmers to over-extract groundwater.

Economy in Water Use

When the natural endowment of water of a region is not good, prudence demands that farmers of the region ought to use the irrigation water in most economical manner. This question of economy in water use has two distinct aspects, both of which are inter-linked to some extent. One pertains to the cultivation of crops that need copious watering and the other pertains to the use of scientific knowledge as well as man-made devices like sprinklers and drippers that substantially curtail water requirements at the field level.

In this region of Punjab and Haryana, the rapid expansion in paddy cultivation with the aid of tubewell water has not been viewed with approval by many persons, including this reviewer. While Dhillon has raised this issue of optimal crop pattern under irrigated conditions, he has given it an entirely different direction, namely, the desirability of mono cropping under each canal outlet/distributory for a more efficient scheduling of water release in a canal system. This idea of uniform cropping pattern is not favoured by R.S. Gill, who draws attention to varied factors that go into the determination of crop pattern by a farmer.

Though Singal does not take up the issue of optimal crop pattern in general and that of paddy cultivation in particular, he appears to subscribe to the basic philosophy that a water-short region better produce crops that need light irrigation. This is suggested by his reaction to reports of over-exploitation of groundwater in Punjab: "Under such a situation, the only recourse left will be to take to low water rate application crops more and more..." (p. 100).

On sprinklers, which economise on irrigation water by 25 to 35 per cent (at field level), Singal is quite ecstatic, whereas Dhillon almost rules them out when he writes as follows:

> The over-head system, in the form of sprinkler irrigation, needs considerable capital investment not justified at the present level of returns. Availability of power and capability of the farmer to operate the equipment are other limitations (p. 49).

This reviewer is inclined to Singal's position which is based on successful introduction of sprinkler irrigation in the water-short, south-western part of Haryana state. Not only 15,000 sprinkler sets have been privately installed on private tubewells (with subsidy from NABARD as well as the state government), but also over 100 large sprinkler sets are being operated by the government.

Unfortunately, the sprinkler mode of watering crops is technically infeasible for paddy crop. Since investment in a sprinkler set is lumpy, the paddy-wheat sequence that has become a favoured sequence of the farmers of Punjab and Haryana (outside the cotton belt) militates against the economic viability of sprinkler irrigation for wheat crop only. Therefore, diffusion of sprinkler irrigation is partly contingent on farmers giving up the paddy-wheat sequence in favour of some alternative sequence that needs lesser irrigation. For instance, the paddy-wheat sequence, as per the recommendations of the Punjab Agricultural University, would require 225 cm. (180 cm. for paddy alone) of irrigation water as against 70 cm. for groundnut-wheat, 85 cm. for maize-wheat, and 90 cm for cotton-wheat sequences and 150 cm. for sugarcane, a crop, recommended in lieu of the paddy-wheat sequence for one-fifth of the land in Punjab by the Johl Committee on crop diversification in the state.

Unless these alternative crop sequences are made as profitable as the paddy-wheat sequence, farmers would not take to them. This is truly a situation of conflict between private gain and social loss in water utilisation. Resolutions of such conflicts are better attempted through policy instruments than through the imposition of physical restrictions on certain crops. This requires action on several fronts. As paddy is procured by the Centre at pre-announced, if not incentive, prices, the alternative kharif crops must have similar price-cum-procurement support. This is particularly essential for the maize crop, the main kharif crop of Punjab prior to the rise of paddy in the post-HYV period. Likewise, the Johl Committee's recommendation to the Centre to sanction 50 additional sugar factories to the state for facilitating the switchover from paddy-wheat to sugarcane is an admirable measure that is in the realm of industrial location policy.

CHAPTER 19

MANAGING WATER RESOURCES

In this chapter we offer reviews of two books. In section I a collaborative study of the Punjab Agricultural University, (PAU), Ludhiana is reviewed, whereas in section II we give some glimpses from a study with a global coverage.

I

The focus of this PAU study*, which is a joint venture across several disciplines, is on the sustainability issue of Punjab agriculture. The distinguished authors, some of international repute, underscore the serious imbalance between demand for water (37.6 MAF) and its supply (24.7 MAF). How the imbalance is adversely affecting groundwater table in many parts of the state is brought out with the aid of a very neat, simple formula.

Before reviewing the book chapter by chapter, two queries come to mind about the huge imbalance mentioned earlier. One, it is not clear if the authors have duly reckoned with additional surface water resources that would become available to Punjab after the construction of Thein dam on the Ravi. This doubt has risen because they have reckoned with existing canal supplies for each of the nineteen zones into which they have delineated the state. Two, what

---

* *Water Resources of Punjab,* by S.S. Prihar, S.D. Khepar, Raghbir Singh, S.S. Grewal, and S.K. Sondhi (1990), reviewed in Indian Journal of Agricultural Economics, Jan-March, 1992.

adjustments have been carried out for the fact that canal supplies, earmarked for Rajasthan but not used by that state because of delay in completing the mammoth Rajasthan Canal, are being presently allowed to be used in Punjab? Do these two adjustments in the contrary directions really counterbalance each other if not carried out in the study?

Whereas Chapter I gives a background view of the growth in Punjab agriculture, Chapter II spells out the objectives of the study, alongwith the genesis of the concern for it. From Chapter III onwards, the plot thickens, so to speak, and complex nature of water unfolded. In this chapter the objective no.1, namely, definition and identification of agro-climatic irrigation zones of the state, is fulfilled.

Chapter IV is entitled 'Available Supply of Water-Present and Proposed Metholodogy and Assessed Status'. Its main concern is with the estimation of annual groundwater availability from the recharge or infiltration from (i) rainfall, (ii) canal seepage, and (iii) return flow, i.e., percolation of groundwater applied to a field back to the groundwater table. The central point being made here is that the 'return flow' is far more than assumed presently as per the norms laid down by the Groundwater Estimation Committee of 1984. Thus net groundwater use is much, much less than gross groundwater use as suggested by the actual or recommended level of irrigation for crops. Such difference is particularly large for paddy whose phenomenal growth is widely perceived as the main cause of groundwater depletion in this state. More specifically, almost two-thirds of water applied to paddy (200 cm. or thereabouts) seeps down to groundwater aquifer.

Having obtained zone-wise estimates of water supply in Chapter IV, the authors build in Chapter V the corresponding demand estimates. Irrigation demand is worked out with the help of (a) crop pattern data for mid-eighties, and (b) evapo-transpiration (ET) needs of various crops. These ET Coefficients, normative as they are, indicate water requirements that are net of percolation loss as well as change in water storage in crop root zone area. From this angle, ET needs of paddy (73 cm.) are not far above those of cotton (65 cm.) and maize (60 cm.), the two other main competing crops of the kharif season. So, one cannot really blame the displacement of maize by paddy as a major factor behind groundwater depletion. Furthermore, since ET needs of sugarcane (180 cm.) turn out to be more than ET needs of paddy-wheat sequence (123 cm.). Curtailment of paddy-wheat sequence in favour of sugarcane crop, as suggested by some concerned persons (including the present reviewer), does not appear to be a sensible proposition from the viewpoint of reducing groundwater imbalance in the state.

In Chapter VI the authors undertake a very interesting exercise, namely, translating the zonewise excess demand (supply) of water into zonewise fall (rise) in groundwater table. Such predicted magnitudes of fall (rise) in water table are then contrasted with actual fall(rise) during 1983-86. The authors' depth of knowledge about water-related matters is revealed in this, zone by zone contrast and discussion.

Chapter VII acquaints us with marked gaps in our knowledge about various parameters about water resource. And the concluding Chapter VIII draws up an agenda for action and policy implications, twelve in number. These deserve due attention both in policy-making and research circles, inside as well as outside Punjab. On the controversial issue of paddy growing in Punjab, the authors have not taken any categorical stand. In their recommendation no. 5 they desire that 2 to 2.5 lakh ha. of marginal land, which has come under paddy cultivation, be better diverted to leguminous, soil enriching crops of pulses and oilseeds. And in their sixth recommendation they appear to be concerned with the Punjab farmers' tendency to do very early transplanting of paddy, thereby giving rise to added pressure on groundwater resource. So, they recommend action-oriented research in this area.

It appears that the authors perceive substantial step-up in intensity of cropping to be a major factor behind the water imbalance in the state. So, they caution against any emphasis on raising further intensity of cropping from its present level of 175 per cent.

The book is well written, and the exposition is truly distinguished by high order of lucidity. But for an economist lacking scientific background it is no easy reading. Yet, it can be commended as a serious reading for anyone interested in acquiring firmer understanding of complexities of water resource, as also appreciating the myriad gaps in our knowledge in this area.

II

The book** under review is sixth in the topical series 'Themes in Resource Management'. These books "provide introductions to key areas in resource management for students of geography, economics, planning, politics and environmental studies". Leading international experts are invited to write these and the scope ranges from "local to international scales, from developed to developing nations, from the public to the private sector and biophysical to political considerations". Mcdonald and Kay, who are senior lecturers in water resources management and geography, respectively, succeed admirably in telling us where the vast scientific knowledge about water resources is "strong and where it is tentative and inconclusive". Political aspects of this knowledge are duly emphasised in their presentation. This is another commendable attribute of this book as the professional water expert is in dire need of such sensitisation, more so in India.

'In one sense it is well nigh impossible to review satisfactorily a book having a global canvas of water-related research material from diverse scientific disciplines. Still, I do so, and without worrying unduly on this score. What has really impelled me to undertake this review task is the high educative content of the book. It is a serious work, one reading of which should be a sobering experience for those

---

** *Water Resources: Issues and Strategies* by Adriant T. McDonald and David Kay; Longman Scientific and Technical, Essex (England), 1988 (co-published in the United States with John Wiley, New York); review published in *Economic and Political Weekly*, December 9, 1989.

who think they know all about water resources. Development and management of water resources is now a complex task, a message that has been exceedingly well conveyed by the authors, who evince a remarkable inclination to delve into diverse research material on water from all over the world.

The book consists of ten chapters plus a very detailed list of references and a useful index — and a short foreword by Bruce Mitchell of the University of Waterloo. Chapter 1 is a brief introduction to the contents of the book. Chapter 2, entitled 'The Physical Resource', deals with physical characteristics of water, the global water balance, and a discussion based mainly on some studies on river catchments in Britain. That afforestation of river catchments enhances water availability is a myth that is well exploded with concrete evidence which points to a significant reduction in river flow. In this regard, the curve in Fig. 2.12 on p. 29 is very instructive. Likewise, we need to know if afforestation really adds to groundwater availability. Being a groundwater economist, I am a bit unhappy that the authors have underanalysed the groundwater resource from the irrigation angle. (In point of fact, the irrigation-related content of the work, globally speaking, is not commensurate with the pre-eminent use of water for irrigation purpose). Also, those who advocate groundwater irrigation over major surface water works in India may be misled by data in Table 2.2 which shows that groundwater resource is far more abundantly available than river water. The estimates in this table are in stock terms, whereas relative abundance, say from the irrigation angle, is to be judged in flow terms, that is, what volume of rain water flows annually into the rivers and into the groundwater table.

Chapter 3, titled 'The Human Resources', examines structures for management of water resource at national and international levels. Water management conflicts in California in the US are analysed, along with a brief discussion on problems of water management in Israel. But for large-scale transfer of water over long distances, demands could not be matched with supplies in both California and Israel. (Detailed plans for such transfers within the Soviet Union are briefly discussed in the subsequent chapter 4). The ecological and the resource costs of such transfers, not to speak of interstate or inter-country wrangles that may arise in the process, are indeed high. Will the benefits from such transfers be commensurate with the high costs? Will it not be more cost-effective to do demand management via investments in water-economising devices in acutely water-short regions? Answers are not of a universal character; each community has to do its own calculus, a point that is well made by the authors later in the book.

The last section of chapter 3 pertains to international aspects of water resource development. Not very long ago, water resources in a country could be developed in comparative isolation, and with little regard for the environmental side-effects. This is no more so. After listing a number of international agencies and their water-related interests and activities, the authors analyse how the water conflicts of the US with its two neighbouring countries, Mexico in the south and Canada in the north, are sorted out in a bilateral framework. It is to be noted that in extremely water-short regions the conflict need not be confined to river flows alone; it can extend to groundwater as well. Thus, the groundwater in the Hucco Bolson aquifer of the Rio Grande river between Texas (USA) and Mexico is a source of disputation. The freshwater reserves here are shrinking at the rate of one per cent per annum as the groundwater table has tended to recede by one foot per annum during this century. The conflict cannot be managed through the simple device of groundwater regulation because groundwater on the American side is a private resource. The arid climate of the area of conflict has really put groundwater resource under siege, giving rise to the usual adverse consequences such as (1) rising pumping costs, (2) damage to property from land subsidence due to receding water table, and (3) intrusion of saline and polluted waters into the aquifer.

The main upshot of chapter 4, entitled 'Water Supply', may hearten those who feel that there is enough water for meeting mankind's requirements. But there is a big rider to this that needs due appreciation: "there are problems in matching supplies to demands at different places and times". While storage works take care of the time element, inter-basin transfers are the answer for water-short places. Here, the element of earth's gravity is not sufficiently reckoned with even by otherwise intelligent people. The cost of moving large quantities of water against the force of gravity for heights above 500 feet can be far more than the resultant benefits from such waters in the agricultural sector of the water-short region. Captain Dastoor's Garland Canals and the Ganga-Cauvery Link thus appear to be pipe-dreams.

It is imperative to draw attention to a couple of other important observations of chapter 4. One, rather large quantities of water are needed for effluent disposal through transportation, an aspect which is not sufficiently appreciated by Indian water planners. As groundwater gets exploited, a river's capacity to regenerate itself below the storage dam/barrage is adversely affected. Without releases from the storage points, the inherent capacity of the river to cleanse the waste waters dumped into it is seriously eroded. Two, the composition of national demand for water is quite varied across countries and with their stage of development. Take India and the United States. According to data in Table 4.2, the *per capita* consumption of about 500 m^3 of water in India is 93 per cent for irrigated agriculture. On the other hand, this sector accounts for 41 per cent of the per capita consumption of about 2000 m^3 in the US, where water demand from thermal and nuclear power stations for cooling purposes accounts for a share of 38 per cent (39 per cent in Canada, 47 per cent in Belgium, 40 per cent in Poland, and 14 per cent in the Soviet Union). Three, though the anti-big dam writings of Goldsmith and Hildyard are occasionally referred to in this chapter as well as in the book, the authors' reservations about these deserve attention. They conclude: "Goldsmith and Hildyard could have produced an even more useful contribution if they had devoted more of their extensive analysis to the assessment of appropriateness of dam projects in different environments and political systems" (p. 96).

The intractable problem of flood control is delineated in chapter 5. The paradox of increase in flood damage despite the implementation of 'engineering' flood control measures is effectively explained. While in the advanced countries the problem is essentially one of the property losses, it is mainly one of loss of life in the poor countries. According to the authors, "the key to effective flood management lies in the design of a plan that combines them all to suit the particular circumstances of the community and the environment. It is not a question of choices between adjustments but rather of the selection of an appropriate group of responses". This brings out the irrelevance of measures like 'floodplain zoning' for densely populated regions like Bangladesh.

Chapter 6 is focussed on the issue of quality of water which is of central concern in advanced societies. The relevance of standards of quality of water emerging from such societies for the developing economies is quite open to question. And this area of concern is not divorced from politics. For instance, "both the British and the US governments have deliberately suppressed research work on acidic precipitation" (p. 170). Acidic precipitation is derived from vehicular and industrial emissions containing the oxides of nitrogen and sulphur. It is the ability of this pollution to travel great distances across international boundaries that has generated intense political controversy between the producers and recipients of 'acid rain'. The three-fold impact of this pollution is (1) major changes in aquatic ecosystems, (2) damage to forests, and (3) corrosion of man-made structures.

Chapter 7 is a short foray into the economics of water as a source of power. The marked cost-effectiveness of hydro power *vis-a-vis* nuclear and thermal power is highlighted. Whether this advantage will be offset when true costs of (1) land and forest submergence, and (2) rehabilitation of dam oustees are fully taken into account needs due examination in our context when the very idea of big dams is being questioned, *inter alia,* on the above two grounds. (In the raging Narmada controversy the department of environment is alleged to have placed the estimated cost due to forest submergence to be one and a half times of the total outlay required for the entire Narmada Valley Development Project.)

Chapter 8 deals with the question of river basin management. The experiences of the much-acclaimed Tennessee Valley in the US are critically reviewed — a case of image being out of alignment with ground reality. The Volta and Senegal river valley development efforts in Africa are commented upon. Experiences of English and Welsh regional water authorities are reported. In conclusion, the authors observe:

> Very few projects encapsulate true 'river basin planning' which S.K. Saha (1981) defines as a discipline combining land and water resources management. More often the management structures established are not designed to take such a holistic view of their role. In both developing and developed nations, river basin management is most often seen as the more efficient allocation of water resources to facilitate irrigation and water supply.

Chapter 9 is titled "Issues and Strategies'. Issues of scale are deemed central to understanding the problems of water resource management. As for strategies, these are outlined separately for the developed and the developing worlds. "Political stability and legitimacy form the pre-requisites for successful resource planning. However, many third world nations do not possess these attributes" (p. 237). In India, there has been stability and legitimacy at the Centre. Yet resource planning is unsatisfactory. Is it because resources like water and forests are under the purview of the states, many of them suffering from political instability of one sort or the other (e.g., the Centre changing frequently the chief ministers of states where the ruling part is the same as at the Centre). The concluding chapter 10 draws some lessons for the future.

CHAPTER 20

TWO GREAT STORIES

Two fascinating narratives on water resource development are briefly recaptured in this chapter. The story in the first section is one of reminiscences of a well known water engineer of India who distinguished himself both at home and in international assignments. In the subsequent section we give the reader a touching account of what it takes to develop water resources in a gigantic manner in harsh environs.

I

This highly readable book* is by one of the most distinguished and much honoured engineers of the post-Independence era of this country. Dr. Kanwar Sain was the doyen of Indian water resource engineers till his death, three years ago, at the ripe age of 90 plus. He lived through those times when gifted possessors of engineering skills were looked upon with awe. One is struck by the ethical content of the reminiscences in the context of the tarnished image of an engineer today, especially when he is in the employ of the government departments like the PWD and the irrigation.

Besides great honours at home and abroad — Padma Bhushan, the O.B.E., Order of the Elephant by the Government of Thailand -, he held high offices with probity and warmth

---

* Kanwar Sain, *Reminiscences of an Engineer,* Young Asia, N-126, Panchashila Park, New Delhi-110017, 1978; reviewed in *Journal of India School of Political Economy,* October-December, 1992.

for his fellow workers. The book provides glimpses of the great rise of the young country lad, from the lowly position of a junior engineer to that of the Chairman, Central Water and Power Commission (CWPC, now CWC) which post as of today is of the rank of the Secretary. In the author's own words, this is not an attempt at writing an autobiography nor is it an engineering treatise giving details of projects mentioned therein. It is not even a memoir giving events in the strict sequence of their occurrence. It is nothing more than reminiscences relating to the author's career as an engineer, *bringing out points which may not find a place in the engineering history of projects.*

Why should non-engineers find this book of some interest? And why is it being reviewed almost 15 years after its publication? The reviewer could not readily procure a copy for his own professional reading till 1990 when a complimentary copy was made available to him at the inaugural Kanwar Sain Memorial Lecture in Delhi. Unfortunately, he could not speedily go through its 37 chapters (nearly 500 pages). The need for a review, belated though it is, was felt because of *inter alia* the contents of the book about the Narmada dams. The book is of some historical value; if only more irrigation engineers commit themselves to writing in a similar vein, we would have an additional source material in the realm of history of Indian irrigation. Its last two chapters are quite instructive in comprehending the Narmada debate of recent years Whereas the Master Plan for the Development of the Narmada for the benefit of Madhya Pradesh State is discussed in chapter 36, the vital question of optimum height of the Navgam dam of the Sardar Sarovar Project is taken up in the chapter 37, entitled 'Narmada Water Disputes Tribunal'. As for social scientists, it is enough to point out that Dr. Sain, as honorary visiting professor of the I.I.T, Delhi, delivered lectures on *economic, social and legal aspects of water resource planning to the M.Tech students.*

The book opens with an interesting anecdote, namely, expulsion notice served on the author as a student at his Alma Mater (Roorkee University) for being a member of the procession in support of the non-cooperation movement of our freedom struggle, While promising the authorities that he would never take part in active politics, he vowed to himself to serve the nation as an engineer as best as he could have done had he entered politics. This is followed by an interesting narration of (i) his first exciting apprenticeship under H.W. Nicholson, the engineer who first prepared back in 1919 the blue prints for the Bhakra Dam Project, and (ii) his courage in standing up to Nicholson's successor, A.M.R. Montague, on a matter of personal honour.

Among the numerous Indian water projects Dr. Sain writes about, the following ones may be mentioned: D.V.C. Project (Ch. 8), Bhakra Dam Project (Ch. 9 and Ch. 28), Rajasthan Canal (Ch. 12 and Ch. 26), Hirakud Dam (Ch. 15), Kosi flood problem (Ch. 17), Nagarjuna Sagar (Ch. 20), Farrakka Barrage (Ch. 25), Narmada dams (Ch. 36 and Ch.37).

Dr. Sain had been abroad on several occasions to different countries, and has left accounts of such visits. His first visit to the mecca of dam building (i.e., the U.S.A) is described in Chapter 5. Visits to China, the Soviet Union, Iraq, Egypt, Italy, Yugoslavia, Israel, and Switzerland are narrated in subsequent chapters. One chapter is devoted to his 20-year association with the United Nations, and another to his developmental work on the Mekong River Basin (Cambodia).

Dr. Sain did not like the idea of adjudication of inter-state water disputes by courts or water tribunals. Instead, he favoured mutual agreements among the disputing riparian states. He does not envisage the possibility of an impasse in such bargaining, and what to do in that event, However, an impasse could arise as much from the political interest as from the genuine differences among experts even on concrete scientific matters such as the quantum of flows in a river. In the case of Tehri dam, the expert opinion on its seismic vulnerability is poles apart; see, for example, this reviewer's 'What is Wrong with Tehri Dam?; *Facts for You,* Vol. 14, No. 4, October, 1992.

In a very discerning note (reproduced in full on pp. 446-55) he tackles the ticklish issue of desired height of the Navgam dam of the Sardar Sarovar Project. It may be clarified that he wrote this note in his personal capacity, while he was still in the service of the M.P. government, in response to a letter from V. Shankar, the then Principal Secretary to the Prime Minister, Morarji Desai, who desired his views on how best in his opinion the Narmada dispute could be settled.

To minimise the crucial costs of submergence arising due to the formation of reservoir, he opted for a height of 440 feet (FRL), full 15 feet less than the level finally indicated by the Narmada Water Disputes Tribunal (NWDT) in its award a year later. He took this stand knowing full well that another very eminent water engineer, Dr, A.N. Khosla (of the Khosla Committee and the founder Chairman of CWPC) had strongly opted for a height of 465 feet back in 1964. In fact, Dr. Khosla had suggested even a still greater height at 500 feet so as to fully harness the hydro power potential of the Narmada Waters whose flows were reckoned by him at 36 million acre-feet (MAF) as against 28 MAF by NWDT as well as by Dr. Sain. Dr. Sain opted for 440 feet because at this height the submergence cost, as reflected in the culturable area lost and the number of persons affected, would be much lower than that at 455 or 465 feet as per his following estimates:

Reservoir level (feet)	*CA submerged (acres)*	*Population Affected (No. of persons)*
440 (Sain)	14,495(56)	12,289(31)
455(NWDT)	26,065(100)	39,636(100)
465(Khosla)	38,000(146)	57,100(144)

Figures in brackets show relative magnitudes, with NWDT height = 100.

These numbers partly do reveal that Dr. Sain, unlike Dr. Khosla, attached far more weight to the submergence costs than to material benefits arising from the use of water resources. This comes out in his following observations on storage dams while drawing up the long-run water plan for Madhya Pradesh in 1970: 'In view of the possibility of using regulated flows repeatedly for power generation and conservation, storages have been provided as high up in the (Narmada) basin as possible. Storage dams involve submergence of land with all the accompanying problems—the loss of land as a development resource, consequent loss of employment facilities, uprooting people from their homes and farms and their rehabilitation involving economic, social and human problems. Whereas some submergence is unavoidable in any storage scheme, an attempt has been made in the (Master) Plan to keep the extent of damage to the minimum. Also, an attempt has been made to avoid undue discontent on account of concentrated dislocation of population in one locality (p. 439).

This clearly shows that Dr. Sain, while subscribing to the big dam idea, was not for mega dams like those built in the United States to impound all river flows (including exceptional floods) without much regard to the submergence angle. It should be noted that the American situation is different from ours where land is scarce and population density is very high, For example, in the building of Hoover dam, which could impound three times the mean annual flow of the mighty Colorado river, the submergence cost was practically nil because no settlements and cultivated lands (nor forests) were involved.

So, 31 big dams (plus thousands of small dams) of the Narmada were proposed in the Master Plan of M.P. Flood moderation was one of the eight objectives of this plan. But the need for flood control is more in the basin outside M.P. So, Gujarat's human interests have been fully reckoned with while drawing up the Plan. He writes: 'The Plan took note of the fact that soon after leaving the boundaries of M.P. and Maharashtra, the river enters the Gujarat plains which offers only a limited scope for conservation storage' (p. 439). According to him, the flood waters of the Narmada would be moderated to about one million cusecs, less than half the exceptional high flood discharge of 2.3 million cusecs recorded in 1970.

Thus, one sees in this book a very humane face of an engineer, both in his professional conduct and personal life, which was imbued with moral values of high order: integrity, unselfishness, courage, and consistency.

II

The history of irrigation development reveals that whenever large-scale irrigation works were contemplated these had been opposed even by well meaning persons. This opposition arose even when such works did not entail construction of a big dam. In recent decades, environmental concerns have added an altogether new dimension of resistance to all mega projects, more so to big dams. Today, dam building for irrigation and power generation no more remains a laudable activity, so much so that big dams are viewed by some as man-made curses, though engineering fraternity continues to look upon them as boons.

The book* under review is an attempt to convey to the lay reader what really goes into the making of a mega dam on a mega river. Its central concern is to sing paeans to the builders of a huge dam, the tallest in the world till recently when it yielded its place of pride to the Russian Nourek dam. Its emphasis is on human aspects rather than on the stupendous, engineering feat of taming a wild river in a hostile setting.

The author amply succeeds in conveying the true costs of building the Hoover dam, transcending beyond its nominal investment outlay of the order of 50 million dollars (at 1930 prices). This account truly underscores that no amount of meticulous costing or shadow pricing of resources can give us a true measure of project costs. This is so despite there

---

* *Hoover Dam - An American Adventure* by Joseph E. Stevens, University of Oklahama Press: Norman and London, 1988, pp. 326; reviewed in *International Journal of Development Banking*, July, 1992.

being no encounter with today's intractable problems of relocating and rehabilitating dam oustees, nor of any submergence of forests and fertile valley lands.

The book under review is much more a readable than a reviewable work. It has all the tell-tale markings of a research study: seven chapters, each one suffused with footnotes (placed at the end of the book in a 30-page section so as not to interfere with smooth reading by most readers), a twelve-page Bibliography, and an Index to important names of personalities, places and institutions mentioned in the text. To create this moving account the author has mined a wide array of source material, ranging from technical project reports and exploratory/investigative studies which preceded the final formulation of the project by the federal Bureau of Reclamation, to media writings of the times, minutes of important meetings, personal memoirs (including unpublished ones, e.g., one by John Meursinge, noted engineer and Hoover dam construction worker). Imaginative, select quotes from persons from all walks of life (including family members of the workers) enliven the account so stirringly written by Stevens.

The Hoover dam on the mighty Colorado river has been built by blocking the Black Canyon near Boulder city, not far from the famed Eldorado Valley of the arid south-western U.S.A., having sparse vegetation and searing winds. In chapter 1 are described the antecedents of this 'monument to twentieth century technology, a symbol of man's triumph over nature', its conception and investigative planning as a multipurpose project. We are introduced to Frank T. Crowe, America's legendary dam builder for whom it was a burning passion to build this dam, who worked for the consortium of six contractors who pooled their financial resources to bid for this high cost, time-bound, risky federal project with a promise of a bonanza of profits, of course.

The title of chapter 2, 'A Deadly Desert', speaks volumes for its contents. Alongside the harshness of the environs of the dam site, we are informed of those who genuinely felt it was an impossible task; about those who feared its vast storage would cause a catastrophic earthquake that would shatter the concrete arch of the dam and unleash a flood of 'biblical proportions'. To this desolate spot arrived a multitude of unemployed persons from all walks of life, thanks to the Great Depression. But for this reservoir of manpower, desperate to eat three square meals a day even at great risk to limb and life, one wonders if the dam building could be completed two years ahead of schedule, with handsome profits to the contractors ($ 10-18 million on a project outlay of the order of $ 50 million). The heat was a terrible foe, averaging 119 F degrees one July in the open and 140 degrees inside the choking tunnels and making workers lose their sanity and occasionally their lives.

The gritty study of constructing huge diversion tunnels (diameter 5-storey building), required prior to be damming of a big river, is unfolded in chapter 3. The austere life of the newly-built Boulder city for the dam workers is described in chapter 4. The danger and drudgery of erecting coffer dams, as also excavating the river bed at the dam site, are brought out in chapter 5, aptly titled, 'Incessant, Monstrous Activity'. This is followed by the penultimate chapter on erecting the dam itself. This is a tribute to the American genius for organisation, under the command of Frank Crowe.

Finally, we come to the concluding chapter 7, titled 'Twentieth Century Marvel'. Besides glimpses of the great dedication ceremony and the radical transformation of the economy of south-western USA, the author apprises us of a conversational snippet between Crowe and Young that tells us who really built the Hoover dam — the workers. The author deserves our thanks for this painstaking but immensely readable account of dam building.

LIST OF AUTHOR'S WRITINGS

I. Books

II. Journal Articles**

III. Mimeo Works

IV. Semi-Academic and Media Writings

V. Book Reviews

Abbreviations

BS	Business Standard[1]
EE	Eastern Economist[2]
EPW	Economic and Political Weekly[2]
ET	Economic Times[1]
FE	Financial Express[1]
FFY	Facts For You[3]
IEG	Institute of Economic Growth
IJAE	Indian Journal of Agricultural Economics
MS	Mainstream[2]

---

1 daily
2 weekly
3 monthly
** These double asterisks relate to writings on irrigation/water resources only.

I. BOOKS (10)

**1. Indian Water Resources Development for Irrigation: Issues, Critiques, Reviews. Commonwealth, New Delhi-2, 1993.
**2. Trends and New Tendencies in Indian Irrigated Agriculture. Commonwealth, New Dlhi-2, 1993.*
**3. Major and Minor Irrigation in India. Indira Gandhi Open University, New Delhi, 1991.
**4. Studies in Minor Irrigation with Special Reference to Groundwater. Commonwealth, New Delhi-2, 1990.*
**5. Big Dams : Claims, Counterclaims (ed.). Commonwealth, New Delhi-2, 1990.
**6. Studies in Irrigation and Water Management. Commonwealth, New Delhi-2, 1989.*
**7. Irrigation in India's Agricultural Development: Productivity, Equity, Stability. Sage, New Delhi, 1988.*
**8. Economics of Groundwater Irrigation in Hard Rock Regions. Agricole, New Delhi, 1986.*
**9. Development of Tubewell Irrigation in India. Agricole, New Delhi, 1982.*
10. Economics of Television in India. S. Chand, New Delhi, 1974 (Ph. D. thesis).

II. JOURNAL ARTICLES (75)

1. INDIAN JOURNAL OF AGRICULTURAL ECONOMICS (10)

**1. Water Resources Management : Issues and Dimensions. 44 (3), July-September 1989.
**2. Economic Linkages among Irrigation Sources. 43 (4), October-December 1988 (with K.J.S. Satyasai).
**3. Water Management in the Mula Command : A Study in the Productivity Impact of Canal Waters. 42 (1), Jan.-March 1987.

---

* Published under the IEG Series, Studies in Economic Development and Planning.

**4. Irrigation and Water Management in India. Perception of Problems and their Resolution. 41 (3), July-Sept. 1986.
**5. Questionable Conceptions and Simplistic Views about Irrigated Agriculture of India. 40 (1), Jan.-March 1985.
**6. Scale Economies in Tubewell Irrigation. 33 (1), January-March 1978.
**7. Externalities of New Groundwater Technology on Small Farmers. 30 (3), July-September 1975.
**8. Demand for Irrigation : A Case Study of Government Tubewells in Uttar Pradesh. 28 (2), April-June 1973.
9. Productivity of Factory Operated Sugarcane Farms in India. 28 (2), April-June 1973.
10. Role of Firewood in the Indian Economy, 22 (4), October-December 1967.

2. ARTHA-VIJNANA (3)

**1. Enhancing Production through Crop Pattern Changes. 33 (2), June 1989.
**2. Unutilised Potential of State Tubewells. 15 (3), September 1973.
3. Location of Agro-Industries : A Case Study of Fruits and Vegetable Processing Industry. 11 (3), May 1969.

3. JOURNAL OF INDIAN WATER RESOURCES SOCIETY (5)

**1. Crop Pattern and Irrigation Planning. 10 (4), October 1990.
**2. Crop Pattern Management with Special Reference to Deccan. 10 (1), January 1990.
**3. Water Resources Development: Groundwater versus Surface Irrigation. 8 (1), January 1988.
**4. Productivity of Irrigated Farming : Survey Evidence from Three States. 7 (2), July 1987 (with K.J.S. Satya Sai).
**5. Income Impact of Irrigation in India : An Empirical Assessment with Secondary Statistics. 5 (3), July 1985.

ECONOMIC AND POLITICAL WEEKLY (36)

**1. Coping with Floods in the Himalayan Rivers, 1 May, 1993.
**2. Impact of Irrigation on Multiple Cropping. 28 March, 1992 (jointly with H.S. Datta).
**3. Benefit-Cost of Tehri Dam Project - A Review Analysis. August 31, 1991.
**4. Developing Groundwater Resources: Merits and Demerits, 23 February, 1991.
**5. Major and Minor Irrigation (Discussion). 29 Sept., 1990.
**6. Big Dams : Claims, Counterclaims (Discussion). July 21, 1990.
**7. How Reliable Are Groundwater Estimates, May 19, 1990.
**8. Major and Minor Irrigation Works : Cost Aspects of the Controversy. Review of Agriculture, 30 Sept. 1989.
**9. Mounting Antagonism towards Big Dams. May 20, 1989, also reproduced in V.S. Mahajan (ed), *Economic Development and Environment* (forthcoming).
**10. Irrigated versus Dry Farming. 19 March, 1988.
**11. Indian Irrigation - An Assessment. 7 May, 1988.
**12. Irrigation's Impact on Farm Economy in High Rainfall Areas - The Kal Project. Review of Agriculture, 24-31 Dec., 1988.
**13. Towards a New Water Policy? 31 October, 1987.
**14. How Stable is Indian Irrigated Agriculture. Review of Agriculture, 26 September, 1987, also reproduced in *Recent Advances in Agricultural Statistics Research*, published by IASRI, Pusa, New Delhi.
**15. Management of Groundwater Resource : Direct versus Indirect Regulatory Mechanisms. 5-12 September, 1987.
**16. Irrigation Impact on Farm Economy. Review of Agriculture, September 1985.
**17. Irrigation Performance during Drought. 13 July, 1985.
**18. Impact of Irrigation on Instability in Farm Output. Review of Agriculture, September 1983.
**19. Underutilisation of Groundwater Resources : A Case Study of East Uttar Pradesh. Review of Agriculture, September 1980.

**20. Trends in Tubewell Irrigation, 1951-78. Review of Agriculture, December 1979.
**21. Tubewell Irrigation in the Gangetic Plains. Sept. 1977.
**22. India's Groundwater Resources. Review of Agriculture, March 1977.
**23. Economics of Groundwater Utilisation : Traditional versus Modern. Review of Agriculture, June 1975.
**24. Utilisation of Groundwater Resources : Public versus Private Tubewells. Review of Agriculture, September 1974.
25. Traditional versus Modern : The Case of Indian Sugar Industry. 15 April, 1967.
26. Comparative Advantage of U.P. in Sugarcane. 2 Nov., 1968.
27. Nationalisation of Sugar Industry : An Economic Perspective. 3 December, 1972.
28. Nationalisation of Sugar Industry - A Comment. 3 March, 1973.
29. Cost of Tax Collection in India - A Comment. 20 April, 1968.
30. INSAT TV Plan : Questionable Features and Parameters. 11 October, 1975.
31. Television in India : What Role in Economic Development? October 14, 1972.
32. School Education Through Television. Nov. 24, 1973.
33. Satellite TV Revisited. April 20, 1974.
34. Economics of Television in India. March 10, 1973.
35. Television in India : Retrospect & Prospect. June 14, 1973.
36. Financing of Indian Television System. May 3, 1975.

4. OTHER JOURNALS/VOLUMES/BOOKS (27)

**1. Role of Irrigation in Raising Intensity of Cropping. *Journal of Indian School of Political Economy,* Vol.3, No.4, October-December 1991, pp.631-71.
**2. Irrigation Development and Its Impact on Foodgrains Production. *Journal of the Indian Society for Agricultural Development and Policy,* Inaugural Issue, 1(1), 1990.

**3. Perspective on Groundwater Irrigated Agriculture of India. *Journal of Soil and Water Conservation,* Vol.35, Nos. 1 & 2, 1991.

**4. Dryland or Irrigation Technology? *Journal of Soil and Water Conservation,* Vol. 35, Nos. 1 & 2, 1991.

**5. Perspective on Groundwater Irrigated Agriculture. *IASSI Quarterly,* Vol.9, No.4, April-June, 1991.

**6. Irrigated Versus Dry Farming: A Case Analysis of Andhra Pradesh. *Agricultural Economics Research Review,* Vol.4, No.1, 1991.

**7. Need for Artificial Groundwater Recharge: Vital Role of Surface Irrigation Works. *Journal of Soil and Water Conservation,* Vol.34, 1990, pp.28-32.

**8. Major Irrigation Dams - A Balanced Approach. *IASSI Quarterly,* Vol.9, No.3, January-March 1991.

**9. Trends in Unutilised Irrigation Capacity in India. *IASSI Quarterly,* Vol.9, No.3, January-March 1991.

**10. Some Aspects of Irrigation Induced - Employment Generation. *IASSI Quarterly,* 9 (1 & 2), July-December 1990.

**11. Canal vs Well Irriation, in G.S. Kainth (ed.) *Agricultural Development in India : Various Issues.* Academic Foundations, New Delhi, 1992 (forthcoming).

**12. Groundwater as a Buffer During Drought, in *Management of Irrigation Systems* ed. by N.K. Tyagi et. al., CSSRI, Karnal, 1990.

**13. Water Resources Development: Groundwater vs Surface Irrigation, in V.S. Mahajan (ed.) *Agriculture and Rural Economy in India,* Deep and Deep, Chandigarh, 1991.

**14. Land Use and Irrigation, in *National Seminar on Conservation of Land and Water Resources for Food and Environmental Security : Lead Papers.* SoilConservation Society of India, Delhi 1990.

**15. Production Augmentation through Canal Irrigation - Empirical Results for Ten Major Irrigation Works. *Journal of Agricultural Issues,* Vol. 1, No.1, 1989.

**16. Some Errors in Cost-Benefit Analysis. *WAMANA,* January 1989.

**17. Economics of Tubewell Irrigation. *Journal of Soil and Water Conservation.* 32 (1,2), March, June 1988.

**18. Agricultural Productivity of Water in India. *Indian Journal of Quantitative Economics.* 3 (2), 1987.

**19. Output Impact According to Main Sources of Irrigation: Empirical Evidence from Four Selected States, in J.S. Kanwar (ed.) *Seminar on Water Management - The Key to Development.* Agricole, 1988.

**20. Conjunctive Irrigation for an Expanding Agriculture, in *National Workshop on Conjunctive Use of Surface and Groundwater.* Water and Land Management Institute (WALMI), Aurangabad, July 1987.

**21. Irrigation Performance in Uttar Pradesh, in R.T. Tewari (ed.) *Development and Change in Uttar Pradesh.* Ashish, 1988.

**22. Differential Income Impact of Public Canal Irrigation in Maharashtra, in Niranjan Pant (ed.) *Productivity and Equity in Irrigation Systems.* Ashish, New Delhi - 1984.

**23. Improving Economic Returns from Well Irrigation in Hard Rock Areas - the Maharashtra Case, in *Proceedings of Seminar on Groundwater Development - A Perspective for Year 2000 A.D..* Indian Water Resources Society, Roorkee, 1983.

**24. Irrigation Strategy for the Deccan. *WAMANA.* Vol.3, No.4, October 1983.

**25. Economic Return to Investment in Irrigation in India. *WAMANA,* Vol.3, No.3, July 1983.

**26. Groundwater Exploitation in India : A Study of Internal and External Economics. *Indian Journal of Power and River Valley Development.* Vol.27, Nos. 6 & 7, 1977.

27. Inter-sectoral Dependence between Industry and Agriculture. *Asian Economic Review.* August 1964 (joint with Waheed Khan).

III. MIMEO WORKS (6)

**1. Groundwater Irrigation in East U.P. IEG, 1978.

**2. Underutilisation of Minor Irrigation Works : A Case Study of State-owned Tubewells in U.P. IEG, 1969.

3. Development of Television in India. IEG, 1975.
4. Productivity Trends in the Indian Sugar Industry. IEG, 1965 (with Dharm Narain).
5. Price Policy for Sugar. IEG, 1963.

**6. Largescale and Smallscale Irrigation, IEG, 1992 (word processed).

IV. SEMI-ACADEMIC-CUM-MEDIA WRITEUPS (62)

**1. Minor Irrigation: Exploding Myth of Low Capital Costs. *FE*, 16 Jauary 1993.

2. On Improving Social Returns from Organised Research in Social Sciences in India. *FFY*, June 1992.

**3. Underutilisation of Minor Irrigation Capacity. *FFY*, December 1992 and January 1993.

**4. Dryland vs Irrigation Technology, *FE*, November 23, 1991.

**5. Perspectives on Groundwater Based Agriculture of India, *FE*, August 10 and August 17, 1991.

**6. Irrigation - Induced Job Generation. *FE*, 20 March, 1991.

**7. Some Comments on Irrigation in 8th Plan. *FFY*, 14(5), November 1992.

**8. What is Wrong with Tehri Dam? *FFY*, 14(4), October 1992.

**9. Issues in Indian Water Resources Development. *FFY*, 14(3), September 1992.

**10. Canal vs Well Irrigation: Myths and Realities. *FFY*, 14(2), August 1992.

**11. Do Big Dams Aggravate Floods? *FFY*, 14(1), July 1992.

**12. Irrigation Development and Its Impact on Foodgrains Production. *FFY*, 13(12), Annual Number, 1992.

**13. Economics of Big Dams. *FFY*, 13(11), May 1992.

**14. Population Pressure, Irrigation Imperative and Environment. *FFY*, 13(10), April 1992.

**15. Big Dam Debate. *FFY*, 13(8), February 1992.

**16. Unutilised Irrigation Capacity in India, *FE*, 18 and 19 December, 1990.

**17. Conjunctive Irrigation : Sardar Sarovar, *FE*, 10 September, 1990.

**18. Groundwater Planning, *ET*, 24 April, 1990.
**19. Artificial Groundwater Recharge, *FE*, 10 April, 1990.
**20. Water Management, *ET*, 30 and 31 January, 1990.
**21. Groundwater Resources and Rural Development, *MS*, 29 April, 1989.
**22. The Way Out of the Narmada Imbroglio, *ET*, 5 December, 1988.
**23. Myth About Minor Irrigation (under Communications section) *Seminar* (on Drought), June 1988.
**24. Canal Irrigation, Waterlogging and Crop Losses, *MS*, 2 April, 1988.
**25. Irrigated vs Dry Farming, *MS*, March 19, 1988.
**26. What Ails Indian Agriculture, *ET*, 9 March, 1988.
**27. Irrigation & Agricultural Instability, *MS*, 26 January, 1988, and *FE*, 19 January, 1988.
**28. Dry Farming : The only Hope? *ET*, 13 Jan. 1988.
**29. Inter-Basin Transfer of Water, *MS*, 26 Dec., 1987.
**30. Groundwater vs Surface Irrigation, *The Statesman*, 7 November, 1987, Calcutta edition (Economic page).
**31. Indian Irrigation (in two parts), *ET*, 2nd and 3rd September, 1987.
**32. The Drought of 1987, *ET*, 17th August, 1987.
**33. Public Irrigation by Tubewells - Some Considerations, *BS*, 6th June, 1978.
**34. Subsidizing Public Irrigation, *BS*, 10 and 11 May, 1978.
**35. Economics of Public Irrigation, *BS*, 7 and 8 April, 1978.
**36. Patterns in Tubewell Growth, *BS*, 23rd and 24th February, 1978.
**37. Tapping Groundwater Resources, *BS*, 30th November, 1977.
**38. Rural Electrification and Tapping Groundwater, *BS*, 9 and 10 September, 1977.
**39. Financial Returns on State Tubewells in U.P., *AICC Economic Review*, Vol. XXI, No.14, March 1, 1970.
**40. Has India Enough Water to Waste, *BS*, May 10, 1977.
**41. Communicating through Satellite, *BS*, February 26 and 28, 1977.
**42. Options in Tubewell Irrigation, *EE*, 12 November, 1976.

**43. Development of Tubewell Irrigation in India, *EE*, 10 September, 1976.
**44. Economies of Scale in Tubewell Irrigation, *EE*, 15 October, 1976.
**45. Social Consequences of New Groundwater Technology, *ET*, July 5, 1975.
**46. Economics of Groundwater Utilisation, *ET*, Bombay edition, April 23 and 24, 1975.
47. Power Requirements of Tubewells, *ET*, Bombay edition, March 26, 1975.
48. Planning for TV Development : Some Financing Aspects, *ET*, Bombay edition, March 7, 1975. The Delhi edition carries a different title (TV needs Ads to spread its wings).
49. Case for Scrapping S.I.T.E., *ET*, March 30, 1974.
50. Reconsidering Place of TV in Changing National Situation, *ET*, February 19, 1974.
**51. Public and Private Tubewells, *ET*, September 23, 1973.
52. The Illusion of a Low-Cost TV Set, *ET*, November 13, 1973.
53. Economics of Running TV Stations, *ET*, October 16 and 17, 1973.
54. Development of TV in India, *ET*, April 6 and 7, 1973.
55. Television versus other Media, *ET*, December 18, 1972.
56. Economics of TV Software, *ET*, January 20, 1973.
57. Why Satellite TV Experiment in India? *ET*, November 26, 1972.
58. Satellite vs. Terrestrial TV Technology, *ET*, October 4, 1972.
59. Satellite TV for India, *ET*, Sept. 15, 1972.
60. The Coal Industry, *ET*, February 1963.
61. Defence Role of Motor Industry, *FE*, February 13, 1963.
62. Fourth Plan Prospects : Indications of the Interim Budget, *FE*, May 7, 1967.

V. BOOK REVIEWS (24)

**1. Krishna Bharadwaj. Irrigation in India: Alternative Perspectives. *Journal of Indian School of Political Economy*, Vol.IV, No.3, July-Sept. 1992.

**2. Vijay Paranjpye. High Dams on the Narmada. *Journal of Indian School of Political Economy*, Vol.4, No.1, Jan.-March 1992.

**3. S.S. Prihar, S.D. Khepar, Raghbir Singh, S.S. Grewal and S.K. Sondhi. Water Resources of Punjab - A Critical Concern for the Future of Its Agriculture. *IJAE*, Jan.-March 1992.

**4. Leslie E. Small and Ian Carruthers. Farmer-Financed Irrigation: The Economics of Reform. *IJAE*, Vol.7, No.2, April-June 1992.

**5. A. Sundar. Managing Public Irrigation Systems. *EPW*, January 16-23, 1993.

**6. Joseph E. Stevens. Hoover Dam: An American Adventure. International Journal of Development Banking, Vol.10, No.2, July 1992.

**7. Ram Bilas. Rural Water Resource Utilisation and Planning: A Geographical Approach in Varanasi District. Concept, 1988. *IJAE*, October-December, 1989.

**8. Adriant T. Mcdonald and David Key. Water Resources: Issues and Strategies. Longman, 1988. *EPW*, Dec. 9, 1989.

**9. Combined Report of the U.S. Dryland Farming Team and the Economics Team Visits to India, 1987. *EPW*, 19 March, 1988.

**10. S.P. Pal. Contribution of Irrigation to Agricultural Production. NCAER. 1985. *IJAE*, Jan.-March 1987.

**11. K.C. Nobe and R.K. Sampath (ed.). Irrigation Management in Developing Countries : Current Issues and Approaches. Westview, 1986. *IJAE*, October-December 1987.

**12. Niranjan Pant and R.P. Rai. Community Tubewell and Agricultural Development : An Organisational Alternative to Very Small Farmers Irrigation in East Gangetic Plains. Ashish, 1985. *IJAE*, January-March 1986.

**13. T. Satpathy. Irrigation and Economic Development. Ashish, 1984. *IJAE*, April-June 1985.

**14. Ian Stone. Canal Irrigation in British India : Perspectives on Technological Change in a Peasant Economy. Cambridge (UK), 1984. *The Indian Economic and Social History Review*, Vol. 22, No.4, 1985.

**15. K. Palanisami. Irrigation Water Management : The Determinants of Canal Water Distribution in India - A Micro Analysis. Agricole, 1984. *IJAE*.

**16. Robert Wade. Irrigation and Agricultural Politics in South Korea. Westview, 1982. *IJAE*, January-March 1984.

**17. P. Kumar. Economics of Water Management. Heritage. *Indian Economic Review*, October 1978.

**18. Role of Irrigation in the Development of India's Agriculture. The Indian Society of Agricultural Economics, 1976. *EPW*, December 3, 1977.

**19. Colin Clark. The Economics of Irrigation. Pargamon, 1967. *EPW*, 10 February 1968. (under the title 'Criss-Cross on Irrigation').

**20. Paul Singh Dhillon. Water Resources Development and Management in North-West India : Some Issues. Centre for Research in Rural and Industrial Development, Chandigarh, 1987. *EPW*, October 22, 1988.

21. G.S. Bhalla and G.K. Chadha. Green Revolution and the Small Peasant : A Study of Income Distribution among Punjab Cultivators. Concept, New Delhi, 1983. *IJAE*, Vol.39, No.2, April-June 1984.

**22. Leslie Abbie, Thames Q. Harrison and John Wall. Economic Return to Investment in Irrigation. World Bank, Working Paper No.536, 1982. *WAMANA*, Vol.3, No.3, July 1983.

23. John W. Mellor and Gunvant M. Desai (ed). Agricultural Change and Rural Development. Oxford University Press, 1986. *Social Action*.

24. Jaya Bose. Impact of Electrification on Indian Agriculture with Special Reference to Bihar. Agricole, New Delhi, 1982. *IJAE*, Vol.38, No.1, January-March 1983.